ANCESTOR
A Carriacou Sloop's Voyage to Vancouver

by

Jon van Tamelen

SEAWORTHY PUBLICATIONS, INC. • MELBOURNE, FLORIDA

Ancestor
A Carriacou Sloop's Voyage to Vancouver
Copyright ©2019 by Jon van Tamelen

Published in the USA by:
Seaworthy Publications, Inc.
6300 N Wickham Rd.
#130-416
Melbourne, FL 32940
Phone 321-610-3634
email orders@seaworthy.com
www.seaworthy.com - Your Bahamas and Caribbean Cruising Advisory

All rights reserved. No part of this book may be reproduced, stored in a retrieval system, or transmitted in any form, or by any means, electronic, mechanical, photocopying, recording, or by any storage and retrieval system, without permission in writing from the Publisher.

Library of Congress Cataloging-in-Publication Data

Names: Van Tamelen, Jon P., 1936- author.
Title: Ancestor : a carriacou sloop's voyage to Vancouver / by Jon van Tamelen.
Description: Melbourne, Florida : Seaworthy Publications, Inc., [2019]
Identifiers: LCCN 2018061538 (print) | LCCN 2019016803 (ebook) | ISBN 9781948494212 (e-book) | ISBN 1948494213 (e-book) | ISBN 9781948494205
(pbk. : alk. paper)
Subjects: LCSH: Van Tamelen, Jon P., 1936---Travel. | Ancestor (Sloop) | Sailing--Caribbean Area. | Sailing--Pacific Ocean. | Caribbean Area--Description and travel. | Pacific Area--Description and travel.
Classification: LCC G530.V367 (ebook) | LCC G530.V367 A3 2019 (print) | DDC
910.9162--dc23
LC record available at https://lccn.loc.gov/2018061538

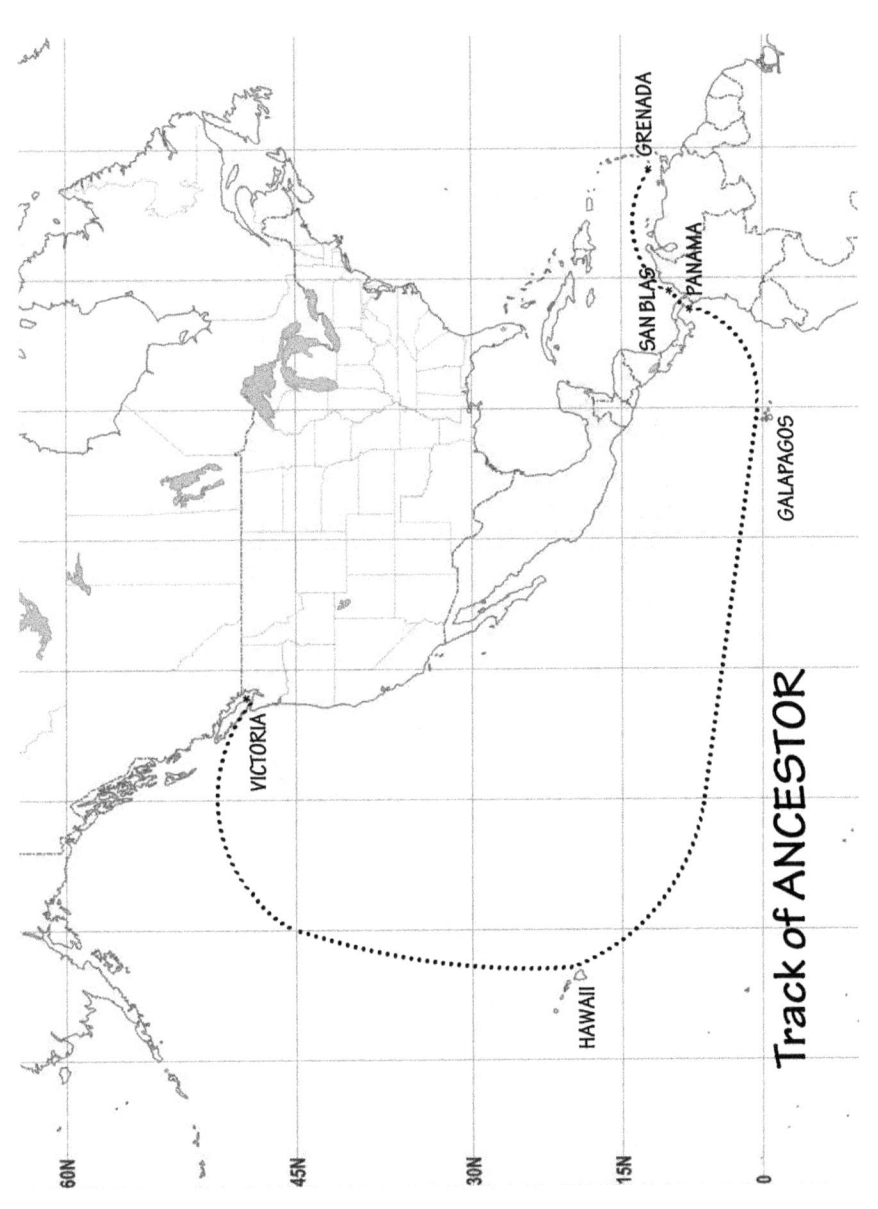

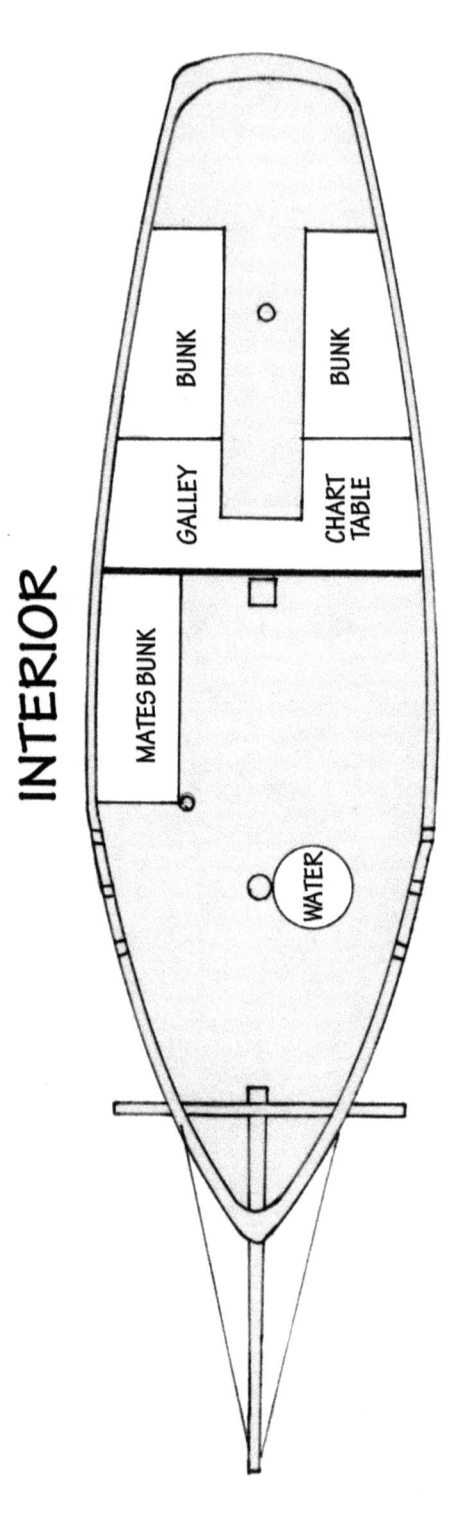

ANCESTOR DECK PLAN

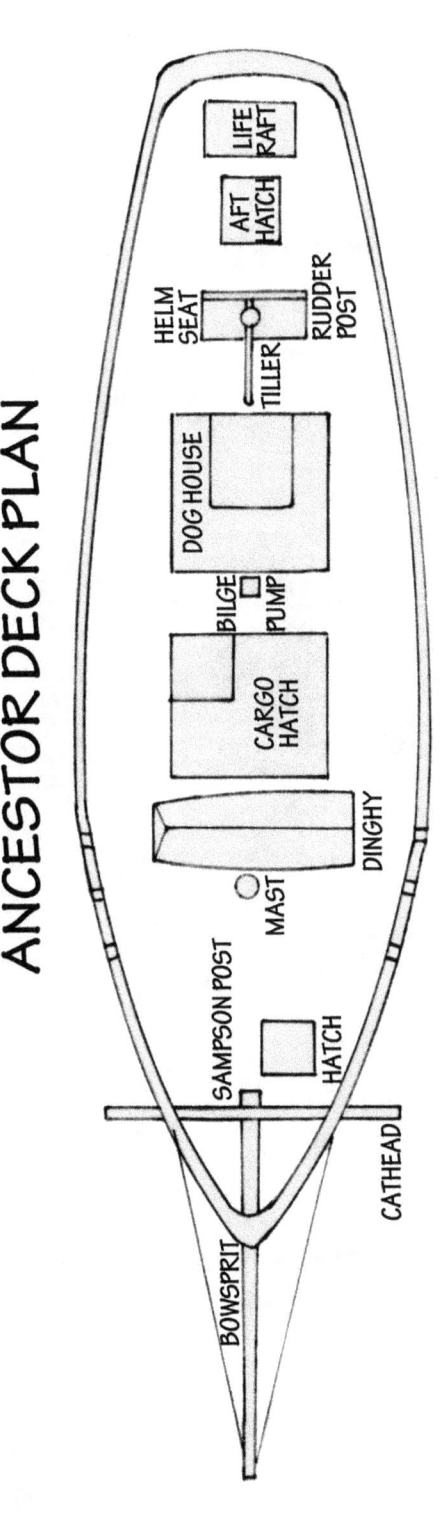

Table of Contents

Track of Ancestor iii
Ancestor Interior Plan iv
Ancestor Deck Plan v
Log Book vi
Tropic Dreams ix
Buying de Boat 1
Port Elizabeth and Anchoring Technique 10
Bequia Work and Play 14
Ice and the Kingstown Harbour War 17
New Crew and Our First Gale 20
Off to Grenada 24
Westward on S/V Carcharias 30
The Colón Caper, a Canal Transit and a 727 Jet 38
Interlude 41
Preparation for Travel 43
No-Name Boats 48
Full Crew Again and Fun Days 57
The Big Shakedown Cruise 62
Forestay 65
Haul - Out, Life Raft, Registry and Carnival 66
Grenada to Panama 74
A Change of Plan 83
Panic at Puyades, Ancestor Island and Molas 86
Cristóbal, ROP and Hilton Beverley Fraser 94
Panama Canal Transit 104
Hijack Warnings 108

The Boys Fly and We Get to Work	110
Galapagos Bound	116
In the Galapagos	128
Galapagos to Hilo	140
Shark Food	146
Onward, Ever Onward	148
Wearing Ship	159
In the Dumps	168
Bureaucratic and Air Conditioner Shock	177
Just Hang Loose	180
Good Job	185
Cat? What Cat?	191
Fearless Forestay	199
Hawaiian Mermaid	203
Barnacle Crew	205
Just Have Fun	207
Tow Job, Shanghaied Crew and Travel	213
Sea Monsters	224
Seal of Approval	229
Jelly Sea	234
X Marks the Spot	236
Wind and Fog	238
The Flotsam and Garbage Blues	243
Victoria to Vancouver	249
Epilogue	256
Post Script	273
Miscellaneous Receipts	275
Glossary	277
Acknowledgements	281
About the Author	282

Tropic Dreams

The Tropics! Warmer weather than one could ever hope for, up here, at forty-nine degrees north latitude. We dream of the tropics when winter winds and rain try to drown us. Sometimes we want to escape to the warmth and greenness of high volcanic islands or white beaches on low islands or to atolls with swaying coconut palm trees. Our imaginings are vivid. Our northern dreams conjure the sweet fragrance of frangipani. One visualizes bougainvillea creeping over stone walls and fences and window sills. Ah, dreams.

When we do break the bonds of the north and resolutely wing or sail our way to those seductive destinations, we are happy and eager to sample those southern climes with all our senses.

I had, on previous occasions, broken the bonds of the north and in 1974, I was escaping again. Air Canada flew me from Vancouver to Toronto and on to Barbados, where I caught a LIAT Airlines (Leave Island Any Time) flight which delivered my jet-lagged body to Grenada.

When I stepped from the airplane into the heat, I was, indeed, realizing my dream. I carried only a small bag containing a change of clothes, sunglasses, sunscreen, a towel, a bathing suit and a toothbrush. When a taxi hove-to at the curb, I jumped in. I was off to Grenada Yacht Services to join the *Ring Anderson*.

Jan de Groot, *Ring's* owner / skipper, had invited me to sail with him that winter.

For the past two years I had been operating the *S/V Anywhere*, a forty-seven foot gaff yawl. Anywhere and I offered passengers scenic, tranquil cruises among the Canadian Gulf Islands and to the northern end of Vancouver Island. It had been a good life but repetitive and it was no longer challenging. The charter business had been gradually dampening my spirits. So I was happy to accept Jan's invitation. My boat was sold to Jan's brother, leaving me footloose and fancy free.

After several trips on the *Ring* between Grenada and Martinique that winter, we anchored one night at the island of St. Vincent. Karma. I will never forget that night.

Buying de Boat

In the magical universe there are no coincidences and there are no accidents.

William Burroughs. American novelist, satirist and painter

The sun had set in Kingstown Harbour on the island of St Vincent. *Ring Anderson* tugged gently on her anchor chain. She was soothed, as were her crew, by the beauty of the harbour and the land-scented breezes drifting from shore.

I sat with *Ring's* captain on the aft deck. The crew had spread white cushions for the comfort of their charter guests, who were contentedly sipping brandy, lighting cigars, enjoying the evening and sharing stories about Martinique and today's passage.

Ring was a Baltic ketch, 120 feet in length overall. All the way from Martinique, she had maintained an easy eleven knots on the easterly trade winds. As a friend of the captain, I was aboard with no assigned duties other than to appreciate the vessel and our ongoing travels through the West Indies.

The Grenadian crew were proud of their ship and loyal to their captain. They were busy setting up steel drums, checking the sound quality and grinning from ear to ear at their guests. The charter clients had not been informed that these men were also accomplished musicians. The vacationers smiled. The air was filled with the distinctive, 'bonk bonk,' metallic tones of the steel drums performing the Caribbean version of some classical music piece.

I felt the magic of the night and waited for something to happen, while a waxing moon winked among the trade wind clouds.

Suddenly there was motion from seaward. A small, gaff-rigged ship, under sail, was beating her way into the harbour, making good time but she displayed no running lights.

Jan de Groot, our captain, said, "Smuggler, I guess." He descended to the chart room for the binoculars, which he passed to me. The smuggler made an impressive sight. She was loaded down and her decks were almost awash. She was snorting into the wind like a thoroughbred race horse: poetry and grace in motion. Closer and closer she came. This vessel tugged at my heart. She had no name. No flag. The hull was light blue, with white bulwarks. *This beauty is the Ancestor of all of the sailing ships that ever travelled the oceans. I have just laid eyes on the boat I will name Ancestor.*

"I'm going to own that boat. I've got to have her." I said out loud.

"Yes Jon." Jan replied, "She is beautiful. Buy her."

So I did and now my story may begin.

* * *

The mystery vessel sailed up to the inter-island dock. There, she was tied-off and her sails were furled. I could see how heavily laden she was.

In no time, people were shuffling down to her with hand carts and wagons. A few small pickup trucks joined the parade. A mid-ship hatch cover was removed: huge sacks were heaved to the waiting hands ashore. This work continued for an hour and gradually the boat's hull rose from the water. I was fascinated and impatient to go over for a closer look. After the offloading was completed, her hungry crew went aft for a meal. Smoke rose from the deck. They had lit a fire and started cooking.

Jan, standing with me at the rail said, "Okay, Jon, take the launch and go. Don't wait any longer." Needing no more encouragement, I hurried to the dinghy, fired up the motor and aimed for the dock.

The vessel's main boom extended six feet over the transom. The main gaff was twenty feet long. The smoke we had seen, was billowing from a three-foot, square box on the starboard aft deck. The box itself was two feet high. I later discovered that the bottom section of a metal drum, inside the box, contained sand and three rocks arranged to accommodate pots and pans. An impressive galley stove!

My dinghy bumped the dock. I tied off the painter and walked along to 'casually' study the boat. The crew's supper chatter ceased when they saw me and I didn't know quite what to do. My time-honoured solution was to load my pipe. I got it puffing, and said, "She a good ship. She be happy and make the good speed."

An old man, who I assumed to be the skipper, checked me over and asked, "You here to vex me mon?"

I smiled and paused before answering, "Not here to vex. Here to appreciate. Can I walk her decks?" Another awkward silence followed, while the skipper and his crew discussed the situation in loud whispers. Eventually, the old man nodded for me to come aboard. His crew again fell silent but they dished out fish and rice and passed a bowlful to me. Now I was really excited. I hoped these men could see the sailor in me and not a spy from the customs office. We ate and smoked and introduced ourselves. The skipper was James Bethel from Windward, Carriacou. At first he was cautious but as we became friendlier, he told me about the trip they just completed.

St. Vincent had declared a moratorium on the import of rice some time ago. So James had waited until he figured the islanders had consumed their supply and needed more. When the time was right, he ran his vessel on down to Surinam and loaded as much rice as could be safely stowed below decks. Then James sailed to Kingstown to offload his valuable cargo. "Supply and demand be the key to life," he declared. "We make a few dollars here and there. Dis da key," he added, pointing at his empty cargo hold. "But dis life not easy."

The night wore on and as I prepared to leave, I took a calculated breath and said, "I want to buy your boat."

For a long time, he said not a word in reply. Then he looked into my eyes. "So, I be thinkin.' Tonight you pass by with the sun and we talk more." I thanked him and returned to *Ring*.

Jan was awake and anxious for my news. He laughed when I finished recounting my story. He said Ring would wait for me to finish my morning negotiations with Mr. Bethel before casting off for Petit St. Vincent. With that guarantee, I strung my hammock under the stern awning and got comfortable to do some serious thinking. Falling asleep was not easy surrounded by the magic of the night. Plans and ideas swirled in my head. I was surprised to see the dawn light and hear the roosters' chorus proclaiming the new day.

With morning coffee in hand, I watched for activity on James's boat. When smoke could finally be seen rising from their galley, I became tense but I forced myself to wait patiently until they were at breakfast. Only then, did I motor over to have my conversation with James.

The skipper invited me to the foredeck, where we could talk undisturbed. He began by explaining that times were 'tough'. With a sly smile and a wink, he proved it by demonstrating how his bowsprit could be pulled inboard to change the vessel's appearance! James would sail to Martinique for spirits and deliver these goods to Isla Margarita under a standard cutter rig! For his next assignment, James would disguise his boat as a knockabout sloop with no bowsprit!

"This life be alright," he said, "but the authorities, they be gettin' wise to my tricks." The skipper figured that one day, he'd probably be caught and that would mean the end of his 'trading days.' I learned a lot about the smuggling business from him but all too soon Jan was blowing the horn and *Ring's* Blue Peter was flying from the spreader. I had to go. James gripped my arm as I was about to leave. "If you pass by Windward next Friday, with $9,000 dollars, the ship is for you."

"I'll be there. What is the name of the vessel?"

"She got no true name. Launch time, I need a name. So he be called *Lucy Anne B* for the launch." We shook hands and I was off, back to the *Ring*. My soul was dancing.

* * *

I stayed with Jan and *Ring Anderson* until we reached Petit St Vincent. Where we enjoyed the Wednesday night jump-up. Next day, I caught a ride back to Kingstown on another charter boat. My eleven-year-old son, Todd, was flying in from Vancouver to spend a couple of months with me among the Windward Islands. I certainly did not want to be late arriving at the airport. Todd needed to see his old man's face when he disembarked. The plane landed. There he was.

The first of our many adventures together over the next months happened when we caught a ride south from Kingstown to Carriacou. The boisterous trade winds gave us a record setting passage - according to the skipper of the *Betty Blue*.

Carriacou is 15 miles long and 5 miles wide. The major town, Hillsborough, is on the northwest side of the island. We tied off at the main dock, said good bye and thanks to our 'ride' and went for ice cream cones in town. Afterward, Todd and I set off to walk across the island.

At Windward, Carriacou

The hike, to Windward on the northeast coast, took longer than anticipated. As we neared the village, we saw reefs extending north and south along the island and there were no marked passages through them! Petit St. Vincent and Petite Martinique were visible to the east. There were buildings along the shoreline, and boats being built along the beach. Some hulls were being planked with pitch pine, others, like white cedar skeletons, were waiting for their hull sheathing. Three island sloops shared the anchorage. We entered the village around noontime, parched and overheated but prepared for some fun. Folks waved at us helpfully as we searched for James Bethel's home.

In the mid-1700s, first the French then the English settled at Carriacou. A little more than a century and a half later, men emigrating from Scotland became this island's pioneer boat builders. They brought a boat design dating from 1893. The layout showed a work boat with a beam one third the length of its hull. There are builders here who still use these same dimensions. The Scots modified the sail plan to deal with the Caribbean's trade winds, which demand lots of sail.

James was waiting for us, although he did seem almost surprised to see me. After meeting his family, I presented him with his $9,000 bank draft. We talked about boats while sipping 'Airport Jack', a white rum from Grenada. Powerful stuff and well known for the fact that, when you pour a drink and add ice, the ice does not float but sinks immediately to the bottom of the glass. James boasted that his boat had won all the inter-island races for the last three years. The vessel

Boat building details, Windward, Carriacou

was famous throughout the Windwards. While sipping drinks in the shade, I was already reconfiguring the sail plan for deep sea traveling with a small crew. The rum did not help with the re-design, so I filed my ideas away for retrieval in the days to come.

Quite a crowd of local folk had gathered to enjoy the view of Petit St. Vincent and Petite Martinique on the eastern horizon. Everyone talked enthusiastically about boat building and sailing and we men puffed our pipes and the hours drifted away.

James's wife produced a delicious callaloo soup for our lunch with dunking bread made from cassava. The meal went down extremely well. It also soaked up the rum, which my body was unaccustomed to. Following the meal, the friendly crowd strolled down to the beach. Departure time.

The boat - my boat now - was anchored off the village shore. Todd and I rowed out with James, his son, and several other islanders who all climbed aboard. I confessed that I did not know the pass through the reefs so James asked his son to guide us. What Todd and I were about to do was impulsive and intimidating. We were going to simply sail away without first familiarizing ourselves with the boat and her gear. To ease my discomfort, I asked James's lad to watch me get her sailing and tell me when I was doing anything wrong. Throat and peak halyards were on the starboard side. I grabbed them both and hauled

Boat building details, Windward, Carriacou

away, keeping the peak halyard relaxed and slightly behind the throat halyard. After belaying the throat, I heaved on the peak halyard and tensioned the gaff to where it belonged. The staysail was aged flax, full of holes, but it worked well enough when set and full of wind. While the locals weighed anchor for us, I adjusted the mainsheet. We were away! Everybody, except James's son, clambered off and paddled or motored to the beach.

After several tacks, we were lined up with the pass, which was, thankfully, visible now. Without ceremony, our guide hopped into his dinghy and headed home. Todd and I were on our own.

Wow. How the vessel moved! How she responded to the tiller!

Outside the reef, we had a beam reach for today's sail to Union Island, on the northern horizon. Our passage was uneventful yet exhilarating. To the east of Union Island, we rounded up in the lee of Palm Island, where we dropped the hook in four fathoms. Todd and I did high-fives and hugged. This was our first anchorage with our dream ship.

We had another magical night. Palm Island was, and still is, a resort area, with coconut palms waving in the wind. The night we arrived, people were strolling along the beach. Pan music drifted from inland. After our sails were furled, we promptly lit a charcoal fire in the cooking pit. Our meagre evening menu consisted of rice and a can of beans with a dash of cayenne pepper to spice everything up. That did the job. After our feast, I made tea, lit my pipe and my son and I sat on the hatch cuddling until Todd nodded off. For his sleeping quarters, I had rigged a hammock between the forestay and the main mast and now I poured him in. Jet lag affects us, one and all.

Already I was thinking of this boat as the *Ancestor*. While Todd slept, I used a rusty tape measure that somebody had forgotten on deck to record *Ancestor*'s dimensions. I'm not sure how accurate I was but here are the results in my notebook:

38' on deck

11'6 beam

~5'6" draught

15" high bulwarks

I added other information that James had shared with me:

Island cedar ribs (natural shapes, trimmed to fit hull shape)

Greenheart keel

Pitch pine planking

Pine mast and boom

Stone ballast

Galvanized iron work from previous vessels

Upper shrouds and forestay of galvanized wire

Inner stay, ¾" manila rope

Sheets and halyards, ½" manila rope

Double topping lifts, ½" manila rope

Mainsail and jib of well-used cotton

Staysail flax, complete with lots of holes

Deadeyes of greenheart wood, lanyards of ½" Dacron

Island lore says that when a boat is ready to be launched, the people cannibalize the previous boat, which has been reduced to a wreck on the beach. They transfer everything of use - the metal work, mast, bowsprit shrouds (whisker stays) and other rigging - to the new vessel.

This new boat begins her life on the sea and the captain and his crew go about their business, up and down the islands, constantly on the lookout for cedar on shore, which they collect for their next vessel. Large supplies of pitch pine planking are harvested from shoreside stockpiles, the remainder of shipments delivered from Nova Scotia years ago. James said that often, these vessels, with transplanted, old boat parts, only survive for four or five years!

While Todd dozed, I also recorded that my foredeck was clear and between the mast and the dog house dwelt the cargo hatch, which measured five feet square. The doghouse itself was smaller; eighteen inches high, with a sliding top hatch. Immediately forward of the doghouse, an eight inch, square, vertical, wooden box protruded onto the deck; the bilge pump. More about that later.

Sitting alone peacefully on deck, I was relaxing. I smoked my pipe with my elbows resting on the doghouse hatch. My senses absorbed everything around me. The western sun blended into the shadowed mass of Union Island. I couldn't believe my luck. I'd bought this boat although many people had insisted that local folks never sell boats to outsiders. The exception to the rule was *Mermaid*, a vessel that had been sold to a doctor, or some other professional, a resident of Carriacou. Why me, then? I had no clue. Maybe it was the combination of circumstances. Firstly, James Bethel had found himself in a compromising position. Circumstances were forcing him to re-evaluate his current situation and my offer. Secondly, a fortuitous, perhaps predestined coincidence had brought me to Kingstown that night when I set eyes on the boat I would name *Ancestor*. These events proved themselves to be providential for sure. And here I sat, happy me, with my son, aboard my own, very recently-purchased boat. I smoked and listened to the night sounds of Palm Island.

Night sounds. The tropics. Friends and family were freezing up north. Ah, contentment. Until I heard crickets chirping, very loudly. My tranquil evening had been interrupted. Why were the crickets so noisy? After all, we were anchored at least two hundred yards from land. I ducked my head into the hatch, thinking that this would mute the sounds from shore but to my surprise, I found that below, the chirping was even louder than topsides. What? Impossible! Were the crickets inside the boat? I slid down and landed on the rock ballast in my bare feet. The critters were temporarily silent. I had startled them. I squatted to listen and soon enough they were chirping again. A jungle colony lived on *Ancestor*! I hoisted myself back on deck. Who would believe me? I couldn't believe it myself. A kind person had left a bottle of Airport Jack onboard. Laughing out loud, I took a hefty swig and saluted our new life and the end of a perfect day.

Port Elizabeth and Anchoring Technique

The morning sun of Palm Island greeted us. Roosters sang. The air held a pleasant coolness. Todd rolled from his hammock and peed noisily over the side while I started the fire, brewed coffee and prepared our oatmeal. No oranges were available but one ripe paw paw with a squirt of lime accompanied the meal.

"Full tummies equal happy times," said Todd, the philosopher. His skin was still showing wind and sunburn from the previous day. We would have to be careful. He did not like the suggestion of a long-sleeved shirt and sunscreen but he did submit to both for part of the day.

Before casting off, we talked over a few details about our new acquisition; *Ancestor*. In much simpler terms than recorded here, I explained to my son that there are no winches. The headsails are adjusted by luffing-up and tensioning the sheets on wooden cleats. The cleats are made of hardwood about two by three inches in section and about three feet long, spanning exposed frames on the inside of the bulwarks. The mainsheet is a five part tackle set on a short metal traveller which seems to be adequate for the job. We also reviewed the route for this day's travel to Port Elizabeth on the island of Bequia. Our main and staysail were hoisted, leaving the sheets loose while I went forward to haul the anchor. This was when our fun really began.

A rusty, old, half-inch diameter chain was attached to an equally rusty, old anchor weighing at least one hundred and twenty pounds. There was no way to haul it to the surface. I considered dropping our sails again to enlist the mainsheet tackle for extra help. I also had a few more ideas but at the moment none of them seemed practical or doable. "Todd, I said, catching my breath, "we don't need this junky old anchor on our boat. We'll figure something out when we reach Port Elizabeth." With that decision made, we untied the end of the anchor chain and let the anchor plunge into the deep. Todd backed the foresail and as the bow came around, I hardened the mainsheet and off we went, whooping and hollering. Crazy. Todd took the tiller while I hoisted and set the jib, which was also old and full of holes, as I have mentioned before and probably will again. The wind was an easterly Force 4, which held all the way to Bequia.

Port Elizabeth is one of my favourite anchorages in the Windward Islands and it beckoned us now as we rounded the headland. About fifty vessels lay at anchor. They would provide a bit of a challenge for us under sail and anchor-less. The wind held, not steady now and with less heft, and prone to sudden, strong gusts which were a little too hefty.

We dropped the jib and carefully tacked amongst the yachts. I recognized a familiar boat, the *Jens Juhl*, a two hundred ton, ex-Baltic ketch, cargo vessel, which traded among the islands. I knew the captain too, and the mate and the cook.

As soon as I saw *Jens Juhl*, I devised a plan. "Todd, we'll sail up to *Jens Juhl's* stern to attract their attention. If we have to, we'll pay-off and make a second run, if we can't raise them on the first try. Or if they're not aboard."

The peak halyard was eased, scandalizing the mainsail, which slowed us down to manoeuvring speed. We approached *Jens Juhl*. Luck was with us. Johnny, the mate, had seen our rig approaching and he had come aft to take a look. We luffed up within twenty feet of his stern. Johnny peered down and said, "Jon, what the hell is going on? Is this your boat?"

"Yes, my new yacht and we have a problem. No anchor. Could you help out?" He laughed and offered us a small anchor and about a hundred feet of line. We would position ourselves under his rail when he was ready. Meanwhile, Todd backed the staysail and we went for another tour of the harbour.

Ten minutes passed before I could see Johnny waving for us to make a second approach. Our boat luffed-up under *Jens Juhl's* stern rail. Johnny had a 50 pound anchor with 50 feet of chain and rope attached, ready to pass over. The transfer of this heavy gear was completed successfully. Todd and I fended off. Happy lads we were when we sailed away to find our own anchorage near the Frangipani Hotel, a very cool place to spend a few evenings anytime in that

Port Elizabeth, Bequia. Jens Juhl to starboard and Friendship Rose careened to port

harbour. The hook was dropped. The main and staysail were backed. The new anchor was snugged into the bottom. It was time to smile, have our customary hug and then get busy furling sails and tidying the deck.

Johnny motored over in his launch, towing a small dinghy for our use. Big thanks there, since I had intended to swim ashore to find something to make do as a tender until I could find a suitable, small boat. We had coffee and then I gathered up the bill of sale, written on a scrap of paper, our passports and a ball point pen. Johnny invited us to *Jens Juhl* for dinner at 1800. He was still shaking his head and grinning when he departed.

Todd remained onboard while I rowed over to the main wharf to clear customs. The port captain was an island man who got a kick out of my documents. The office staff had watched our arrival manoeuvres and the antics we needed to perform in order to get Johnny's anchor onto our boat deck.

Our cargo manifest declared "2.5 tonnes stone ballast, nil cargo." With the clearance documents in my back pack, I rowed to the boat to stow our paperwork safely away. A few minutes later, we were ashore at the Frangipani, sitting in the shade, drinking ice cold fruit juice and eating roasted peanuts out of old coke bottles.

The remainder of the day was spent walking in the village and buying provisions; lots of paw paws and limes and peanuts. I even treated myself to a Greenie (Heineken beer) that went down very smoothly. My watch indicated that it was close to dinnertime aboard *Jens Juhl*. Soon we were watching Janey, the cook, preparing a stir fry in a large wok, over a hissing gas-burner.

The skipper was in Kingstown on business. He would be returning the next day on the *Friendship Rose*, a 90 foot, local island schooner, which served as the ferry between Bequia and St Vincent. Over dinner, many stories were shared until Todd fell asleep. Janey added generously to our provisions, which we gratefully accepted. My sleepy boy and I returned to our crickets, our beds and our dreams of tomorrows.

Bequia Work and Play

The following days were filled with activity and making plans. We walked up the hill to Tulleys, the local marine supply shop, to buy a 45 pound CQR anchor, 50 feet of chain and 200 feet of nylon rode. Afterward, a kind stranger offered to haul everything to the Frangipani Hotel. When we returned to the boat we were surprised to find that someone had placed an old fisherman-type anchor on deck! It weighed about 30 pounds and was properly coated in rust. We never did find out who had decided to make the gift to us.

Our sails were dead, and anyway they were much too large for a long ocean trip. I had already decided to make it back to Vancouver; ten thousand miles of deep sea travel. Therefore, I had to make new sails, cut the boom off at the transom, and shorten the gaff by eleven feet.

I found Mr. Simmons, Bequia's local sailmaker, in his sail loft, of course. Unfortunately, he had no time to take on our job. He suggested that I investigate the island's hardware store, which stocked ten ounce cotton. Mr. Simmons offered to supply our needles and thread. I thanked him and returned to the hotel to begin drawing our new sails and calculating the quantities of material we would have to purchase. My design called for a main, a staysail and a jib. The hardware store did indeed stock the amount of cotton canvas and bolt rope we required and there was a bonus for us tucked away on the store's upper floor, where we discovered two by six inch by sixteen foot lengths of Purple Heart timber at a cost of seventy-eight cents per board foot. This was just what I needed to lag down the ballast in the hold. (Coincidentally, years after I bought this timber, I learned that it had been imported by my friend, Jan de Groot, to be used for new bulwarks on his boat, the *Ring Anderson!*)

Todd was kept busy scraping our bulwarks and decks. The seams would need re-caulking too but we'd do that later. I agreed with my son. "Dad, let her leak awhile longer. The crickets and other ballast dwellers need water too." Speaking of ballast dwellers, there was also a healthy population of cockroaches aboard, some up to three inches in length. For Todd's amusement, I made him a wooden cockroach mallet so he could hunt them down and bash them. On the first night, when the rains forced us below decks, I was surprised to see, in the glow of our kerosene lantern, that centipedes were aboard for the ride as well. The largest creatures were about five inches in length and a half inch wide! A veritable zoo was our new yacht.

The days and then weeks passed in a frenzy of work. Rock was shifted around to level out the ballast. Our beautiful Purple Heart wood was cut and fit athwartships to lag down the ballast. Edge timbers were placed longitudinally along the hull; these were secured by lag bolts fastened into the frames. Out of smaller dimension tongue and groove, we constructed a bulkhead just forward of the dog house, below decks. We installed storage shelves, food preparation counters, a small chart table and two quarter berths running aft under the side decks. My boy and I had great fun making do with our humble set of tools. We had a regular hand saw, a manual auger to drill holes and a screwdriver to secure the timbers. Purple Heart is a difficult wood to work with when one has no power tools, and in the evening, I felt justified in soothing my tired muscles with a beer at the Frangipani. By morning all of my aches would be gone. I would sharpen the saw and get back at it. Todd was a super helper and also a good swimmer. We plunged overboard many times each day to cool off. Occasionally, he swam over to the *Jens Juhl* to sample their goodies, knowing that Janey always had a good supply of treats.

On shore, I was happy to see Todd making friends with the local kids his age. When I pulled him out of school for two months, which turned out to be three months, I had asked him to bring his math and science text books along. He spent several hours each day reading and making notes and doing the exercises. I also made a deal with him. Together we would study the places we visited and the local people. Our curriculum included the islanders' culture, habits, the flora of the island, and the racial heritage of the people. This routine proved agreeable for both of us. We learned a lot. When Todd returned to school in Canada, his teacher asked him to give a ten minute lecture on what the Caribbean islands had taught him. My son ended up presenting daily talks for a week. His teacher was pleased. Eventually, Todd's school principal contacted me. He said something like, "The next time you sail to the islands, I have three hundred students to send along with you!"

When we were ready to start cutting and sewing sails, I went to Mr. Simmons's loft and spread out my canvas. He helped me with the layout by ensuring that the match marks on the seams were properly positioned so I wouldn't make a mess of the job. Mr. Simmons was also good enough to sew a longitudinal seam down the centre of each canvas panel to add stiffness to the mainsail. I had done some sail designing and sewing previously on *Corine*, a 47 foot gaff yawl, out of Townsville, Australia. On *Corine's* return trip to Australia from Rapa Iti, we stitched up an entire replacement mainsail, by hand, while we were underway. So, this current sewing task was no mystery to me, just hard work. Busy with my sail needles, thread, a leather hand palm, and a block of beeswax, I could easily imagine myself back aboard *Corine*, setting up a hook-line to tension the material, then stitching and stitching, seemingly forever. A week later, I was working on the bolt ropes and installing cringles for head, tack, foot, reef points, and finally, I was done. Phew. Now for the new jib. But first, a change of plan. I decided to keep the old staysail. It would serve the purpose after all even though it had holes. The seams were okay and the flax cloth was resilient. I patched the staysail with canvas then I went back to work on the jib. In another week, it was almost finished too. Progress. Our little ship was shaping up.

A fellow ashore had an ancient lifeboat compass with a four inch square copper housing. I gave him five dollars for it and then, using copper nails, I affixed the compass to the deck, starboard side, immediately aft of the dog house. On the *Jens Juhl*, Johnny had a small bag of tube-shaped, magnets, which varied in length and diameter. He gave them to me so that I could swing the compass.

This operation was fun. First, I reviewed the chart of the harbour and picked out landmarks which could be used for range markers, verifying this visually from the shore and from the boat. Then we bent on the sails, upped the anchor and went sailing back and forth on a light breeze in the harbour, with a hand-bearing compass, shouting out bearings, taking back bearings, and recording all the information. We made another pass with our magnets strategically placed and then slowly adjusted the needle until the bearings matched. On and on. The sails looked great and we were quite proud of our performance with the reduced sail plan. Finally it was done. I made up a deviation card. Hey, we had direction now!

Ice and the Kingstown Harbour War

*A*ll work and little play was making us restless, but fortunately an opportunity arose to provide a bit of excitement. Jens Juhl was heading for Tobago in several days. She needed to take on ice prior to departure. Jan asked us if we could sail to Kingstown and bring them a shipment of ice. Of course we could. We were given the contact information and supplied with a pile of old jute bags to put in the hold and we were off. The trades were kind to our new sails; not too strong as to cause undue stretching, but enough heft to sail up to St Vincent at five knots. When we reached Kingstown's anchorage, we managed to get to within about three hundred yards of the inter-island dock before the wind died. Time to start kedging. I climbed into our borrowed dinghy, loaded the anchor and gear, then rowed and stretched the chain out to set the anchor. This is how we pulled the boat toward the dock. From our new position, we managed to get the anchor line to the dock and soon we were alongside.

On the way into the harbour, a small incident occurred when a forty foot, fibreglass charter boat, a Beneteau, cut in very close to us. She was under power and in a hurry to get to the dock. The vessel was on a collision course with us and so we tried to manoeuvre ourselves out of the way, all the time waving and shouting to get the attention of the people onboard, who were drinking and having fun and not watching their course. The inevitable happened. The Beneteau glanced off our port side forward bulwarks! The crew of six were laughing, speaking very slurred French, and obviously drunk. Their antics annoyed me and we gave each other the international finger signal. They roared away, plenty pleased with themselves. Warping-in calmed me down but I made note of where they dropped their hook in the harbour, after they had discovered there was no space for them at the dock.

The iceman had seen Todd and I arrive, and in a few minutes his five man crew was loading fifteen, two-hundred pound blocks of ice aboard our little freighter. I signed the manifest and battened down the hatch, having covered the ice with our burlap bags I was certain this cargo would be content to wait for us while we had lunch. Therefore, satisfied that all was well, we went ashore for a sandwich and a drink.

Kingstown is an interesting place. We had a relaxing time on an upper, open-air balcony, studying the folks and the island vegetation surrounding the restaurant. Learning. Both of us. After we finished our sandwiches, we saw that the wind was blowing a comfortable Force 3 out of the east. Exactly what we needed for our departure.

Back onboard, we spent a few minutes discussing our sailing route 'home' to Port Elizabeth, a route which would first involve a lively run out of the harbour. Mainsail up, jib up and we were off with the wind on our tail. I steered a course for the wayward Beneteau that had abused us on her way in. I adjusted the mainsail by topping-up the boom in order to just clear the decks of our pals' plastic boat. At the last minute, they finally noticed our approach with much yelling and gesturing and spilling of drinks. We were on to them. I managed to steer perfectly - if I do say so myself - and the end of our boom struck their standing rigging a great whack. Their boat heeled almost fifteen degrees. They were falling and screaming and having a bad time, precisely as we had hoped. Sailing away, Todd and I backed up to the transom and gave them a good old 'moon' and that was it. Although we expected to see them again in Bequia, they never showed up. Thus ended the Great War of Kingstown harbour.

Following lunch, when we had returned to the boat, we found a note wedged under the doghouse hatch from a man named Douglas Steele-Lamy. He had observed our arrival manoeuvres. His message said that he was interested in our vessel. Mr. Steele-Lamy was in the West Indies with his son Doug. Could they do some travelling with us? They did join us, later on, for a few weeks in Bequia, contentedly sleeping on deck, swimming and sailing.

Douglas was a real sailor. He was familiar with gaff riggers. Fortunately for us, he was also a super diver. I will always remember the day when our anchor was not happy about coming to the surface. It was stuck in fifty-five feet of water. I have free dived to a maximum depth of forty-five feet, so I chose to make a quick trip down to investigate myself but I could not reach the anchor. Back on the surface, I explained my problem to Doug, who was already in the water. He offered to give it a try. I watched as he ventilated and folded his body and almost without a ripple, slipped below. *He learned that from a seal.*

Minutes later, Doug reappeared, gulped some air and said, "Okay Skip, she's ready to be weighed!" But back to hauling ice.

On our return trip, our little ship, about six or eight inches deeper in draft, cruised along without a fuss. Great! In little more than an hour, we were beating into Port Elizabeth. *Jens Juhl's* crew spotted us. The boys promptly secured fenders on their starboard side to enable us to come alongside without damaging either vessel. We approached on a slight angle with our scandalized main fluttering and Todd standing by to let go on the jib halyard. A soft landing. Our sails were furled, the hatch was opened and everyone began offloading. Their main cargo boom swung out over our deck. Below, two of us worked the slings and the ice was efficiently transferred to *Jens Juhl's* hold. Kenny, the skipper, was onboard and very happy with our delivery service. He said he'd pay us but I refused his money and assured him that we would always be grateful to him and his crew for their friendship and help and generosity. We did, however, accept another meal invitation.

At dinner, Todd related the tale of our Kingstown Harbour wars. Roars of boisterous laughter accompanied his story. We discussed the too common problem of boaters drinking and driving. Everyone agreed, over cool beers, that such behaviour was just not on. Hmmm. Our sailboats remained rafted up for the night until my boy and I moved to our own anchorage early the next morning.

New Crew and Our First Gale

*W*ork continued. *We passed pleasant days getting to know the locals and learn more about their skiffs and two-bowed sailing craft. I made a deal to buy one of these old double-enders from a young fellow's elderly papa. That's how we finally acquired our tender.*

Bequia is a busy community with lots to do and see. There are many skilled local carvers producing precision boat models. Marvellous examples of their craftsmanship can be seen throughout the island. One fellow paddled alongside and said he would build a miniature copy of our boat. Sadly, we could not afford such a luxury and had to decline. Other sellers and barterers came by with fresh fruit. Superb eats were available at reasonable prices and there was always a good supply onboard. We also made weekly excursions to the local farmers' market where lively vendors set up stalls displaying fresh vegetables and crafts. One Rasta guy only sold peppers; he delighted in slipping some truly hot samples into our basket; our lips burned whenever we prepared these fiery vegetables for a meal. Bread was purchased every second day from a lady whose stove and oven were a couple of old metal drums. Tasty bread and only fifty cents a loaf. In the evenings, we could be found at the Frangipani listening to guitar music and socializing with other sailors. There is nothing like a good guitar, a good beer and laughter. One night, much to Todd's embarrassment, I was handed a guitar and asked for a sailing song. I gave them *Blow the Man Down*. That was a mistake. The crowd insisted on my whole repertoire. Everyone sang and danced, and from that time on, we were accepted as 'folks.' We made even more friends. Happy days indeed.

But the time had come to go head out among the Windward Islands. Our new crew member was arriving. Todd and I took the *Friendship Rose* to Kingstown and went to the airport to pick Brigid up. She had relatives who owned a property on the east side of Bequia. We had first met her years ago in West Vancouver when I was Brigid's sailing instructor. When her courses were completed, she became a regular cruising customer, along with her friends, on weekend excursions among the Gulf Islands. *Friendship Rose* delivered the three of us back to Bequia. Where else in the world could you travel, under sail, and bash through the trade wind seas on a ninety-foot schooner, with decks loaded with cargo lashed under tarps and passengers (traffickers) crowded together on the leeward side to avoid the worst of the spray. Everyone loved *Friendship Rose*.

On the Friendship Rose en-route to St. Vincent

A few more days were spent at Bequia, showing Brigid around, hiking, picking tamarinds off trees and coconuts off the ground and letting the trade winds blow our cares away. Then it was time to go.

One day, midmorning, we set sail for St Lucia. I expected to reach the Pitons, at the south end, by eight or nine that night. Unfortunately, we did not have a marine radio to tell us about the gales that were expected that afternoon. Also, without a barometer, we were not aware of the weather change, so we travelled on, towing our Two-Bow tender astern. The dinghy was too heavy and awkward to pull on deck. This fact added to our woes later on.

The voyage started out well. We held about six knots, right on course. Three hours into the trip though, the wind changed direction, backing into the north. The sky and cloud cover were still unchanged. There were no visual signals to alert us of trouble. I let the boat fall off on the starboard tack and as the wind increased, we put a reef in the main and dropped the jib, keeping all sail inboard. Within the hour, we had a Force 7 gale to deal with and it was rougher than hell. I could see the tender taking on water and knew it would be parting company with us soon if this weather didn't improve. One hour later and the wind increased to a Force 8 (forty knots) and I decided to heave-to. I did not know our vessel well enough yet to have confidence in my decisions under these conditions. The winds continued to howl. At sunset they veered, which suggested a weather change. Todd kept an eye on our now swamped dinghy. He reported her status every few minutes but the poor little boat had become such a heavy drag astern, I knew we would be compromised if the wind increased any more. Axe in hand, I chopped the painter and sadly, that was the end of our two-bow tender.

We had been blown a long way to the west. I thought we should continue under a reefed main and staysail toward St Lucia, which was still not visible in the darkness and these gale conditions. Gradually, we started to make headway into ten foot waves. Hour after hour, we banged and crashed into our first gale at sea. This was certainly a wet, rough way to learn about how our new vessel handled but as we proceeded, I gained more confidence in *Ancestor*'s sailing abilities. This storm was a bone in her teeth and I let her chomp away at it. We managed to eat some fruit and sea-biscuits to maintain our strength. At dawn, the wind settled to a Force 4 from the north east and we could see our island on the horizon. The reef was taken out of the main, the jib was hoisted, and we beat toward land through the confused seas. Exhausted but happy, we congratulated ourselves and our boat for riding out the storm when *Ancestor* tacked into the harbour at the Pitons at about midday.

The anchorage there is deep. The steep bottom slopes away from shore. We went in until about two chains from the beach and then let the anchor go and sailed it into the bottom. Sails were furled and I immediately lit a fire to cook up a much needed meal.

At the Pitons, the normal routine is to drop anchor and row a line ashore to tie off onto a palm tree. By adjusting the tension on this line one can ensure the anchor will hold. We were unable to do this. Before I could even swim ashore with a line, the boat was dragging her anchor and drifting out of the bay. Sails went up, anchor too, and we began manoeuvring to what we hoped was a better spot. But it wasn't better. We repeated this trick a few times. On the fourth try, Todd, with a wrench on a line acting as his depth sounder, called out the depths in his hearty young voice, and now sure of the water depth we sailed the anchor into the bottom. We got it right. A fast swim to the beach with a light gauge rope and we were properly tethered.

That described *our* arrival to the Pitons. Several years later the situation changed. Locals would come out to the boat as you approached the bay and these lads would negotiate a price for tying your shore line to a tree. But in *our* day, they hadn't twigged to this lucrative business and we had to do it the hard way.

The Pitons are spectacular conical peaks. To the north, Mont Soufrière emits sulphurous fumes which tend to sweep down to the coast and perfume the air for the sailors anchored below. Fortunately, the winds do not swing into the north very often; one usually enjoys nothing but clear air and cool sea breezes.

We spent two days here with five other boats in the anchorage. One fellow, after scoping us out for some time, rowed over to get acquainted. When he heard our story, including the fact that we had lost our dinghy, he generously offered to take us ashore anytime we desired. We accepted on numerous occasions.

So far, our sailing plan was to continue southward; maybe check out Palm Island again and Petit St Vincent, and anchor wherever we found ourselves at the end of the sailing day. I was eager to get going. I wanted to make sure our new mainsail had not been stretched out of shape in the gale and so early next morning, we were off on the trade wind and sliding south. Great sailing it was, and the mainsail was just fine.

Todd and Brigid at the Pitons

Off to Grenada

*A*s an upgrade on the boat, I wanted to replace the parrels on the luff of the mainsail. I wanted to use metal so that they would be inclined to rush down the mast when furling the sail, and metal parrels would allow easy hoisting of the mainsail on a downwind course. That was my plan anyway. We stopped again at Bequia to see what could be found for this purpose. I met with Bluesy Simmons, the son of the sailmaker, a renowned sailor and all-round, fine fellow. After thinking for a few minutes, he took us to meet another sailor who had recently done salvage work on a wreck. This gentleman showed us a whole pile of stuff. He had lengths of half inch diameter copper rod, which until recently had been electrical bus-bars on some unfortunate ship! They were precisely what I had in mind. I bought enough to make up our new parrels. Onboard, I measured, made a sketch, and then took the rods ashore to a machine shop to make up the shapes. When they were installed, they worked well, sliding smoothly up and down the mast. Next, we walked to the windward side of the island to visit a fellow who sold deadeyes, bullseyes, and lizards for local sailing craft. His were well made with Greenheart wood. I bought some lizards for fair-leading the jib sheets. Things were progressing nicely. We might soon have everything we needed for efficient sailing.

The two Dougs had joined us in Bequia and we had many fine times together. Their plan was to be dropped off on one of the Tobago Cays to camp for awhile. On the day we parted company, Doug senior gave me two wonderful gifts. One was a chronometer, about three inches in diameter, in a brass casing. The other gift was a bamboo sail-needle case. As I write these words years later, I still have the needle case but I cannot recall what became of the chronometer! Thanks Doug.

Doug and his son found their dream island in the Cays. We all swam to the island in shallow water, with the camping gear held above our heads, and our finned feet working overtime. Nothing important got wet. It felt like we were abandoning them but they were obviously quite content to be left alone. Doug was already assembling his spear gun when I swam back to my boat.

Our southerly travels continued. The magic had not dimmed since the night when I first set eyes on *Ancestor*. Ideal sailing winds; tropic sunsets; occasional green flashes, and fathomless night skies turned even breathing into a mystery. There were markets to visit, sailors from all over the world to converse with and warm pristine seas to soak and dive in. Here were amazingly clear waters which allowed me study how our anchor sets in a sandy bottom, how the vessel reacts to wind gusts in a variety of conditions, how she veers or backs, and how much she heels.

One day, on our way into the Carenage at St George, we sailed past Kick 'Em Jenny, a submarine volcano off the north coast of Grenada. Once inside St George harbour, we altered course southward and drifted with full main and jib through the narrow channel leading to a lagoon anchorage. It was a busy harbour, considering the traffic on the road surrounding the lagoon, the hustle and bustle business of the Grenada Yacht Services going full speed ahead, and all the boats around us. We needed to adapt to Grenada's fast pace.

Our first priority was to acquire a new dinghy. Swimming ashore to small islands is fine and dandy but it was time to indulge in a little

On a mooring, St. George, Grenada

luxury. Our nearest neighbour was a thirty footer called Banana Boat and when I realized she had two small dinghies alongside, I wanted to find out if we might get lucky. I swam over and hailed her skipper.

Bill Colon was from Nova Scotia. He had been diagnosed with terminal cancer ten years earlier in Halifax and his reaction to his diagnosis had been to buy a sailing vessel, head south, and die in the sun. Two out of three. Had he been cured by his positive attitude and his tropical life style? He ended up staying in Grenada, building dinghies, making oars, and doing all sorts of woodwork on transient boats. He was more than happy to sell us a dinghy which I bought on the spot. The name on its transom was *Full Speed Ahead*. I rowed her back to my boat at half throttle, feeling very pleased with myself.

Other than Bequia, my favourite port in the West Indies is St George, Grenada. Everything is to my liking here, except for the traffic, which goes with Grenada's growing population I suppose; I always spent too much money there too!

We went ashore for showers at Grenada Yacht Services and then had a snack at the GYS restaurant, before heading back to the boat for a lazy and lovely evening. All around the lagoon there were musicians tuning their 'pans', and playing a few warm up melodies and not too far away, there was an evangelical jam session adding to the mix. Competing for souls perhaps? I suspected that it was an uphill battle for the evangelical folks.

We always slept on deck, with the sleeping mind on the alert for possible rain showers, which would have us occasionally scurrying for the hatch. We scurried on this night and our crickets, centipedes and cockroaches quit snoring when we dashed below. In the morning, *Ring Anderson* was motoring into port. What a sight she was. Her skipper and crew waved and gave us the thumbs-up greeting. It was good to see our friends again.

St. George is Ring's home port. She slipped into her berth at GYS. We gave them an hour to get settled before rowing over to say hello. David Collier invited us aboard and soon we were sharing travel tales. David was from British Columbia. It was interesting to compare notes on the different paths which had brought us to this same destination in the West Indies. David was in charge of Ring's tender and he seemed to be super busy, going to the shops and markets to buy provisions for their next charter trip. We stayed late.

In the morning, a red-hulled, fifty foot Van de Stadt sloop, named *Carcharias* - which is the Greek word for a great white shark - arrived and dropped anchor nearby. Her last port of call was Las Palmas in the Canary Islands. The *Carcharias* crew was ready for some shore leave. John and Peggy Grey, Canadians, were heading back to Vancouver after a five year stint, working in the Middle East; their most recent assignment was in Ankara, Turkey. We were destined to become well acquainted over the next months but none of us knew that then.

Work continued on our boat. A second coat of enamel paint had the cap rail looking tidy again. Two more days were spent building a crutch for the main boom. Brigid and Todd often went to Grand Anse beach to swim and get into mischief. There were fresh water showers close to the water so they would return looking clean and spiffy and making comments about my sweaty, unwashed appearance and holding their noses and things like that. Snobs is what I called them. While they were off playing one day, I came upon a piece of hardwood on shore and trimmed it down to replace a bad old cleat. I shaped it and bedded it in red lead, lagging it in position on the port side bulwarks, ready for a jib sheet.

I checked out the bilge pump. Could I make it more efficient? Despite the fact that the pump was amazing in its simplicity and worked well, the thing was also a man-killer. Imagine a vertical square box made from two by eight inch planks; its top protrudes a foot above the deck; a two inch diameter pole extends upward from the box. The top of the pole has no appendages but on the bottom, there is a square piece of thick rubber (ex-car tire) fixed perpendicular to the pole. Operating instructions: 1. Grab pole firmly with both hands. 2. Lift pole quickly and lower it with a drop motion. 3. Repeat step two until water spills over the box and onto the deck. 4. Continue until the bilge is dry! Not what you'd call a model of efficiency. Furthermore I had to fortify myself with a generous bowl of oatmeal prior to using it!

The rudder and tiller were rather different as well. The rudder and rudder post consisted of one piece of wood and the rudder itself was small; maybe four square feet. The post was rounded and four inches in diameter. A rectangular hole had been cut into the rudder post near the top, with a slight taper in it and with smaller dimension at the rear of the rudder post. A short tiller, from a crook of island cedar, was shaped to fit the tapered hole. I rammed the tiller into the hole and placed a square boat nail through the end to hold it in place.

The rudder post housing was fashioned from two pieces of wood which had been painstakingly carved with half circles on each piece. When both sections were fixed together, I had a square box shape with a circular hole over four inches in diameter running through it. "Dis de old way mon," a man had told me in Carriacou.

In other news, *Jens Juhl* also arrived in port and arranged to be hauled out on the large screw-lift. They needed to redo the bottom and check out a few leaks which had started on a trip from Barbados, when *Jens Juhl* was heavily loaded and pounding her way through heavy seas. So, our friends were here, which cheered this skipper and his crew, especially Todd, who was already looking forward to Janey's galley-baked goodies. When *Jens Juhl* was settled on the lift, her transom was twenty-five feet out of the water. Todd hurried over with his pal Graham. I watched them diving off the transom, trying their best to splash all the water out of the lagoon. Quite a sight.

One day I went for a walk alone, through the botanical gardens, to remove myself from the activity in the lagoon and to do some serious thinking. Let it be known. I don't do serious well. Especially when it involves timing and resources. April was upon us. We had been expecting a wire in the amount of five thousand dollars to arrive at Barclays Bank in St. George. This would be the last instalment from the buyer of Anywhere, the forty-seven foot yawl I had sold in the fall of 1973. We needed the money to continue our rambling ways among the islands but the funds had not come and it became apparent that I would have to fly to Vancouver and find employment to build up the cruising kitty once again. I smoked my pipe on a bench surrounded by teak trees. I watched their big, heart-shaped leaves crackling together in the breeze. That calmed me. It'll all work out, Jon. When my pipe was done, I jumped into the dinghy, rowed to the boat and tackled my chores. In my absence, Todd and Brigid had painted the port side deck and bulwarks. I complimented them and teased, "Should I go ashore more often?"

That evening we were invited to *Carcharias* for dinner. Peggy had boiled up a large pot of pasta, to which she added vegetables and spices aplenty. The Greys said they were planning to weigh anchor on the following Monday. Until then, they were waiting for engine parts and they wanted time to complete their repairs before sailing to Vancouver via Panama. A couple, who had intended to help them on this next leg of the voyage were unavailable at the last minute. John Grey asked me, "Would you and your crew consider sailing with us?" The crew who had done the trans-Atlantic crossing with John and Peggy, had prior commitments and could not do the Panama and Canada portions of the trip. Furthermore, *Carcharias*' owners did not feel competent enough to handle their vessel by themselves on such a long passage. The Grey's son was hoping to meet them in Panama but nothing was definite. I conferred with my own crew and they were thumbs-up and eager. It was a win-win situation. I was strapped for cash and here was a free ride home. We clinked wine glasses to seal the deal.

With this sudden change in plans, we had three days to get organized. In the morning, I rowed ashore to look at an abandoned engine block on the beach. Exactly what we needed for a mooring block. At the marina, I enlisted a couple of enthusiastic volunteers to help me. They were game for my mooring program. We borrowed a twelve foot long work platform with a motor on it, went over to the engine block and winched it aboard.

Next. I attached fifty feet of chain onto the block with a float for the top end of the chain. We motored out into the lagoon, and in an area free of boat traffic, we dumped the block overboard with a great splash. *Ancestor* was towed over and tied off on her new mooring. She would wait there obediently until I returned in the early weeks of January 1975.

Next. Our sails were dried thoroughly, unbent, loaded in the dinghy and rowed ashore, where I stored them in one of *Ring Anderson's* lockers. Next. We brought over all the other worthwhile gear that was removable. My poor ship looked naked and forlorn. I promised her that this was a temporary inconvenience and I'd return before she knew it.

Next. I paid a visit to *Banana Boat* and asked Bill if he would do some work on *Ancestor* while I was up north. We needed a forward hatch on deck ahead of the mast, with a good, hold-down feature to secure it from below. We also needed a small access hatch built into the main cargo hatch. Bill offered to sell us a Primus one-burner, kerosene stove, mounted in full gimbal rings on a cast bronze stand. He would also keep his eyes open for a forty gallon water cask for us. He agreed to all of this and he would wait for payment until next January.

Thus ended our sojourn in Grenada.

Westward on S/V Carcharias

*L*ater that same day, we took our passports to John Grey so he could prepare his crew list for the customs people and get his clearance documents. On Monday morning, we rolled up our sleeping bags and along with our personal stuff, the three of us moved aboard Carcharias and signed on for the voyage.

We cleared the harbour, hoisted sail and slid away from Grenada. "What a great boat!" I exclaimed, just before John started to explain that *Carcharias* would not go downwind under genoa alone. No matter what he tried, the jib overpowered the performance of the auto helm. Being a cheeky fellow, I responded, "I can make her sail properly."

Although reluctant to undertake anything new, John said, "I'll give anything a try. Once."

I suspected that, whenever the genoa is set on the whisker pole, there is too much weather helm. My solution? Attach a swivel block to the end of the main boom and lead the jib sheet through the block, securing the boom forward with a guy rope and a downhaul to hold it in position. We did this and adjusted the sail, which now set with a belly of wind. We trimmed everything until the strain was off the helm. When John engaged the electronic auto helm, it steered like a charm. Our skipper shook his head, muttered thanks and off we went. Two days later, we raised Curacao and made our first stop, at the Spanish Waters lagoon on the south shore.

From Spanish Waters (Sari Fundi Marina) we strolled around the bay and hailed a taxi, which consumed us and all the additional bodies it could hold. We arrived at Willemstad, where there are several offices that must be visited in order to complete the customs formalities. Only when our duty was done could we indulge in tourist time.

In the inner-harbour of Willemstad, small vessels, draped with colourful awnings, tie up to peddle fruit and vegetables. They pull in early every morning from Venezuela. Willemstad is a gorgeous city with a safe harbour; a miniature replica of Amsterdam. The tall, narrow buildings have the Dutch style booms, extending from the peaked roofs that hoist goods up from the street to various floor levels. The city is an expensive place to shop, but one must buy what is needed even if one is a poor sailor. Other than the Dutch language, Papiamento, the local language which is a blend of many languages, is pleasing to the ear. To my mind, it is a happy sound.

Two days later we made the short run from Curacao to Aruba and anchored at Oranjestad. This city is laid out in a circular pattern with the centre at the hub. The heart and soul of the community. It was fascinating to walk the streets, take in all the sights and look at the expensive wares in the windows. Oranjestad's ornate buildings are themselves deserving of lingering looks and appreciation. We agreed that, on another voyage, we would spend a few weeks here.

As usual, we met with other cruising sailors and as usual, we enjoyed exchanging stories about the wonders of Aruba and the fun of travelling under sail.

After spending several days here, we did the paper work and set sail for Panama. The winds were very gusty, at Force 6, on that first day out. *Carcharias* was making eleven knots under a small jib. What a ride! Safe but exhilarating. The following day, when John started the engine to charge his batteries, he encountered a problem. A high pressure hydraulic pipe, which feeds the transmission, had corroded and was spraying oil all over the engine room! The engine was switched off and we scratched our heads. John decided to continue under sail only, to Cartagena, Colombia, the nearest port. I unscrolled the large scale chart and studied the approach. If Francis Drake could sail here, we could too. And so it was that we beat our way into the bay where Cartagena sprawls along the northern shore. Many sand bars and a poor buoyage system made our entrance challenging but we managed and eventually our hull kissed the dock, at the Club de Pesca, in the heart of the city.

There was an unsettling hint of revolution in the air. The local officials were being very cautious about visitors. It took hours to get clearance to go ashore, and when we did, we were advised to carry our 'Permisso Para Desembarco' clearly visible in our hands at all times on shore. Every few minutes, we encountered an army patrol, usually a pair of troopers, with guns at the ready. When confronted by these uniformed fellows, we learned, do not reach into a pocket to find your pass, because that might cause your immediate death. Raise your hand and display your pass. Simple as that.

Other than this silly inconvenience, we were free to partake of the city's sights, and this is what we did every day. The skipper had to find a marine engine dealer who would have the part needed for our dead 'iron jib'. On the third day, he and Peggy rode the bus to Barranquilla where they were lucky enough to find a replacement pipe.

While in Cartagena, the weather was balmy, with only an occasional rain shower in the early morning hours. Which meant we could sleep on deck. Great! I had found a bronze belaying pin on the beach and when we got into our sleeping bags one night, I gave it to Todd, explaining that there were a lot of thieves around and he might need the pin to defend himself. To an eleven year old boy this was exciting stuff and he placed the 'weapon' close by before falling asleep.

A noise woke me at 2:00 a.m. in the morning. I looked toward the bow. A couple of guys in a dinghy were trying to steal *Carcharias'* anchor. They were finding this to be a difficult task and now they were moving toward our stern, gripping the rail to pull themselves along the hull. I jiggled Todd awake and pointed in their direction. Quivering, Todd grabbed his belaying pin and prepared for battle. Our location was obscured from the robbers' line of sight. On they came until they were right beside us. Todd looked at me, wide-eyed, waiting to take a swing. At the right moment, I nodded and he whacked a hand clinging to the railing. The resulting scream was painfully loud in the stillness of the night. We watched our thieves frantically paddling away. Todd sat there, still in his sleeping bag, with a smug look on his face, and still holding the brass pin. I wondered how many broken bones the one fellow had suffered, but I did not dwell on the incident. We had a hard time getting back to sleep.

The Club de Pesca, where we were moored, has a thick wall surrounding it. Several cannon balls are embedded there for local colour; a reminder of the grand old days when the Spanish found themselves under attack by the British. I later re-read Francis Drake's very entertaining account of one siege.

A vessel sharing our dock was a thirty-five foot Sea Runner trimaran, the *Scrimshaw*, with the designer, Jim Brown, his wife and sons aboard. There was also a twenty-five foot trimaran with a teenage, single-hander aboard. Todd and the Brown lads went sailing with him one day. They returned at dusk sporting awful sunburns. *Crazy kids!* I shook my head, hosed Todd down with fresh water, dried him and applied oil to his blistered torso. I suppose the boys were too preoccupied with their sailing adventure to worry about protective clothing. Todd had tender skin for a few days and I think he learned an important lesson. His sad little face reminded me of my laxity as a parent too.

Two days later, with the engine repaired, we were ready to go. The harbour chart was stowed in the cockpit, for easy access. John took the helm to negotiate the entrance himself. I did not object, of course, because it was his vessel. Brigid, Todd and I sat on the forward cabin to watch the scenery. This had been a fun stop since none of us had been to Cartagena before.

When I glanced ahead at our track, while Todd, Brigid and I were talking about all the fun we had here, I saw that we were off course for the first marker. I went to the cockpit and mentioned this to the skipper. He was annoyed and said, "Not to worry. I know exactly where I'm going." I shut up and returned to my perch.

As we neared the sandbar, I suggested to Todd and Brigid that we all hang on for the crunch, since we were sailing at 8 knots. When we hit the bar, our abrupt stop was quite a shock. We barely managed to hold on without being thrown from the deck. I asked Brigid to check on Peggy below, and then Todd and I went to the cockpit to confer with our skipper. "Look at this chart, Jon. I was right on course, wasn't I?" I understood how John had gotten confused and spent a few minutes with him until he could see the course error.

He wanted to call the coast guard immediately for a tow but I assured him that we could get off the sandbar by ourselves if we got right to work. He agreed. We launched the dinghy, put a small Danforth anchor, chain, and rope into it and I rowed out to set the anchor as far away from the boat as possible. Then I rowed back to *Carcharias* and took the main halyard and attached it to the anchor line. We took the tail end of the halyard to a sheet winch and started cranking. The boat heeled about forty-five degrees to starboard and we let it rest there for awhile to see what would happen. Evidently, we did not have sufficient power yet to skid her off the bar. John raised the genoa and sheeted it in to provide a bit more force. *Carcharias* started to move a little and we gave the genoa some more belly and applied more power to the anchor. It took an hour and I had to reset the kedge anchor once more but finally we were afloat.

Once the boat was shipshape again, *Carcharias* headed south once more. I stayed in the cockpit for a few minutes to make sure John was on course and then I went forward to join the others. The skipper, a bit out of sorts, had asked me to leave, so I figured he was okay.

The second grounding was a repeat of the first. We used the same technique to re-float the vessel. I was getting exhausted from the kedging work and the skipper became more reluctant to see reason. Once again I was told not to interfere and so I returned forward to Brigid and Todd. John's behaviour was puzzling. Todd wanted me to physically remove him from the helm. I informed my son that such an act is mutiny. A marine court of law would do more than slap my wrists. Earlier, when Brigid had checked on Peggy in the salon during the first grounding, John's wife commented quietly that we could now understand why they needed crew. I chewed on this information for a few minutes, trying to figure out why a professional engineer like John Grey, was unable to find and follow a marked channel, even if, as in this situation, the markers were only wooden stakes. But with binoculars and a reliable chart, how could there be a problem?

We were now close to Isla Boca Grande, which was separated by a narrow channel from a smaller island to the south. The Spanish, in a past era of marine warfare, had laid chain across this channel, attached to the larger island by a hidden windlass. They would tighten the chain when an enemy ship approached and the chain would rip the bottom of the enemy ship and sink her within minutes. An efficient scheme. During our passage, there were different dangers to avoid. While we were in port, a very bad incident occurred exactly at this spot. An American sailboat had anchored for the night in the channel, near shore, and next day, a marine patrol found all three crew members murdered; bandit territory. The sooner we were far from here the better.

A half mile east of Isla Boca Grande, when the tropical night was closing in, our boat ran aground again in these dangerous waters. We used the same procedure as before, but with another anchor added to the mix. The locals were keeping an eye on us and as the sun kissed the western sea, several boats put out from the shore. Not good. They came, not to assist us but to estimate our strength before trying anything. I kept on cranking the winches and set the anchors for another pull.

It was hard work, but adrenalin and hard work are better than being attacked. I asked for all hands on deck and we positioned a search light to blind anyone who got too close. Peggy, Brigid and Todd carried broom handles and boat hooks to make it look like we had weapons. The sailors who had been killed were butchered by machete and knife. If this was the case, we stood a good chance of defending ourselves in a brawl. The locals kept their distance, a hundred yards away, waiting for an opportunity to get the upper hand on us. Our situation was tense but fortunately we were soon free and as the curtains of night dropped from the heavens, we were able to leave.

Completely exhausted, I told John that he had better go below right now since I could not take any more of this interesting workout and if he refused then I would most likely get violent and that was something I didn't want to do. He went below.

Brigid, Todd and I organized three-hour watches, then the jib was boomed out and away we went, masthead light on for other traffic to see. I could not sleep because I was mentally and physically drained. I took the first watch. Todd took the second. He is very capable on a boat. Although he has a tendency towards motion sickness, he overcomes his wooziness when there is a job to be done. On this night, I had been observing the planet Venus and our course, and when he took over I showed him how to steer by this bright planet; since Venus moves approximately fifteen degrees every hour, I instructed him to adjust his course every half hour to take the planet's relative motion into account. He was comfortable with this routine. Todd didn't use the compass once during his watch. Brigid did the same. The automatic pilot stayed off all night.

I was worried about an encounter with John but he came on deck, said good morning, and appeared to have forgotten yesterday's disagreement. Both Peggy and John were fine people and I liked them a lot. After a hearty breakfast we discussed the rest of the trip to Panama. I really wanted to stop at the Archipelago de las Mulatas, (the San Blas Islands), for a day or two. I spoke about the island inhabitants, the Kuna, who manage the coconut groves there. Plus I was hoping to purchase some of the very colourful molas which are made by the women and girls. My suggestion appealed to everyone. I altered course for Puyades Island, my favourite anchorage in that archipelago.

Fortunately we arrived before sunset and dropped our hook in thirty-five feet of water, in the island's lee. Paradise! On the island's windward side, reefs breast the ocean waves with a muted but crashing roar. It was a perfect evening to sit on deck and allow the magic of the place to envelope us.

Our other crew member was a white cat. The Greys adopted her in Turkey. We have all seen white cats before but this one was totally deaf! No problem says you. So what? This is what. If that cat was sleeping below and you approached her from behind where she could not see you, she would explode, claws out and striking and she never missed. I learned a painful lesson our first day aboard when this little feline punctured my right leg. The wound bled freely and hurt a lot. From that time on, I moved cautiously around our white, four-legged friend.

Next morning, we were all ashore wandering around. I showed them the local well, an excavation about eight feet deep, set back from the tide line. The sea water, which fills this depression is somewhat filtered by the sand and it is diluted by rainwater falling into the well. The water is brackish but drinkable. Everyone took turns tasting using a convenient section of bamboo as a cup.

In only ten minutes, we walked across the island to the windward side. We listened to the thunder of the breakers on the reef as they curled and crashed. The shoreline is gentle sand with succulent plants creeping towards the coconut palms. It is a beautiful place, a spa, to be savoured by the visitor who should not even care about tomorrow. Naturally we unanimously decided to stay for one more day.

John was a good swimmer. He speared fish for our dinners as if there was nothing to it. There is nothing as delicious as fresh fish for dinner.

I recalled my last attempt at spear fishing back in Grenada when I spent about an hour trying to get close enough for a clean shot. The fish were easily spooked and I was unlucky. I remember diving twenty-five feet to where I might find a parrot fish lurking under an overhang of coral. I poked my spear into a hole and a moray eel shot out at me. Startled, my heart rate accelerating, I back-paddled and gave him a flip of my fins. So much for my fishing.

Our next stop was Holandes Cays, a small group of islands to the west, where we spent several fine days. There was always fresh fish on the table, we had beer, and no one was eager to go anywhere else, as we knew we soon must do.

On the first morning at Holandes Cays, two canoes sailed up to us. The Kuna Indians are historically known as the Cuna. These people had molas for sale. Peggy invited them onboard for a cool drink before they left for Puyades Island. This encounter was a highlight of our stay.

The Panama Canal is only one hundred and twenty miles away. After a few days, we set sail. Our passage was swift and comfortable.

We entered the north end of the canal system and sailed into Limon Bay. When he was satisfied with the anchoring, the skipper went ashore to clear customs and make the necessary arrangements for transiting the canal. The first step is a survey to establish the vessel's tonnage measurement for the transit. With this data, the authorities calculate the costs, give you the regulations and determine the date and time of each vessel's canal transit. When this had been finalized, we moved to the Panama Canal Yacht Club and took a berth to wait for our transit day. The yacht club caters to transient small boat traffic; the PCYC has all the amenities, including an excellent bar where the beer flows freely, and free advice for any questions one might have. The twin cities of Cristóbal and Colón occupy the east shore of Limon Bay; Cristóbal spans the waterfront and Colón occupies a more easterly setting.

Cristóbal is much calmer than its 'twin' city. Both are very lively, overcrowded, and impoverished. During the daytime, either city should hold no dangers for the traveller but at night both cities can get rather dicey.

The Colón Caper, a Canal Transit and a 727 Jet

In my opinion, throughout history, adventure is something inflicted upon you, not something you seek and certainly not something you pay for!

Todd, Brigid and I decided we would walk to a Chinese restaurant in Colón. Sailing gives anyone an appetite because of the constant motion and exhilarating fresh air. Anyway, at sunset we walked to Colón and found the recommended restaurant where the food was delicious and we did justice to it. The eatery was packed with a cross section of races and languages around the tables. It was dark outside. And peaceful.

When our meal was done, I left my son and Brigid to check out the front of the building. At street level there was a facing wall set at an angle to the entrance and in this recess there was a long counter with coffee machines. I thought I would buy a coffee and bring it back to our table. When I was paying the salesgirl, I saw a lot of people on the sidewalk and four fellows were standing apart from the crowd. Two of the young men held knives and they were coming in my direction. My first sip of coffee tasted bitter. Adrenalin flooded my body.

Weapon. What can I do? I went to the coffee machine and picked up a full, hot Pyrex pot of coffee and flung it squarely at my assailants. The scalding liquid sprayed the faces of the knife handlers. That stopped them. Momentarily. I grabbed another pot, of boiling water, and this time, I managed to do a better job of dousing the four men. I could hear the cafe manager yelling to me from the doorway, "Come in!" I needed no further encouragement. In the restaurant, the patrons were jammed against the far wall and as soon as I was safely inside, the door was locked and bolted. Todd and Brigid had not even been aware the confrontation on the street. I joined them at the back of the room.

The manager had made an emergency phone call and a few minutes later, a siren wailed and an American jeep arrived. One MP driver and a pair of armed marines emerged with their firearms at the ready. A welcome sight. We were hustled to the jeep and away from danger. Back at the yacht club, one of the marines warned, "Never, never, go into Colón at night unless you want trouble." We thanked the soldiers and I ordered a second coffee at the yacht club restaurant having spilled my first coffee on the streets of Colón. After an hour, my heart beat returned to normal and my muscles relaxed. Adrenalin is useful when it is needed, but it's slow to be absorbed back into the body, and then one experiences a kind of sickly feeling along with fatigue and lassitude. I slept well that night and by morning I had recovered.

News came that John and Peggy's son and his wife would be joining *Carcharias* in Panama. This meant that the three of us had to revise our own, ongoing travel plans. We researched the possibility of signing on to another vessel bound for Hawaii or the Pacific Northwest but there were none advertised and so we agreed to fly back to Vancouver from here.

We took the isthmus train to Panama City, one of the best train rides in the tropics, with glimpses of Gatun Lake through the trees. At a travel agent in the city, we made flight reservations and then trained back to Cristóbal and the yacht club in time to be *Carcharias'* line handlers on her trip through the canal.

Small vessels transiting the canal are required to have four line-handlers aboard, plus the skipper and a pilot. Canal men, standing on the walls high above, shouted, "stand back," when they tossed monkey-fists, attached to thin ropes, onto the decks. Four thumps, two on each side and the lines were at our feet! We fastened the mooring lines (one hundred feet each), and they pulled them taut from the sides of the lock to secure the boat and control her position as each lock flooded. Great sport and a fun ride with all that turbulent water rushing in! Safer at sea, I think.

Midway through the series of locks, Gatun Lake is a beautiful stretch of fresh, warm water, (average 84° F), with stunning views in all directions. Ships follow the designated channels and their propellers stir up the lake water, keeping the resident crocodiles at bay. You never see these creatures close by. Crocs prefer the shore edges where life is tranquil and easy.

Our passage from the Atlantic to the Pacific lasted twelve hours. We arrived at the Balboa Yacht Club and found a mooring before dark.

The pilot was whisked away on a canal launch and we were free to contemplate the Pacific Ocean and all the ship traffic sliding by only a hundred yards away from our boat: cargo carriers, automobile carriers, cruise liners, oil tankers. We saw them all.

Next day, we signed off the ship's documents, grabbed our passports, hugged John and Peggy, hopped into a taxi and said, "Tocumen Airport, please." We suddenly found ourselves hanging on to one another desperately. Our driver set a new speed record for the fastest ever flight to the airport. He was totally nuts, blowing his horn every few seconds, racing through red lights, weaving from side to side across the road and all the while telling us how great a certain Panamanian boxer was and what his chances were to win a world title. Miraculously still alive and in one piece, we found ourselves screaming to a stop at the departures area. I believe anyone going to that airport by taxi will have a similar adventure and the passenger is extremely grateful to have survived.

At Guatemala City, we changed planes and flew to Los Angles where we transferred to yet another flight. Eventually the three of us landed at Vancouver International Airport, feeling shell-shocked and dopey, but we agreed; nothing goes to windward like a jet aircraft. Todd and I said farewell to Brigid and headed home.

Interlude

On the coast of British Columbia, the month of May is gentle. Fruit trees are in bloom; spring flowers too. Inland, the first trees are in leaf; aspens cast a beautiful light green colour and add their sweet scent sap to the air. Crocuses have been in bloom since March, and other early-rising shrubs, in protected areas, are budding. Interlude

One can forget the tropics for awhile and appreciate the welcome and changing seasons. Northerners are busily getting ready for summertime and planning vacations in the mountains and on the lakes and rivers. Preparations are sometimes as exciting as the holidays themselves. In the meantime, we earn a living to make it all happen. I found it somewhat difficult to shift gears from the romantic tropics to a structured work ethic-based lifestyle; but I made the effort, became a technologist again, and faced my present reality.

Work was okay. My only complaint was that I had to transition from 'laid back' to 'high gear' in short order. My current employer had received a communication from a nuclear pump supplier out east. The supplier would ship a Volute Case pump to Gam-X Inspections Ltd., in North Vancouver and my job would be to prepare a revised radiographic inspection procedure, developed ASAP. He and his company were of the opinion that the existing procedure was not revealing all of the casting defects in the pump casing; this resulted in leaks when under pressure. My name had come up and my boss began grinning as soon as I walked in the door.

That was the start of a few busy months for me. When the nuclear pump procedure had been accepted and signed-off on, I found myself travelling across the province, performing x-ray and ultrasonic weld inspections.

Perhaps working for a living is a noble pursuit. It is definitely easier than robbing banks and spending time in prison, but there are limits, in my view, to the happiness of such endeavours. For me, work has mainly been about making enough money to finance my next sailing trip.

The term used by most sailors is 'cruising kitty.' As summer turned into fall, I deluded myself into believing that my cruising kitty was fat enough for another trip to the tropics. I was to discover that the 'kitty' was still somewhat malnourished but my financial situation sure looked adequate to me as the coastal weather went into its winter phase and warm southern breezes beckoned.

Arrangements were made, airline tickets purchased, and I was eager for a blast of tropical air. Todd and my nephew Brian would join me in a week. Our hope was to sail west this year and see what Mother Nature had in store for us.

Preparation for Travel

Slack her sheets to the evening breeze.

Let her run toward the green flash.

West is good for now.

Dream dreams of horizons with webs, of longitude and latitudes.

Pick steering-stars to guide us through the night.

Watch for meteors and satellites in the heavens,

and mermaids in the sea.

The stop in Barbados was long enough for me to discard my northern garb and find clothes more suitable for the climate. LIAT Airlines lived up to its moniker and was two hours late leaving for Grenada. I didn't mind. I had automatically switched into 'Don't worry. Be happy.' mode.

Stepping off the plane in Grenada gave me the same euphoric feeling I'd had the year before. The air held the same perfume and the heat was unchanged and soothing; the only change was the weight of my bag. I had brought a hand-made, ugly, stainless steel gudgeon/pintle fitting for the bottom of *Ancestor*'s rudder. Also I was lugging a set of binoculars, a short wave radio for time checks and weather reports, marine charts for the Caribbean, Panama Canal Zone, Galapagos Islands, Hawaii and the North East Pacific Ocean, a taffrail log, a plastic sextant, a nautical almanac, Sight Reduction Tables for northern latitudes, and code flags. I had anticipated trouble clearing Customs and Immigration with this load, but the Passport Control fellow remembered me, stamped my documents and said, "Welcome back to Grenada, Skip."

A little apprehensive about *Ancestor*, I had visions of a neglected boat losing faith in her crew. I shared a taxi into St. George. My boat had been tethered to an engine block for months and I had not been in contact with Grenada during all that time. She came into view as we rounded the lagoon on our way into town and my pulse accelerated. "I'm back," I whispered to her. "A few minutes more and I'll be with you again."

When the other passengers got out, I asked the driver to take me to Grenada Yacht Services. As soon as we arrived I lugged my heavy bag to the harbour master's office. He was pleased that I had stopped by. He wanted to know what I was intending to do next. My explanation carried on for some time until he said, "Is *Ancestor* for sale? There have been many inquiries. One *very persistent* French lady has returned many times asking me when the owner would be back." I thanked him for the information and especially for the implied warning about this woman.

Outside again, I checked *Ring Anderson's* storage locker to see if all was well. *Ancestor's* sails had suffered no rat damage and everything was exactly as we had left it months ago. I wandered down to the docks and I was greeted by sailors and Grenadians, whom we had met last year. This was a cheerful homecoming.

I hitched a ride out to *Ancestor* and before I could blink, I was climbing over her bulwarks and heaving my bag onto her deck. Apart from a dirty bottom, she looked super. I slid open the doghouse hatch to see if I could hear crickets, but there were no welcoming sound. I settled on deck, in my favourite position, lit my pipe, and did a proper visual inspection. Bill Colon had done excellent work building a small hatch into the top of the main cargo hatch, and he had also installed another hatch, as promised, in the forward deck and he had cleaned the boat thoroughly. A paint job was still necessary but she looked fantastic. The sun-baked decks revealed many open seams, so I walked over to the bilge pump and gave it a few priming strokes; the bilges were dry. Bill had indeed taken care of *Ancestor*.

A few minutes later, Bill, appearing to be in fine fettle, steered *Full Speed Ahead* alongside. We spent a few hours on deck going over everything he had done and how he had done it. Two of the heavy items in my bag, which I have not previously mentioned, were a bottle of sparkling white wine and a bottle of Bill's favourite rum. We sampled the rum but kept the wine for an ice-bath at some later date.

Bill had located and steam-cleaned a forty gallon plastic water barrel for me. He had also fashioned a spare oar for the dinghy and he was willing to sell his Primus stove and gimbal ring stand as we had also previously discussed. I escorted him back to *Banana Boat*. We would settle our account on the morrow.

I rowed my own dinghy over to GYS to grab my sleeping bag from the locker, along with whatever other articles I could haul in one trip. Then onboard, I went below and checked everything by the light of a small kerosene lantern. My boat was quiet and there were no bad odours. For my last pipe of the day, I sat on the bulwarks and listened to the steel drum band practicing for the upcoming Carnival. Silently, I thanked them for the Caribbean concert, knocked the ashes from my pipe and had a long drink of sweet water before going to sleep in my hammock. No rain showers pestered me.

I was at Ring's locker again early next morning, gathering and ferrying gear back to the boat. It didn't take too long and as the dawn was finally showing signs for another agreeable day, I climbed the mast to check halyards, stays, topping lifts, and to lubricate the wooden-cheeked blocks up there. Everything was in order.

When I had descended again to the deck, a small boat dropped by and I was handed a papaya (paw paw here) plus a green lime for my breakfast! The fruit was from a neighbouring sailing vessel at anchor whose crew had been watching my activities. Guessing correctly that I did not have food onboard yet, they kindly delivered breakfast.

By 10:00 a.m. I had the sails bent-on, sheets attached, and I was ready to visit *Banana Boat*. Bill and I came to an agreement and I paid in U.S. cash. With our business done, we jumped into the dinghy and went shopping.

I love open air markets, and in Grenada they are special. The sellers, ladies mostly, cry out "Here, my dear!" or "Here my love, buy you from me." Half an hour later, we staggered back to the dinghy with our loads of produce. I had also purchased local nutmeg, mace and cinnamon. Back on *Ancestor*, Bill placed a bottle of Jack Iron rum on deck. "Thanks for the money, Jon. You might need this one day."

Next, I needed to make a list of what would have to be done on the boat before we could sail west. My idea was to sail for Panama before mid-February. My list was composed with that time-frame in mind.

In the afternoon, I had visits from a number of sailors. Some we had met last year, and a few were newly arrived cruising folk. I accompanied several of them to the GYS restaurant for a beer or two and got caught up on the latest gossip about recently completed Atlantic crossings and other topics of interest. A group of Grenadian guys came over to welcome me back and to enquire about Todd. My son was a favourite with these dart players. Todd had the ability to do subtractions instantly, a skill which impressed them. I told them my boy would be returning in a week or so.

Down at the dock where the dinghy was tethered, another young Grenadian stopped me to pick my brain about Canada. We had a friendly conversation but I had to watch myself when he asked, "Dis island, Canada, is it big as Grenada?"

Tactfully I answered, "Most likely a bit bigger but I don't know for sure." The fellow seemed satisfied with my reply. We shook hands and parted company.

Evening was approaching. I rowed to the GYC to watch the sunset with a few folks. The clubhouse is small and that establishment and its members harbour no pretentions. With cool beers in hand, we sat on the northernmost point of the property to watch the spectacle. The sky was clear. Only a few trade wind clouds drifted past. The cloudless western horizon formed a perfectly curved line, exhibiting the roundness of our planet.

If you have never seen a 'green-flash' at sunset, you must put this on your 'to do' list. It is a phenomenon which occurs only when the visibility is unlimited. As the upper limb of the sun passes below the horizon - at that exact moment - there is a brief but distinct vertical green flash. A rare and awesome sight!

* * *

I pulled out a can of tar the next day and spent hours caulking deck seams. While I was working, I was mentally calculating my financial situation, which needed my urgent attention. The five thousand dollars I had expected to have for this trip had not yet arrived at Barclays Bank. This was worrisome.

Before leaving Vancouver, I had been in touch with an old canoe-paddling friend, Hilt Fraser, who lived in Sarnia, Ontario. He had agreed to meet us in Panama where Todd and Brian would be leaving the boat. He offered to accompany me to Hawaii and Vancouver. This would be more than satisfactory. I was fairly certain that he would be able to add some resources to the voyage but I couldn't depend on it. I was still mulling this over when I re-stowed the tar can in the hold.

* * *

Another idyllic tropical morning was dawning. I ate an entire paw paw and watched an island schooner tacking into the St. George Carenage, with just enough wind to reach the seawall.

Her sails came down and she was tied off to the bollards. I couldn't make out her name at that distance, even with my binoculars, but I knew that I had seen her last year at Windward, in Carriacou. Vessels like her are unforgettable. Their designs are rough but workable; their sailing capabilities are amazing, old-school sailing simplicity. *She's like my Ancestor. I'll go over later and check her out.*

No-Name Boats

Kerosene worked well to clean the tar off his hands, followed by a lathering of soapy water to remove the fuel smell. As he sniffed his palms, he noticed a two-bowed dinghy approaching from the direction of the Carenage. A pair of Carriacou Schooner sailors were onboard.

They rowed around my no-name sloop, whispering together until one of them shouted out a common island greeting, "W'ap' nin Skip?" Skip answered, "Wa gwan Skip? How de man?" The sloop's young foreigner did not know much of the local dialect but he was eager to improve his conversational skills.

"No - name boats be good," the local gent confided. "We got a no - name boat too. Is best way of doin' business." He then went on to address his opinions concerning 'value stretch' and the unfortunate fact that Grenadians were suffering from a serious lack of benzina (gasoline) and cooking-gas (butane) and the fact that he and his companion, here beside him, could sail to Port of Spain, in Trinidad, and bring a supply back for people. His second question got to the point, "Could your no-name sloop haul cooking gas? She be the right size to carry a big load."

"But what about coast guard patrols and police in Port of Spain and Grenada?" asked the sloop's skipper, not at all sure that he was receptive to this idea. "Oh, that all fix, no problem. Just you follow no-name schooner and enjoy the seas, the winds and the mermaids. We sail tonight. Reach Port of Spain tomorrow night." And with that the Carriacou boys rowed away.

The sloop's skipper found himself in a quandary. Was he going to get involved in a smuggling run between Trinidad and Grenada? The words "what if" interfered with his thinking processes. He tried to direct his mind toward 'yea' or 'nay' regarding the whole crazy plan. He could lose his boat. End up in jail - if he got caught. On the other hand, here was a chance to engage in an age-old tradition of the seas, and to make a few dollars. His current financial circumstances were definitely not good. Perhaps he should say, "Yea." If only to hear the mermaids sing.

With these conflicting thoughts percolating in his skull, he decided to distract himself with some much needed scrubbing and scraping. He fetched his mask and snorkel, his gloves, scraper, and a belt with lead weights that some generous stranger had donated the day before. He re-positioned the dinghy beside the hull and soon he was in the water, removing five months of accumulated marine growth from the hull.

His sloop was overdue for a haul-out but he would wait until the crew arrived. Right now, at least, his boat needed a shave and a haircut. That is, if she was sailing to Trinidad. Had he made a final decision? Yes. Follow the schooner with no name. Simple!

His cleaned-up hull looked a lot better but the guy holding the scraper looked worse. And certainly he did not smell very good, with a coating of dead barnacle slime covering most of his body. A shower would help.

Almost before his dinghy nudged the dock at GYS, three stalwart Grenadians approached and announced that he would need a crew for the next couple of days, and, what a surprise, they were willing to be that crew! Wow, these guys are clever! How did they hear about his chat with the no-name schooner? He thanked them politely for their offer but sorry, he only needed help sailing to L'Anse aux Épines for a haul-out later in the week. And sorry again, but his own crew would be here by then. They all exchanged a high five and parted company. The three Grenadians were not fooled but that was okay.

* * *

I have heard the mermaids singing, each to each

      - T. S. Eliot. British essayist, poet and publisher

The sea, once it casts its spell, holds one in its wonder forever.

- Jacques Cousteau. explorer, conservationist, filmmaker and author

Fortunately the wind chose to get involved with the departure of the no-name boats. Fresh breezes rattled their mainsails as they were hoisted up and tensioned. The sloop's jib complained about being stretched too tightly after months of lying about in a locker. Her sloop's skipper released the mooring line, hauled sheets, and his boat gathered way, heading for the lagoon entrance. The bowsprit pointed like a finger at the big schooner ahead which had left the harbour with the wind on her tail and her main and foresail boomed-out to help push her large hull. The moon shone between the trade wind clouds.

The skipper of the little sloop was happy. Prior to leaving, he had smoked the obligatory pipe and mentally charted this voyage. If he could see the route, and the end of the journey clearly, before this departure, all would be well. Once he clearly envisioned both no-name vessels tying up at the seawall in St. George, he was content to sail in the schooner's wake.

As the two vessels neared Point Saline, the schooner flew 'wing on wing', with her mainsail on one side and the foresail on the other. The sloop preferred broad tacks to keep her main and jib drawing wind. When they rounded the point, they were side by side. One hundred yards apart. The schooner's crew was laughing and gesturing, showing the sloop where it was supposed to be! Glorious sailing! Phosphorescent spray lit the dark water. Both vessels assumed their new course, southeast by east. The schooner added a working jib to the sail plan. They were bound for Trinidad.

The wind settled into a steady Force 4 and the sloop's captain / crew adjusted his sheets until his vessel could steer herself. The short tiller, with its upward crook, received a steering rope, a piece of half inch manila with an eye-splice. The opposite end extended to the windward bulwarks and attached to a small wooden cleat. A piece of shock chord from the tiller to the lee bulwarks completed the arrangement. The steering rope was adjusted to add resistance to the slight weather helm which the mainsail applied. When the weather helm eased, the tiller was controlled by the steering rope and the gentle tug of the shock chord. This combination allowed the rudder to return to the pre-set angle. These adjustments proved to be suitable for the selected course.

With the 'Christmas wind abeam,' the sloop heeled comfortably into the swell, throwing enough spray across her decks to remind the skipper that he might get wet. The dog house hatch was shoved forward, creating a perfectly comfortable place to relax and enjoy the voyage. The skipper donned a yellow oilskin jacket, provided by the mate of the *Jens Juhl*. He hunkered down, with his legs and torso inside the doghouse and his head and shoulders outside and both arms resting on top of the doghouse for lateral support whenever the boat rolled from side to side. He settled into his night-watch posture. His tobacco, matches and pipe were close at hand. A flask of tea was within easy reach. The schooner was in sight, the sloop was steering herself and Trinidad was ahead, luring both vessels onward. The moon completely approved of the adventure. She winked between the clouds.

Has there ever been such a magical night in the history of sailing? The skipper asked himself. He refilled his pipe with a local leaf tobacco. The sailor was keenly aware of life and of a sense of his place in it. The ocean guided his thoughts.

* * *

On this night, the planet's ocean waters were conjoined with the man's. The skipper was unaware of a physical or mental change, but rather, he passed into a zone of being, a merging, so real, so perfect, that he was unconscious of the transition. His thoughts became the ocean's thoughts. His movements mirrored those of the water world surrounding him. He sailed on, humbled by the intensity of his emotions. The ocean said, "I was never man's enemy; a sailor never has to fight with me. Only stay with me. In peace. When gales, storms or cyclones occur, I am not angry; I am dancing in the infinity of time, balancing life in my embrace, in my depths and heights."

The sailor heard sounds that he had never heard before. Mermaids were singing, each to each, and they were sharing their songs with him now. Was it ocean spray or tears of joy he tasted? Or both? He answered the mermaids with his own song, a song he would never remember. The ensouled cries of unseen whales, the click of crabs on the ocean floor, the melodies of seabirds - these mingled with the ballet of flying fish breaking through the waves to soar on journeys only they could understand. Is that the scent of the Krakken? And are those dolphins leaping skyward and beyond? "Yes and yes," the ocean answered.

* * *

Had minutes or hours passed? Or did time matter in this ocean world?

Questions hovered and beat against the wind. The sailor became once again attuned to his boat, gliding on the bosom of the sea. Dawn's light spread across the sky. He shook his head and awoke to the reality of the present; a voyage to Trinidad. His body was stiff. He focused his eyes on the schooner ahead. *It is there. Leading me. But where have I come from? Where have I been?* He laughed out loud, knowing he would never be the same again.

* * *

The schooner was a mile distant, her sails hard-trimmed on a slacking wind. In just a few hours, the vessels were abeam of one another. The small sloop was nimble in the soft winds, while the larger vessel slowed and craved a stronger breeze to hurry onward.

Displaying what he considered to be proper form, the sloop's skipper placed his boat abeam of the schooner on its windward side. Good morning greetings echoed over the now gentle sea. The skip of the schooner advised, "Wind too strong is comin' in by light de day by Trinidad. Dark be bes' for us no - name boats" This made sense to the sloop's one man crew. He could appreciate the problem. After all, what was a fast passage other than a satisfying journey for the sailor and a memorable performance for the boat? Of course, arriving at night was best, if they wished to remain undetected! His growling stomach forced him to attend to more practical matters. Was that nerves or was it hunger causing those abdominal gurglings? He went below to pump and ignite the stove, realizing, as he puttered in the galley, that he was apprehensive. Who is fond of breaking the law? Or is it breaking the law? While the coffee water boiled, he dissected a paw paw, scooped out the seeds and sprayed lime juice over both halves. Breakfast and a new day. Why worry?

Hours passed. The westerly-setting current was not as strong as he had suspected it might be. The schooner's chosen course was good: local knowledge. The sloop resumed her position behind the schooner and aimed her bowsprit at a smudge of land on the horizon. Trinidad was rising from the water, beckoning the no - name boats.

The sloop's hull had dried out on her Grenada mooring but at sea, her hull planking was being seasoned by the ocean waves whenever she rolled from side to side. The skipper had pumped his bilge south of Saline Point - forty strokes! And now he counted another twenty-four strokes to pump her dry. Thankfully, the timbers were swelling and she should soon be as watertight as any boat of her kind could hope to be.

They closed with the Trinidad coast at sunset. No green flash occurred, because the sun had an early appointment in Venezuela, where the heat haze blotted out what might have been another fine display. There was an adverse, north-setting current in the Bocas del Dragon, the strait between Venezuela and Trinidad. Both vessels nosed into it at five knots and waited for the tide to turn. The sloop's skipper had never been to Trinidad. Nor did he have a chart for the area. So he could do nothing but laugh at himself. Here he was, acting on blind faith, raising his sails and following the unknown crew of Carriacouans, in their big schooner, on a trading mission to an unknown destination. "Trading mission" sounded credible and he relaxed and let the words slide over his tongue.

During the early night hours, the navigation lights of two tankers were spotted only a few miles away, one inbound to Trinidad and the other outbound. Other navigation lights were observed, but none were close enough to worry the no - name boats. After dark, the skipper saw a white, flashing navigation light and the schooner made a slight course change.

The breeze held and the reversal of the north-setting current pulled the vessels south, clear of danger. Having rounded the western tip of Trinidad, both boats hardened their sheets. A new course was chosen.

The wind dropped to no more than a light land breeze. The vessels were ghosting. Gaff and boom jaws creaked. They had very little steerage.

As the wind retired for the day, a single, pale white glow, like a lantern light, advanced from shore. No, it was not the Coast Guard, but a small tug boat, low in the water and spewing greasy smoke through a large funnel. What it lacked in looks it made up for in manoeuvrability and efficiency. Both schooner and sloop were taken in tow and pulled landward.

An hour later, in a great flurry of activity and amid light-hearted laughter, both vessels were secured alongside the quay. The skippers were escorted to a shed where strong hammocks were slung. "Relax," they were told. "Leave the cargo to us." Sweet water and ganja were placed on a nearby table.

The skippers shared the joint, a pleasant sleeping pill of sorts. Before he left, their guide said,

"In de mornin', you be towed to where the tug met you. The mornin' mist will hide you from shore. Use the trade wind. Bes' route to Grenada."

The weary sailors went to sleep. Too soon, it was time to return to the wharf. He could see that there were dozens of vessels rafted together all along the docks and wondered again how it was possible that they were able to get alongside in such a busy place. He stood in the dark and gazed down at his boat in amazement. His decks were scarcely six inches above water level! The main cargo hatch was closed and tarped. The deck was chockablock with 'twenty pounders,' wedged and lashed together, supposedly to maintain order in the bottled ranks of the newly stowed cargo.

He shimmied down a makeshift ladder and crawled over to the tiller, trying to avoid breaking his bones in the process. How would he rearrange the gas containers to sail the boat with any kind of comfort? He scratched his head. Lads hailed him from above and passed down two wide planks, to be used, obviously, as walkways to the mast. These would give him stepping space to raise, lower, or reef the sails. For plank ties, bits of plastic rope fluttered to the deck. There was more than a hint of urgency to these machinations. The time had come to get out of town. As a final gesture, one dock hand hastily tossed an old cushion aboard to lessen the danger of the skipper acquiring a 'ringed bum' on the uncomfortable journey to Grenada. The tug pulled the no - name boats away from shore and any prying-eyes.

The entire loading operation took less than three hours. Now the two cargo vessels were towed southwest, slowly, slowly. The shoreline became a dim flickering of lights against Trinidad's shrinking and shadowed mass. Lines were pulled in. Following a few final moments of chatter, the dark, unilluminated tug turned north, leaving traces of poorly burned fuel in her wake. Her job was done.

Beyond the morning mist, the sun creeped above the horizon, and with it came an adequate breeze. A flurry of activity occupied the crews aboard the no - name boats. Blocks creaked, gaff jaws squeaked, muscles strained, and white canvas formed vertical wing shapes against the dawn sky. Aboard the sloop, the skipper watched his boat come alive. Hesitantly and almost imperceptibly at first, her overburdened hull began to move until it was being propelled through the water. The skipper nervously imagined his boat in these trade wind seas, maybe sailing into a deep wave trough and unable to rise again. He tried to block out these calamitous thoughts. Obviously the schooner's crew was unconcerned. All the same, he moved the dinghy closer to the stern. He lashed oars to the rowing seat, tied a two gallon water bottle to the thwart and collected whatever emergency items he could find, in case he had to abandon ship.

The schooner and the sloop passed through the narrow Bocas del Dragon with the encouragement of a north setting current. The schooner was not as deeply laden as the sloop. She showed three feet of hull above the waterline but she did not move ahead any faster than her small companion. The crews stared anxiously into the sun toward shore but no one appeared to be paying them any attention. The cargo vessels remained invisible as the slog to Grenada began.

The ocean was kind. A Force 4 easterly, which would normally afford a perfect sailing wind for an on-the-waterline boat, instead put a noticeable strain on the rigging and sails, which had to provide both drive and stability for the almost submerged hulls. The sloop's skipper settled in for what might become a tense passage. He could hardly believe that his boat could and would rise to the crest of the next wave and the next and the next, endlessly. He cringed whenever his vessel dropped into a deep, nerve wracking trough. Minutes passed. Hours passed. He appealed to the waters, asking for leniency. He studied the hull's motion and the straining of the rigging. Eventually the skipper understood. Even though the port side bulwarks were buried in water as the sloop surged through each trough, the boat would rise again and shake off the excess water like a wet dog. Here was a hull designed and built for hauling heavy cargo or, as in the present case, far too much cargo. His boat was performing to her design capacity. The sailor was thrilled.

It had taken longer than usual to get the steering adjusted, but the balance was found and the steering ropes were put in place again. The next order of business was food. Considering the explosive nature of his cargo, he dare not use the stove. He unwrapped a wax paper parcel, which he had received from a stevedore just before departure and prepared a meal of sticky rice, maple syrup and raisins. The rice was sweet and filling and the strong craving for a mug of hot coffee was offset by draughts of water poured from a jug at his feet.

Initially, the bilge pump had been difficult to access but when he finally rearranged the deck cargo, it was clear that he had done so none too soon. He found himself pumping with long, tiring, heavy strokes. Sea water gushed everywhere. The decks were awash and the newly caulked seams were not completely watertight. Yet. His back complained with each stroke. His calloused hands developed more callouses. When he rested, he sat on his bottle seat, rubbed his sore fingers, and promised himself that he would look for a new, modern pump as soon as possible.

Grenada loomed on the horizon, a dark smudge on a sharp, curved line of the ocean, beckoning, but still far away. The schooner was a mile to windward, slogging toward the same target. The course was fine considering the west-setting current and the persistent easterly wind. All one could do was enjoy the ride and light a pipe, even though one was squatting on a bomb. The wind, the water, and mermaids sang for the sailor's pleasure.

More cold food for breakfast. Morning revealed Point Saline on the bow. The wind, lighter now, maintained enough power to move the no-name boats along, but the wind lacked the strength to let them beat eastward to St. George with style and grace. The sloop's skipper drowsily fantasized about a spanking breeze to drive the sails and deliver him into the carénage, and a snug berth on the seawall. The dream continued throughout the day. He slept in spurts, between tacks and snacks.

Around here, the breeze normally died off an hour or so before sunset, but it opted to behave differently that day. A gust of wind alerted the sloop's skipper. Harden the sheets! Take the tiller! Within the hour the schooner led him into St. George. Crowds gathered along the seawall. Conch shell horns blew. Sails came down. Many hands caught their mooring lines. The daydream had become reality.

The sloop's skipper held one brief conference with the skipper of the big schooner before he climbed the stairs to the upper floor of a building immediately next to the no-name boats. The Nutmeg Café. Local folk came to him for high fives and to grin and exclaim, "Alright mon." Everyone knew him now and before he could order a meal, fresh fish, fried to a crisp, rice with saffron (or was it turmeric?), mixed island vegetables not cooked to death, and cool beers were delivered to his table!

From the restaurant balcony, he watched the off-loading and devoured his food. The police were the first to claim drums of benzine. Everyone else waited while these first drums were piled onto low truck-beds and hauled away. Then there was a swarm of people eager to buy. An 'official' recorded quantities and collected the signatures of each recipient. Gradually, the schooner hull rose out of the water.

The sloop's cargo similarly disappeared and the tarp, followed by the hatch planks, were set aside to expose the larger bottles below decks. By the time the skipper had finished his delicious meal, lit his pipe and accepted a hot coffee, the sloop was back on its waterline, looking almost forlorn. God, he was proud of that boat.

Sometime during the party, sometime past midnight, sometime when the breeze was exactly right, the skipper hoisted his mainsail and staysail, cast off the lines, hardened the staysail sheet to get her bow around, and coasted over to the lagoon where he picked up his mooring line and secured it to the sampson post.

* * *

Full Crew Again and Fun Days

An enormous, black, mother-raincloud announced herself by sending a blast of cool wind to wake me in my hammock on the foredeck. 5:00 a.m. Still dark. The cloud formed over the Grenadian highlands and swept westward, dragging skirts of water behind her. I rolled out immediately, grabbed my sleeping bag, headed for the galley hatch, smiled and hastily tugged my jeans on. The rain hitting the sea and the deck sounded like a high-speed train rushing past. "Hey! Time I got up anyway, and thank you for the water," I shouted to the clouds. A dramatic beginning to another day in paradise.

If the weather improved, I hoped to work on the boat. Otherwise, I would simply continue planning the trip to Panama and beyond. My friend, Hajo Hadler, once told me, if I remembered his words accurately, "The biggest adventures in life happen in your head." Perhaps he was correct, and I philosophized on that concept and prepared my paw paw breakfast. I did indeed thrive on visualizing passages and landfalls and making provision lists for the next leg of a voyage. The mental and physical exercise are always fun. Stimulating. It keeps me keen and focused on the possibilities of the journey ahead. Today I began by listing the equipment onboard and determining what was missing. I had the following:

1 four inch diameter lifeboat compass

1 box bilge pump

1 40# CQR anchor, chain and rode

3 kerosene running lights; red, green and clear

1 radar reflector

3 kapok life jackets

1 well used old boat cushion

1 taffrail log, c/w spinner

1 plastic sextant

1 three-inch chronometer, in box

1 HO 249, nautical almanac, sight reduction tables

1 portable SW radio for time checks

1 portable RDF, working, (from junk heap at GYS)

1 set of code flags

1 Primus stove c/w gimbal rings

1 old pressure cooker, not working but good for an oven

1 misused and ancient bilge pump, complete with handle, (from junk heap at GYS. I had high hopes for the bilge pump but was unable to bring it back to life.

We were shy of a VHF radio (which I couldn't afford), a life raft (which I couldn't afford), spare sails and rope and fittings (which I might possibly scrounge up somewhere).

I puffed this morning's pipe, waiting for the rain to stop. I amused myself with the unoriginal idea of using bamboo for a life raft. I would need two large bundles of bamboo poles lashed together with a six foot gap between them, bamboo crosspieces, second-hand plywood for the deck, a bamboo spar for a mast, and another fifteen foot long bamboo spar for a flagpole. I thought about drilling one inch diameter holes in the bamboo floats, between the nodes, filling them with sweet water and driving in wine bottle corks. My imagination was running wild but this was a serious matter and I filed the raft design away for future and careful consideration. Provision lists could wait until the crew showed up and we were about to sail.

A more immediate concern involved getting *Ancestor*'s bottom done, which meant a haul-out and a lot of paint. Tropical climates are hard on paint, and if one does not constantly work at it, a boat begins to look shabby after a few months. Another concern was getting my vessel registered. I could hardly wait to see her name on the transom and bows. I had contacted the Ships Registry in St. George and I had applied for the name *Ancestor*, but so far I had received no response. The first step in the registration process was to have an Admeasurer come aboard for a survey to determine the vessel's tonnage. So far this gentleman had not put in an appearance.

Someone who did make an appearance though, was Anthony Collier. There he was, waving from the GYS docks. I went over to pick him up with the dinghy. Anthony was a local character, approximately thirty years of age, and always looking for 'a day's work.' We got on well together, repairing, mending, hauling etc., while he kept us both entertained with stories about his family and local culture. He tried to teach me the regional lingo, which was also a lot of fun. And so our work and conversation crept along at an 'island time' pace.

* * *

Todd and Brian arrived in Grenada on January ninth, looking very white and completely excited.

It was great to see their smiling faces again. They were whisked through Customs and Immigration and soon we were hugging each other. In the taxi, Todd was telling Brian about Grande Anse beach and swimming all day and how to mooch drinks and fresh water showers before returning to the lagoon and . . .! As Brian's northern eyes focused on frangipani and bougainvillea and coco palms, I knew he would not regret coming here. We rattled toward the docks.

At Grenada Yacht Services, we stopped at the restaurant for a treat. Todd's dart-playing pals surrounded our table with their, "Wag wan?" or "W ap'nin?" greetings. If my son was embarrassed or flustered by their attention, he did not show it. Brian was introduced to everyone as the newest crewman of the no-name sloop, which is how people still referred to *Ancestor*.

Full Speed Ahead was seriously overloaded on our return trip to the boat, but we managed to make it without having a swim. Brian cast his young, critical eye around the vessel. He liked what he saw. Meanwhile, I prepared supper.

The sun was doing its good night performance on the western horizon and the steel bands were on shore, getting ready for their evening practice. Carnival festivities would be starting soon. Grenadians love the prospect of an exciting, super parade with costumes and music. Carnival is part of the Easter celebrations and this year the festivities were to be held in February. The push was on. Despite the discordant, distant sounds of the various bands warming up around the lagoon, the overall effect of tinkling music was very agreeable to *Ancestor's* crew.

For the next few days not a lot of work was accomplished on our boat. The crew was young, including myself, and we were very much under the magical spell of the tropics. We roamed around St. George, up steep streets and down narrow lanes, over to the market in the old town and on each occasion, without discussion, we ended up at the Nutmeg Café in the harbour.

The café is on the upper floor of a building that hugs a south facing seawall. There is only a narrow roadway between the building and the water. The café's ambiance held us captive even when we knew we should be going. One more of those fabulous chocolate ice creams please. One more lingering look over the busy harbour and the schooners coming in under sail to tie-off along the seawall. There passengers get off and get on and cargo is craned or man-handled to the shore or to the deck. All of this is accompanied by West Indian banter - music to our ears - and odours that waft upward from the dock. We watched the boats returning with their catch in the afternoon. We listened to conch horns announcing that fish is now for sale. Come and buy! Women came, swinging their baskets, eager for fresh fish.

The island's botanical gardens were a treat for our senses. We walked amongst exotic trees, learned about their pedigrees, touched their barks and skins and listened to the music of their rustling leaves.

I strolled over to Grande Anse beach with the lads one day. We swam in the sea or baked in the sand. The coins in our bathing suit pockets were spent as soon as we became thirsty. The fresh water showers at the end of the day were a bonus.

So our sailing preparations continued sporadically. When we weren't wandering the island, we put our noses to the grind stone to get *Ancestor* ready for our trip. One of the problems on a gaff-rigger is chafing. Canvas sails can rub against rigging wire or topping lifts. We made baggywrinkles to eliminate, or at least reduce, wear on the mainsail. The staysail and jib do not suffer from this kind of damage. For those unfamiliar with baggywrinkles and if you wish to make them, follow these instructions; find old three-strand nylon rope that is no longer useful to anyone but you, and cut it into eight inch lengths. This creates a heap of yarn strands. Then take ten feet of tarred marline, double it in the middle to make a double line, and attach both ends to fixed points. Next step. Hold a piece of yarn at both ends, centre it transversely under the marline, hold tight and pass the ends through the top of the marline and tug downward to cinch it into position. I believe this hitch is called a railroad sennit. When you have about four feet of this drooping fringe hanging there you untie the ends of the marline and attach the marline to the rigging at strategic places, usually where the seams of the sail would rub against wire or rope. You seize the looped end tightly to the wire and coil all of the fringe you've made upward around the wire until it is all used. The final thing you must do is tie the loose ends of the marline around the wire using your best hitches or knots – and there it is, a big, hairy cylindrical shape ready to protect your canvas sails.

Ancestor had double topping lifts on the main boom, which is proper rigging. Both topping lifts needed baggywrinkles attached even though they were not always touching the sail. The leeward lift was eased off while the weather lift was used to adjust the sail for shape when travelling. The boys and I manufactured lots of baggywrinkles.

Five or six cruising sailboats were coming into port each week. It was always a pleasure to meet these travellers and swap tales. One day *Silver Streak* anchored near us and we got acquainted with her South African sailors. They just happened to mention that they had too many sails onboard and they had to dispose of some of them before leaving Grenada. Could I use any of their cast-off sails? Without hesitation, I assured them that they had asked the right person. Through this serendipitous meeting, we acquired a storm trysail for the main and an old spinnaker which still had some good upper sail material left in it. They were happy and we were happy. A win-win, as they say, and I was extremely pleased to cross 'extra sails' off my 'to do' list.

The Big Shakedown Cruise

By the middle of January, work on the boat was progressing well. The tonnage measurement would take place soon. Both Jens Juhl and Ring Anderson were in port. Days were full and fun and we were smiling and eager for more of the same.

Bluesy Simmons, a well-known sailor from Bequia, had come to St. George to check out *Ancestor*. He suggested that we take her for a shakedown cruise. Everyone agreed. We could leave next day when the adults were sober and ready for action.

And so, at 10:00 a.m. in the morning, the boat was boarded by Bluesy from Bequia, Kenny, the skipper of *Jens Juhl*, with his mate Johnny and his cook Janey, a French lady who had an interest in *Ancestor* (because she had sailed an old workboat from France and been shipwrecked), and Todd, Brian and yours truly.

The wind was light by the time we prepared to weigh anchor and I got into a discussion with Bluesy about the best strategy to exit the lagoon. He immediately said, "We should leave 'Petite Martinique' style. It's the only way to go." 'Petite Martinique' style involved getting underway using only the jib and hoisting the main and staysail later as needed. I argued that there wasn't enough wind to get *Ancestor* to pay-off for the lagoon entrance in the room that was available. Everyone joined in the debate and I ultimately gave in. We would do it Bluesy's way. I made him honorary skipper for the day, saluted and awaited his instructions.

The anchor was up in a jiffy and secured to the stem in fine, seamanlike fashion. The jib was hoisted and tensioned while Bluesy manned the helm and trimmed the sheet. We were moving - for about one hundred yards - until Bluesy's crew had to quickly grab whatever they could find as *Ancestor* sailed firmly onto the bottom, slewed around fifty degrees and stopped for a rest!

Bluesy sat there with a strange look on his face and for a few minutes we were very quiet. Then there were huge guffaws and we all chimed in at once, Bluesy included, trying to explain what had happened. Great fun. When we calmed down, the jib was furled and the dinghy was launched. Kenny rowed over to *Jens Juhl* to organize a tow. While we waited for assistance, a bottle of Jack Iron rum was passed around. We saluted Bluesy and thanked him for providing the morning's entertainment. One of us asked what his next instructions might be. He was a good sport and when pressed further, he elected to appoint me Admiral of the Fleet for the remainder of the day. Unfortunately, in order to become Admiral, protocol demanded that I be doused with a generous portion of our overproof rum. The aforementioned liquor was ceremoniously poured over my head!

Thirty minutes later, a large, inflatable dinghy with a powerful motor, was on the tow line, pulling us backward into the lagoon. Our crew moved to one side of the deck to cant the hull over as much as possible, and in a few minutes *Ancestor* was floating again. The dockside committee at GYS applauded and it was clear that we would be subjected to some friendly criticism when we returned to port later in the day.

We got the mainsail sweated up and kept the jib on standby. This time *Ancestor* answered the helm and we sailed sedately out of the lagoon. All hands cheered and laughed as we shook her down. With no further difficulties, we left the harbour and slid nicely out to sea, singing sailing songs and revelling in the weather.

We shared taking tricks at the helm, including Brian and Todd. I occupied myself forward, examining our sails and rigging, searching for whatever might need repair before we sailed from Grenada. While I was alone on the bow, the French gal (no names please) came to initiate a conversation. She told me, in exhausting detail, about finding her thirty-eight foot, ex-sailing fish boat in northwestern France, purchasing the vessel and eventually sailing for the West Indies with a friend. They had a tough voyage. Equipment broke and the hull leaked. Her list of problems was endless. Their landfall in the West Indies included running onto a reef and losing the boat. Fortunately they both made it to shore. Her lady friend left her to crew on another sailboat back to France. 'La Française' batted her eyelashes and said she was hoping to find passage westward to Tahiti. She employed some creative body language, to inform me that she was a very friendly person indeed but I still wasn't taking her bait. 'La Française' whispered in my ear, "I f***ie f***ie." and other words to that effect, in order to make it perfectly clear to me that she could be a real asset aboard *Ancestor*.

The situation was awkward but I repeatedly insisted, "This voyage is a 'men only' trip. I have no intention of changing my mind." Madame (Mademoiselle?) became rather huffy and said that she would not sail on 'some yacht' with a bunch of Americans or, worst of all, with a bunch of Brits. I did my best to avoid further dialogue on this topic. Kenny, noticing my dilemma, and having heard much of our conversation, took it upon himself to cool the woman off. He came forward and emptied a bucket of seawater over her head! Kenny was not going to waste our good rum! A momentary and deathly silence ensued until everyone in unison, including our French sailor, began laughing like crazy. The situation had been skillfully defused.

Shakedown cruise

Forestay

Several days after the famous shakedown cruise, Todd and Brian came back from Jens Juhl. Todd said excitedly, "Dad, wouldn't it be nice to have a ship's cat?" Jens Juhl's cat had borne a litter six weeks ago off the Surinam coast. Janey wanted to find homes for them and of course, Todd had already selected one beautiful, black kitten.

"Male or female?" I enquired, and Brian, being somewhat older and more knowledgeable than my son in such matters, said he had looked; the kitten was female. I put on a stern face and reminded them that it had been decreed. Females were forbidden on the upcoming voyage. Furthermore, as their supreme admiral or commander, or whatever, I was not about to change my mind.

Our exchange was fun. I recounted the many problems sailing folks have had quarantining their pets and placing bonds for the animals with the port authorities. Pets, I concluded, were a pain in the ass for travelling sailors.

Brian said, "Maybe so, Uncle Jon, but who will eat all the flying fish and squid that land on deck?"

Pause. "Have you named the creature yet?"

Pause. "Forestay," they chimed in unison.

I pretended to think long and hard about their request. I checked the rice pot on the stove. I lit my pipe and puffed for awhile. "Okay guys, but you have to take full responsibility for diaper changes and all that. Bring her aboard and introduce her." They were beaming from ear to ear as they aimed the dinghy toward *Jens Juhl*. When they reappeared, hours later, with the new deckhand and a plastic dishpan full of sand, they assured me that no diaper changes would be required.

My nickname for Forestay was Rusty, a label I also used to refer to a piece of wire up forward that was showing the effects of years with no protective coating. We got along well and this happy arrangement continued until Forestay/Rusty signed off the ship's papers many months later.

Haul - Out, Life Raft, Registry and Carnival

*R*ing Anderson returned from another charter trip to Martinique. Her arrival promised to add pleasurably to our hectic social life. Jan's daughters, Michelle and Karen, were aboard and they enjoyed Brian and Todd's company. I was on Ring Anderson, their beautiful sailboat, one evening, admiring the thick varnish on the woodwork and the spotless white cushions spread around the fantail stern. *Ancestor's* barely adequate paint job and her unassuming cockpit seating area paled by comparison.

Jan asked about our sailing preparations. I made a comment about my idea to make a life raft. "We'll build a raft with bamboo bund . . ."

Mid-sentence, he stopped me cold and smiling he said, "There is no way you are going to build a bamboo-bundle-rafty-thing, Jon. This is not adequate. Or safe. Far too risky."

"It's a financial decision, Jan. My crew and I have talked it over. We think we can take our chances using a bamboo raft." He frowned. "Jon, I have a spare, eight man life raft in storage. Just been re-certified. Take it. I'll pick it up in Vancouver next year." Wow! I offered my hand and we shook on the deal. Jan's life raft would be the newest and flashiest piece of equipment on my boat.

January slipped away. I was therefore very relieved when the Admeasurer showed up on the twenty eighth, with his tape measure and notepad. I helped him with the survey, joked with him about the non-existent engine room space and we were done. *Ancestor* received her tonnage measurement: a rating of 10.7 tons, her cargo volume capacity. I was elated. The Ship's Registrar could proceed with the official registration and I was able to scratch another item off my 'to do' list. Everything was falling into place. Our scheduled sailing date would not be compromised.

Haul-out day arrived. Earlier in the week, we had walked across to Spice Island Charters, having arranged to use their marine ways.

On January twenty-eighth, *Ancestor* sailed in light winds around the southwest tip of the island. We tacked up to L'Anse Aux Épines, locally known as Prickly Bay and dropped anchor at 9:30 pm that night.

In the morning, we sorted our tools for an assault on *Ancestor's* bottom. From shore, we watched excitedly. Our boat rose dripping from the sea and displaying her rather hard chine and the shallow deadrise on the underside of her hull. Her stem timber had a definite crook to starboard, mostly above the waterline. We assumed that the timber had a memory of this shape, given to it by the constant trade winds as it grew to maturity on Carriacou. The rudder was ridiculously small. It must have been designed back in Scotland and modified in the Tropics over the years to perform its steering job correctly. There was no doubt about the rudder's efficiency. The worthiness of its design was proven over the next ten thousand miles of deep sea sailing.

We attacked the hull's bottom with scrapers until the marine growth was gone and then I stopped for awhile to examine every seam and plank, searching for soft wood or tender butt joints, fastenings, and any other problems that might call for our attention while *Ancestor* still rested on the ways. Happily, she needed no major repairs, although I noticed that the cranse iron on the bowsprit did not look healthy. Maybe I could replace it if there was time and money to do the job, or perhaps we would have to wait until Vancouver.

That night we camped on deck. A steel band on shore entertained us while they rehearsed their repertoire for the big parade in St. George in a few days. The magic of the night was mesmerizing as was the classical music played on the steel drum 'pans'. But what was most amazing was the band's rendition of my favourite Spanish song, "El Relicario," the Shrine of Love, or as I knew it in English, 'Memories of Love.' I turned away from the others so they would not see the tears running down my cheeks. I was so moved by this music that I even forgot to puff on my pipe.

The following day was a blur of activity. The hull was completely wet-sanded. Minor gouges in the planking were treated with Polyfilla. The seams were filled with brown seam cement. I had hired two Grenadians, John Coren and Carl Lawrence. They were good boat men. While they prepped the hull for painting, I worked on replacing the rudder's gudgeon and pintle fittings. The massive stainless steel fittings, which I had fabricated in Vancouver, fit well and the installation went without a hitch.

Copper bottom paint was applied that afternoon and the topsides received their first coat of blue. When the tropical night descended, we settled down for rice and fish and beer and another evening of steel band music. There is no way to plan for, or purchase, such excellent entertainment. Impossible.

On the morning of February first, we applied the second coat of anti-fouling bottom paint and the second and final coat of blue to the topsides. My, she looked spiffy. We cleaned our water containers and filled them with fresh water from a tap on shore. At 9:30 am, *Ancestor* was lowered into the mother ocean. A light offshore breeze filled the mainsail and pushed us a short distance to where we anchored in five fathoms. We relaxed until lunch time and then Todd and Brian took the dinghy to find some trouble and have some well-earned fun. This left old dad / uncle alone on the boat with a spool of waxed thread and a needle, repairing the boltrope attachment to the clew of the jib. When this job was finished, I tensioned the standing rigging lanyards and lashed them to the deadeyes. *Cross those jobs off the list, Jon. Pat yourself on the back. Don't bother with the list again until tomorrow.*

We hoisted anchor early next day and a Force 4 easterly took us past Saline Point. We short-tacked into a falling breeze, which died out completely close to the harbour. We waited patiently. Brian and Todd tried to outdo each other in whistling-up a wind. Their efforts were successful too! We dropped the anchor on the south side of the

Ancestor on the ways at Prickly Bay

carénage, in front of the fire hall. A stern line to shore tethered *Ancestor* in position. The Ships' Registry was above the fire hall. Very convenient.

The lagoon is an ideal place to anchor or tie-up but it is also interesting to move around once in awhile to get a different view of the world. Also, we wanted a ringside seat for the Carnival parade which would take place soon.

In other news, I had managed to cut my right index finger at the shipyard. As a result, I was plagued with blood poisoning. The next morning, the injury hurt and I had developed an unsightly, black, poison vein from finger to elbow. Todd and Brian rowed ashore to buy Epsom salts while I sharpened the fish-filleting knife and boiled a pan of water. When they returned, I lanced the wound to make it bleed freely, then with a deep breath, I placed my hand in the near-boiling salt water, cringing from the heat and the pain and I massaged the swollen black vein. I had to push the poison out of my body. After the second boiling salt water treatment, the black vein was just about gone and luckily for me, Dr. Tom de Roos, master of the *Peter Storm*, came over and gave me five days of Tetracycline pills. The meds aided in my recovery. *Jon, add to your list. Top-off the first aid kit. You need painkillers and antibiotic salve.*

While we waited for the registration process to be completed, we replaced the turnbuckles on the whisker stays and the forestay. Brian was selected to do the seizing of the turnbuckles so that they could not loosen under repetitive motion at sea, and when this was finished, he packed them with grease and covered them with canvas. He stitched the canvas cloth tightly, before he served the whole lot with marline. We also went over our provisioning requirements to determine what food we should purchase prior to departure. We took turns dictating a grocery list of all the 'goodies' we would like to munch on as we sailed to Panama. A few revisions were necessary until a jumble of food items covered the paper. Our choices did not reflect a balanced diet and the crew obviously craved chocolate and more chocolate. Please. Our finalized grocery list was set aside.

We had to seize baggywrinkles onto the rigging at predetermined places. Brian went aloft often. He enjoyed the work as the steel bands and brass bands continued their rehearsals ashore.

And then it was Carnival time! The crowing roosters' dawn announcements were drowned out by a large brass band upstairs at the

The skipper takes a break

firehall. Calypso indeed. I had never heard so much brass music in one place and it was blaring within one hundred yards of *Ancestor*! After a fast breakfast, we hurried ashore to stake out a position on the south side of the road. Thankfully, we managed to find a spot away from the racket of the brass band. We had a good view of the parade, which was already marching toward us from the lagoon.

People who wanted to participate in the Carnival parade, had been designing and making their costumes all year long. Now they were whirling and shuffling past. Between every steel band, there were revellers showing off their fancy footwork and crooning to the music, which reverberated off the nearby walls. Fantastic! We were all 'grooving' to the persistent beat of the drums. Without warning, Todd was pulled into the parade by a huge devil-like creature. No harm done. The devil was a well disguised dart player, a buddy of Todd's from GYS. They posed while I snapped a photo and the merriment continued. The parade was huge. We couldn't believe the energy of the participants who would be performing music and dancing all the way to the old town and back to the lagoon. We assumed there were judges positioned along the route but we could not identify them as we followed the parade. We knew many of the people along the streets and we could tell from their genuine laughter and high-fives that we

At anchor, St. George. Brian at masthead

were accepted members of the community on that Carnival day.

Suddenly, or so it seemed, it was February 12th and on my morning visit to the Ship Registrar's office, everyone smiled when I was presented with *Ancestor V*'s 'blue book'; her registration certificate. In their research, the registrar's officials had found a vessel in Nova Scotia also named *Ancestor*. This could have posed a problem but being practical West Indian folk, and according to their custom, they had modified my vessel's name by adding the first letter of my last name to the title. We were now British registered; *Ancestor V*.

A local flag maker entered the room and presented me with a new, small, beautiful Grenadian flag. Grenada had become an independent nation in 1974 and they were very proud of their new flag. I was too.

Clutching the document and flag, I raced back to the boat, jumped into the dinghy and immediately started painting capital letters on the transom and both bows, and there she was! No longer a no - name boat! When Brian and Todd returned from their daily excursion, I introduced them to the latest member of the family; *Ancestor V*.

It was time now for our final provisioning. We had rice, potatoes, onions, hot sauce, spices, flour, baking soda, baking powder and three loaves of hard-crust bread. Because butter doesn't last long in the tropics without refrigeration, we bought only two pounds. A brisk walk around the Carénage and through the famous tunnel led us to the market. A stalk of bananas became ours followed by paw paw, guavas,

Todd and dart-buddy, carnival parade

limes, granadillas, dried fish, leaf-tobacco (for me), several large and bumpy wild lemons, coffee beans, a sack of peanuts and I cannot remember what else!

Brian looked swarthy and capable, steadying a stalk of bananas over his shoulder with one arm, while his other arm was wrapped around a bag of fruit. Todd and I were also loaded to capacity, and we must have appeared to be sweaty slaves of yore staggering back to the boat that day.

With everything stashed in hammocks and boxes, and having hung the bananas where they belonged - in the rigging - we were ready to get underway. Our anchor was tied to the stem, the stern line was coiled aboard, the jib went up, and *Ancestor V* was sailing 'Petite Martinique' style out of the harbour. Our destination was Grande Anse beach, only a short distance from town, where we anchored in five fathoms. Grande Anse was a bit lumpy so we had a wet and laughing dinghy ride to the beach.

Jan de Groot's wife, Elise, was in Room 191 at the Holiday Inn, right near shore. We had been invited to a farewell party, which included a movie and lots of delicious food, and cake of course, to end the feast.

Brian and Todd

Everything was stowed next day before we went swimming in the surf and had fresh water showers. I uncorked a bottle of rum and liberally sprinkled the decks; an old Grenadian custom guaranteeing a safe voyage. *Ancestor V* had waited contentedly for us in the gentle breeze. She was quite happy when her anchor came up and was secured for sea. We were off!

Grenada to Panama

The cure for anything is salt water, sweat, tears or the sea.
  - Isak Dinesen. pen name for Karen Blixen, Danish author

Force 3 wind. I had decided we didn't need to go bashing off on the first night of the voyage and so we hoisted only the jib. Our departure was logged as 1745 hours, course 293 degrees. This allowed for two degrees leeway and one degree of drift. No deviation on a westerly course. The magic was back and the lads were in no hurry to sleep. Forestay was carousing, running and jumping up the mast and daring anyone to interfere. The sailors spoke about sailing superstitions, while *Ancestor V* steered herself. I recorded today's date, Friday, February 13th. Oops!

One of the most enduring superstitions I know of, warns that it is unlucky to begin a voyage on a Friday since Jesus was crucified on a Friday. Friday the thirteenth, even to a landlubber, has never been a good day. Don't take any chances. Cast salt over your shoulder while you watch for weird stuff to happen. Also, I knew, it is bad luck to hang bananas from the rigging. Black cats aboard ships, however, are supposed to bring good luck. We joked about our small ship's cat and wondered if she was able to guarantee us good luck for this voyage. Could she counteract the bad joss of bananas hanging in the rigging? Could she fend off the dangers of Friday the thirteenth? Well after sunset, on the sea of the Caribs, these questions were answered.

A tremendous bang was heard up forward. Without warning and with no help from us, the jib and the attached forestay were flailing around in every direction, tethered only at the masthead! Our vessel lost way almost immediately. Which added to the boat's erratic motion and our confusion. *Ancestor V* wallowed in the turbulent seas.

"All hands! Panic stations," I shouted, fighting my way forward to the mainsail halyards. "Gaskets off the mainsail quickly. Brian, take the peak halyard and follow my lead." It was necessary to regain control before trying to capture the jib. The mainsail would provide the necessary stability. Fortunately I had made some small, what I call, 'panic lines', before leaving Grenada. These are strands of rope, in various diameters and lengths, with eye splices in one end of each or a bowline installed, depending on the type of rope. I grabbed a panic line and went forward in the darkness, trying to figure out how to get a line onto the flailing sail to secure it. I recalled how, several hours earlier, while still at anchor, during my safety talk with the boys, I had stressed the importance of caution and patience when sail handling at night. And here I was, out at the end of the bowsprit, being pushed into the gap between the whisker stay and bowsprit by the violent thrashing of the offending sail and the plunging hull. I laid on my back, rope in one hand, while the other hand gripped the bowsprit, which was stabbing at every wave and leaving me spluttering and cursing in zero visibility. I hadn't put on my safety harness and therefore I was both wet and dumb!

Brian had hauled in the jib sheet to help control the sail and at some point in time, I have no idea how but I managed to grab the tack of the sail and poke my panic line through the cringle while holding both ends of the line. After a few more dunkings, I passed the bitter end of the line through the loop and under the bowsprit. I tensioned

Departing St. George

this simple tackle and the flogging sail calmed down enough for me to pass more line through the cringle. The sail was tamed.

I staggered back to the cabin to find a coil of galvanized wire. I cut a length of it and returned to the end of the bowsprit to lock the turnbuckle and prevent a recurrence of the evening's entertainment. I was exhausted.

Todd was on the tiller, steering the boat. Brian was standing by the sheets. They were finessing the course to make the best use of wind and sea. I was lucky to have such a cool crew. Until they started cracking jokes about my appearance. They couldn't resist. I had a number of interesting bruises and a colourful gash across my skull. I was not yet convinced that salt water was a cure for everything. "Does it cure stupidity?" I asked the wind, as salt water stung my skin. Half an hour later, with several cups of tea to warm our innards, and long-sleeved cotton shirts to warm our torsos, we bantered more about superstition. The conversation focused on the failure of the forestay turnbuckle. I suggested that Brian should prepare himself to be keel-hauled at first light, or with a rope knotted around his ankle, perhaps we could simply throw him overboard and yank him backwards through the ocean for an hour or so. I said this because, while we were doing repairs in Grenada, Brian had wired the whisker stay turnbuckles correctly but he had forgotten to wire the forestay turnbuckle. He had applied the canvas covering and secured them properly, and he had even applied a coat of white paint to the completed job, but the banging motion of the vessel and the resulting torquing of the turnbuckle had caused the darn thing to loosen and fail. With the boat on a steady course in Force 3 conditions, the turnbuckle had rotated and eventually come unthreaded, allowing the jib to dance in the wind. Our turnbuckles were not made to yachting or marine standards. They were poorly galvanized devices best used for tensioning a clothesline pole but they were what I could afford. We took a vote on Brian's punishment and it was unanimously resolved that he would have to take over the watch immediately until the sun peeked over the horizon. He got off easy. Todd and I went below and crawled into our sleeping bags in the quarter berths. I heard a thud on deck and Brian softly announced that a flying fish had hit the boom, glanced off and landed on top of Rusty. For the next while the cat batted the fish around the deck. I fell asleep, like a silly sailor who dares to tempt fate on Friday the thirteenth. *I hope the bananas ripen and cause us no further trouble.*

At noon the next day, I calculated our latitude to be twelve degrees thirteen point nine north, and the meridian passage of the sun showed that we were at sixty-two degrees, fifty-six minutes west longitude. We had covered sixty-three miles since leaving St. George last evening. Not too bad considering our bad luck bananas and yesterday's calendar date.

Brian was suffering from sea sickness and although he was still woozy at noon, he coped with the discomfort and did not miss his watch. Todd and Rusty were content. The cat had been born on a boat and so far, she had never been ashore. Good sea legs.

I had cranked up the old direction finder earlier in order to take a bearing on Puerto La Cruz. The azimuth was one hundred and ninety degrees from our location. It fit nicely on the plotting sheet. A light wind stayed with us until late that night.

While performing rigging inspections the following day, I found that one jib sheet needed replacing. The events of Friday the thirteenth had caused a lot of chafe. This task took me only a few minutes and gave me something to do other than smoke and swap stories with the crew. I was pleased with the way we were settling in to life on the high seas, and as a reward, I made an extra-large pot of rice to celebrate. The

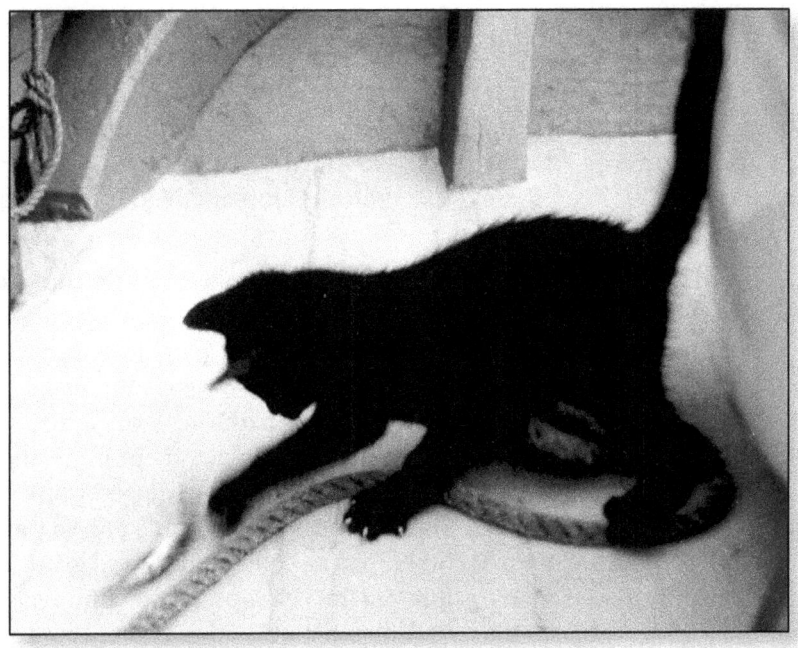

Forestay with her first flying fish

Forestay cuddling

rice went well with some bony but tasty flying fish. Rusty had eaten her share of fish that morning and now she was making kitten groans and favouring her protruding belly. Raisins and a can of Carnation milk was added to the left over rice and with a dusting of Grenadian cinnamon, we had rice pudding: snack food for the night watches. Good stuff.

In the next twenty-four hours, we made another one hundred and two miles. The breeze held at Force 3, northeast. The ship's creaking gaff and boom jaws on the mast spoke to us, while the manila halyards and sheets vibrated on their wooden blocks aloft and below; the voices of a wooden sailing vessel at sea.

On the third night out of Grenada, Brian woke me. He could see the lights of two ships on the horizon. One would be passing close by if it held its course. We needed running lights. Our three kerosene lanterns were sufficient but the port light had no lens and we had to make do with a piece of a red plastic bag in the lens opening. Oh well. Light those wicks, boys, trim them and place them in position. We were doing fine with the light winds until the closest ship was about a mile off and the wind rose unexpectedly to Force 5. We found ourselves reefing the main, stumbling around in the dark and grunting. As soon as we had *Ancestor* sailing again, on course and comfortable, I noticed that our port light had blown out, which prompted a few comments from myself. We needed stronger tape to hold the plastic bag lens in place. I added that item to the ever expanding list of things to do in Panama.

From the log:

Starboard light, starboard light,

Burning greenly in the night.

Your red port friend has just blown out

(Hear the skipper fume and shout)

Did you lose your flame in envy keen

Jealous of a shade of green?

Or did this breeze, which now's a gale

Cause your fickle friend to fail?

Okay, I will not indulge in writing poetry too often. My excuse is that light verse fits my mood in life and the words are rarely profound. Often they flow from my pencil and I can't stop them.

On the third day, we sailed one hundred and thirty-nine miles, thanks to stronger winds. By evening, we were once again under full canvas with Force 3 and Force 4 winds, sailing well, and in twenty-four hours we gained another 145 miles.

You might ask, "Where is the magic in this hum-drum sailing for a few miles each day?" I can tell you. Magic is manifested when the bowsprit fences with the moon, low on the horizon; when the port side shrouds chase Sirius, our guide, on its westward path, fifteen degrees each hour; when flying fish soar from wave to wave leaving their signature smell on the wind; and when the tropical sea, in the black night, causes *Ancestor's* phosphorescent wake to glow for the mermaids. So much is magical. Daytime is for navigating, for repairing anything that breaks or wears out, for eating, and visiting my number-one son and my favourite nephew.

And for getting knocked about from time to time. After noon, the wind stopped and then nailed us from a different direction, which resulted in an accidental gybe. We clawed the mainsail down and did a rough furl to the boom. It was a wild Force 9 gale (>45 knots) and we had to let *Ancestor* run off with a slack jib spilling wind while we bent on the storm trysail. This task was not exactly fun since we had only set this sail once, back in Grenada and this was the first time raising the storm sail under rough conditions. Eventually it was set. *Ancestor* galloped along on a broad reach. We were not on our intended course but we certainly were moving! Heavy rain lashed the boat and the air temperature plunged five degrees. We shivered, laughed, and asked ourselves, "How did this squally, foul weather develop?" There had been no clues until the trade wind clouds abruptly turned into one black, ominous mass. Without a barometer to consult, we were not forewarned of the startling, sharp drop in barometric pressure. I told the boys that it was just Mother Ocean playing with us as she is wont to do on occasion. I don't think the crew were convinced. Anyway, in three hours the trysail was removed and the mainsail was sleeping aloft, in a good Force 4 wind.

There was, we were discovering, a lot to learn about *Ancestor*. Short-handed sailing on a schooner had taught me that whenever the wind is abaft the beam, it is best to furl the main and travel slower and safer, under foresail, jumbo and jib. With a young crew like ours, *Ancestor's* huge mainsail can pose a problem; it can be a dangerous when running-off in a building wind. I had to keep this fact in mind even though we had a new and smaller mainsail. Over the next few days, we experimented with various sail-sets in a variety of wind and sea conditions. Slowly, slowly the boat was teaching us. On the day of that full gale, we covered 145 miles. That made us smile.

At daylight, during my routine a.m. inspections, I found that the clew cringle on the jib had begun to shift and was compromising that section of the sail. Rooting around in the junk box, I found a bronze, two and a half inch diameter ring. This would be a better fit in that corner of the sail. Jib down. Staysail up. I set to work using extra patches of heavy flax cloth, on each side of the clew. I positioned the ring, sewed it in place and added a patch of elk hide for chafe, and the jib was ready. I was fortunate to have kept the extra sail material and old cast-off gear that Mr. Simmons, our benefactor in Bequia, had given me.

Forestay, aka Rusty, was in cat-heaven these days. Four to eight inch long flying fish landed on deck every night and this meant good hunting for felines. Whenever we found a larger fish on deck, we measured it and the longest one recorded on the Grenada to Panama run was eleven inches. Rusty pulled a big one out from under a coil of rope one morning, batted it around a few times, crawled onto my lap and dropped the fish on my knees! Thank you, Rusty. I cleaned it, fried it and ate it. Better than oatmeal in my opinion.

Regarding navigation, we were getting better time-check, shortwave signals from WWV Hawaii than from Boulder, Colorado. Our chronometer was a bit unreliable. There were days when it was two seconds slow, and other days, it was six or seven seconds fast. Without the little transistor radio, we would have had difficulty tracking our position. Frequently, we had morning rain squalls, cloud cover and no chance of getting a sun shot. By noon it was usually clear, with only the trade wind clouds marching along on our course. Then I could calculate local apparent noon and get the approximate meridian passage of the sun. I would sit in a comfortable position on the doghouse cabin. Brian or Todd would stand by at the chronometer and I would take sights five minutes apart before the calculated meridian passage. I'd shout, "Mark!", the exact time would be recorded and I would call out the sextant altitude which would be entered opposite the time. I would shoot again and record the data. At some point the altitude readings would stall out and differences in the sextant angle would remain the same. My readings would decrease as we made notations at a five minutes intervals to balance the data. Using this method, it was easy to calculate the exact time of the sun's passage over our position. We would add the increment value to the Greenwich hour angle to determine our longitude. The difference between the sextant altitude and the calculated altitude, with corrections, were recorded, zenith distance and declination was obtained, declination subtracted and there was our latitude. For our slow moving surface vessel, the noon sight was enough to track our position accurately, to within about a nautical mile. Sometimes I would take star, planet or moon sight but I was in my lazy phase and most of the navigation was done at noon.

Dead-reckoning is another interesting subject. A sailor should be aware of ocean currents, drift, leeway and how these forces influence the vessel. A sailor might have several days of total cloud cover. If the sailor possesses a taffrail log, he can at least keep track of mileage. When seamen become attuned to the ocean, they can make quite accurate guesses on the apparent position. With the system of navigation I was using (HO 249), I always started from an assumed position, took my sights and calculated the intercept on an azimuth of whatever celestial body I was using. I called the assumed position the WAG (Wild-Assed Guess) and I always labelled it that way on the plotting sheet so as not to create any confusion.

A sailor should also be knowledgeable about celestial bodies which are navigational aids in the latitudes being traversed. Planets are better than stars because they are brighter and the navigator can take sights of them later in the evening or earlier in the morning. For instance, if Venus is your morning star, and you can see the horizon clearly, you can pop off a sight in the early hours to update your longitude. The scope used for star sights gathers enough light to give a good horizon, making it easy to complete an altitude measurement of a star or a planet. My habit is to watch the progression of constellations during the night and thereby know the azimuth and approximate altitude of the available stars for the early morning fixes. Night skies are beautiful and sailing beneath them makes humble seafarers keenly aware of who and where they are on the sea and in the universe. Mermaid songs also explain the mysteries of ocean travel. Enough about navigation.

A Change of Plan

On February nineteenth, we altered course from 285 to 225 degrees, aiming for the Archipelago de Mulatas, the San Blas Islands, off the coast of Panama. Todd and I were there last year and we loved this region. Brian was not hard to convince about the course change. We were over 700 miles from Grenada now, making about 130 miles each day. Todd had been a bit under the weather for the last while, eating only crackers and drinking tea. But having the San Blas Islands as a close destination seemed to restore his health. He was definitely in favour of walking on a sandy beach again.

Our noon longitude position next day verified that the one knot current had stalled. You could feel it on the tiller and see it in the wind pressure on the sails. The extra twenty-four miles a day would be missed. Fluctuating winds also contributed to our sluggish progress. It was as though *Ancestor* was dragging more than our taffrail log.

We were just south, and parallel to, a main shipping lane out of Panama, regularly sighting and passing other vessels. During the night hours, our starboard navigation light had consumed several tanks of kerosene since we left Grenada. Day or night, whoever was on watch checked our east and west directions carefully about every fifteen minute. We knew that a vessel under way at eighteen knots could be on top of us in no time at all, and if the bow-watch on an approaching ship was not keeping a sharp eye out for slow moving objects like us, we would be easily sunk. I could picture someone on a huge ship's deck, perhaps hearing a crunching sound and taking a curious look over the railing with a dismissive shake of the head. A vivid imagination helps to keep a sailor safe. Paranoia is not needed thank you.

From the log:

Cranse iron broke during the night. Skipper on the bowsprit applying extra lashing to keep everything together. Todd and Brian both feeling sick. Force 5 northeasterly winds and gale force at noon, estimate 38 - 40 knots. Main furled. Sun sights unreliable due to rough sea conditions, which wipe out the horizon. Wave doused me and the sextant. Too much fun all at once. Days run has been approximately 139 miles. At 1730 took radio bearings on Cartagena and Turbo which puts us at 11 ° N, and 76° 57' W. About 130 miles from San Blas Islands.

* * *

By morning the winds had moderated and they continued to decrease until we had only five to eight knots to work with. We sensed we were near shore and so we scanned the southern horizon with binoculars, looking for mountains above the morning haze. A 10:30 a.m. sun shot placed *Ancestor* ten miles east of our WAG position. This finding confirmed that we were dealing with tricky currents. Fortunately the sky was clear enough at noon for us to update our position, which was reassuring.

All hands were healthy once again. We prepared an evening meal of onions, potatoes and fish, with a dash of hot chili pepper; a tasty meal, washed down with the last of our Grenadian beer.

At 5:30 pm Brian shouted, "Land ho!" And we saw our first smudge of green above the white cloud cover on one of the San Blas islands!

Sunset was almost upon us. Rather than trying our luck on anchoring before dark, we hove-to until morning. The log rotor was pulled in and coiled on deck. The mainsail was furled and the trysail was set in its place. *Ancestor* sat comfortably with the sail slightly cocked to windward and the tiller lashed to the weather side. All was well and each person was alert on his watch and listening for the unwanted pounding of surf on the unseen reefs.

After midnight, around 1:30 am, we heard the unmistakable roar of breaking waves. Through the binoculars, I could see a line of reefs within a thousand feet of us. All hands were called on deck to turn *Ancestor* northward under full sail. A two knot current from the northwest was pushing us toward a nest of reefs bearing to the south and east. The wind was only Force 3 from the northeast, but it was enough for us to sail at two and three knots. Within the hour, we were in the clear.

The morning sky was hazy and I could not get star sights or a shot of the sun. Lack of a visible horizon was the problem. The same navigational dilemma was still with us at noon; we were unable to get a meridian passage shot. Frustrating! We spent the whole day tacking into a light, northwest wind that tried our patience. *Ancestor* barely made any headway; tack on tack against wind and current. My dead-reckoning put us twelve miles off the still unseen mainland shore. I had doubts about getting into the islands. By mid-afternoon, the wind had died off and we were becalmed with sails slatting.

My crew suggested whistling for a wind. The lore tells that whistling at the helm is bad news for the sailor. Such foolish behaviour could cause a storm to appear. No problem. We tied the tiller off and the three of us began our whistling act. After all, we were on a Grenadian boat and Grenadian sailors are excellent wind-whistlers. Why not us? It was an amusing pastime and whistling took our minds off our not-too-comfortable situation. Besides, it worked! The northwest breeze returned and we continued on our way with smug smiles. Each one of us wanted to claim full credit for the wind's return.

Overnight the wind veered to the northeast and everything changed again. At first light, my star sight verified our longitude, allowing us to proceed with confidence. Our target island popped up out of the ocean suddenly at 9:00 a.m..

With the mainsail furled and the jib pulling us along at a slow but acceptable pace, we neared Puyades Island, tucked in on its southern shore and dropped anchor in eight fathoms, onto a white sand bottom. We were eleven days out and twelve hundred and eight miles from Grenada.

Todd and Brian jumped into the water faster than their skipper could blink. They swam down deep and then surfaced to announce that our anchor was well set. After I took a quick dip, we assembled on deck and I mixed up a batter of 'Panic' for our late breakfast.

Panic at Puyades, Ancestor Island and Molas

*M*y Panic recipe comes from northern Canada. In 1957, my brother Hank and I made a November canoe trip down the Smokey River in northern Alberta. The low water level was tricky, especially since the air temperature was scarcely above freezing and we were exhausted after a long day of canoeing. Our goal for that day was a trapper's cabin at the bottom of a seven mile rapid. I was bow-paddling and as we closed in on the rapids, the wind, carrying the first snow of the season, began to blow upstream, directly into our faces. Visibility was close to nil and it was too late to abort and find a safe landing somewhere on shore. I did my best to guide us, but with my eyes full of stinging snow, it was difficult to see anything. We were striking rocks and glancing off them and the canoe was taking on water. A mile would have been too far for us to continue under these conditions but we had no alternative but carry on or drown.

When we finally reached the end of the rough water, we moved into a back eddy. Hank and I developed good swivel hips during that last hour. The gunwales were hardly above water and in order to stay afloat and not capsize, our bodies from the waist down, had to become part of the canoe, while our upper bodies remained vertical, or leaned slightly to either side to prevent the canoe from rolling over. Slow-paddling to shore, we beached the canoe below John Dikuck's cabin. I can still recall how hard it was for me to get out and pull the canoe up. Although soaked and almost hypothermic, Hank and I managed to offload our gear, turn the canoe upside down in a safe place and stumble to the cabin.

Now we get to the recipe.

Like all good trappers, John Diduck did not lock his cabin door. Inside was a stack of dry firewood and kindling, which was soon crackling away in the barrel heater.

In twenty minutes we were warm, our clothes were steaming and we were hungry.

I had seen a flock of grouse near the cabin, so after I dried out the .22 rifle, Hank opened the door and despatched a couple of them. "Hunting at its best," he claimed as he cleaned the birds and I searched for more food to add to our meal. The list of what I found is humble: five pounds of flour, (no weevils), a tablespoon of caked baking soda in a tin and a spoonful of cinnamon in a glass jar. That was it.

"Okay" says I, "I'll whip up a batch of bannock."

"Nah," says Hank, "I'll make pancakes." A heated debate developed about the relative merits of bannock and pancakes but we needed to fill our stomachs and the birds had already been breaded and they were sizzling in the pan. "Ah hell," says Hank, "let's compromise. We'll make part pancake and part bannock and we'll call it Panic!" From that day on, anything remotely resembling either mixture was Panic to me.

* * *

The version of Panic I prepared in the lee of Puyades Island included vanilla flavouring that had been given to us in Bequia the year before. We sniffed the vanilla and agreed that it smelled sort of like it should smell and so it was tossed into the bowl with brown sugar and a can of Carnation sweet cream poured on for the topping. We devoured our Panic and watched the haze clearing and the South American mainland coming into view. In the distance, there were several cayucas sailing toward the island and we hoped they would bring molas to trade with us.

That afternoon, the skipper and his crew snorkeled and went exploring. There are three other islets in the Puyades group, and the reef on the northern side protects them from the mighty ocean's waves. The healthy coral, the prolific marine life, and the overall beauty of the area were incredible. As amazing as anything I had seen on Australia's Great Barrier Reef. The boys and I also made brief but fascinating excursions to the outside reef where we collected five helmet conch for meals and for making conch horns.

Aboard *Ancestor*, we rested, compared stories and fought with the cat. The cayucas we had seen earlier had arrived at the island. Six Kunas waved to us, went ashore and set about collecting fallen palm fronds. Obviously they were the caretakers of the island's coconut trees. Short in stature, the women were colourfully dressed with their mola blouses and huge ear rings. The men were somewhat less decorative, clad in cut off trousers and ragged shirts.

Our peace was interrupted when *Bellatrix*, a CT-41, sailed in, hove to and inspected us and everything else. I said to Brian and Todd, "Okay guys, intense, non-wavering stares are in order. Repel them. Use your telepathic powers. Push them away. Let them know they are not welcome." On the one hand it would be nice to swap tales with fellow sailors but on the other hand, their boat was totally out of place here beside this idyllic tropical island, an old smuggling cutter, and a small flotilla of traditional, dug-out, sailing canoes. *Bellatrix* did not fit in and we successfully willed them away. The CT-41's big genoa was raised and she took off in a southeast direction, while we cheered and thumped *Ancestor*'s deck with our tough, bare feet.

Suppertime approached but our supplies were sparse and uninteresting. No worries. With the help of my capable and hungry crew, we came up with a dinner menu: macaroni and cheese, and a can of beans, all hot and steamy and served on freshly cut banana leaves, and sweet water and very ripe bananas for dessert.

Our Kuna neighbours had burned their pile of coconut fronds to a heap of ashes. They had eaten their meal too. The people now settling in for the night and their soft voices floated above the rumble of waves on the reef. Aboard *Ancestor*, we were silent, in awe, breathing in the tropical night. The sun had dropped into the sea, tugging indescribable filaments of sheer vapour, the colours of the Aurora, into the water with it. I tried very hard to avoid worrying about all the work to be done on the morrow. *Keep in the moment. Tomorrow will take care of itself.*

My young crew unrolled their sleeping bags on the deck, the ship's cat snuggled alongside, and quiet reigned. Except for my pencil writing my thoughts across a scrap of paper.

A sweet night in the tropics.
Ancestor snugged to her anchor,
Nodding
Then dropping off to sleep.
I peer over the bulwarks
In anticipation,

On Puyades Island

Like a Duke in the Royal Box
At Covent Garden-
Waiting for the show to begin.
It begins.
A waxing moon leaps into view
Stage centre,
Coconut palms are eyebrows rising
And the white sandy shore,
Like the gleaming ivory teeth
Of a beautiful ballerina who
Smiles at me and says
"Welcome home Jon"

Midnight arrived before I dozed off. My mind was full of poetry and I scrawled many lines while the distant, hollow roar of the surf sang of the interface of ocean and land. My longing to stay in the Puyades Islands forever, was bittersweet. We had to sail on, soon, before our provisions ran out.

* * *

In the morning we had a huge feed of pancakes, washed down with coffee. Our waists bulged when we were done, but we agreed that this was acceptable at the start of another work day. Todd and Brian hopped into the dinghy to continue with their explorations ashore and I lit my pipe, puffed contentedly, and reviewed my list of things to do.

The chores did not take long. First, I retied one baggywrinkle on the port side topping lift, then I re-lashed some of the ratlines which needed attention. *Is Brian trying to wear them out?* Ratlines done, I secured the radar reflector which was a bit floppy, and then I had to secure the forestay to the bowsprit. The top loop on the cranse iron had broken and a crack had appeared on the body of the iron adjacent to the loop. That fitting was a complete failure and I wrote 'replacement fitting needed' on my Panama to do list. Conveniently, in a hoard of junk we had aboard, I found a piece of three eighths galvanized, seven by nine lay, wire rope, and matching cable clamps. After whispering a thanks to Johnny on *Jens Juhl*, I went forward and positioned myself, comfortably this time, at the end of the bowsprit. Daylight and no dunking in the ocean when working on the bowsprit was my new sailing mantra. To begin with, I put a five-eighth inch stainless steel bolt through the bottom fork of the forestay turnbuckle, then two loops of wire through the fork and around the bowsprit, followed by the application of clamps to finish the job. At first, I was pleased with the result. *It might work fine all the way to Vancouver . . . No, I don't think so. Ancestor doesn't deserve a 'good enough' attitude. I'll get her a proper fitting in Panama.*

The junk box also contained a small fitting that could be adapted to make a flagstaff holder on the taffrail. This I screwed into place and when the crew returned with a length of bamboo, we found that it was a perfect fit in the socket. Bingo – we now had a staff and we could fly our colours proudly.

The Kuna Indians paddled over to *Ancestor* at noon and we invited them aboard.

They were very friendly. A pleasure to have onboard. And even though we had no useful language between us, we managed to communicate with a few words in Spanish and a lot of sign language. These folks were mostly interested in snorkelling gear and fishing equipment. Their molas were gorgeous and we wanted them all of

At anchor, Puyades Island

course, but we traded a face mask, a pair of flippers and one hundred feet of monofilament fish line for three of their artful cloth creations.

Trading now completed, the conversation changed. They indicated that the shape of the most easterly islet of the group was important. They had noticed us spending most of our shore time there and they appreciated that it was our favourite place. The Kunas made hand signs to illustrate how the islet and our boat were similar in shape. We finally understood that they were naming the islet '*Ancestor* Island'! When they realized that we finally got the idea, they were very excited and we laughed together. I unfolded the chart and pencilled in the name '*Ancestor* Island.' They approved and we were humbled and happy that they would suggest such a thing.

The Kunas carried their fresh water in one gallon glass jugs but it was brackish because their fresh water sources were shallow. I persuaded them to bring their jugs aboard, and we replaced their poor quality island water with our water from L'Anse aux Épines Bay in Grenada. They tasted our offering and smiled. When they left us, we talked among ourselves about how blessed we were to have met them. A short time later they waved farewell as they raised sails and headed for their home island.

Following a not-very-tasty lunch, we reviewed our situation with respect to where we were on our trip and how the provisions were holding out. Todd did an inventory and called out, "Three onions, one potato, a half-pound of macaroni, five teabags, one half pound of coffee, one pound (estimated) of rolled oats and forty gallons of water." Hmm.

"Okay guys," I said, "we'll go ashore and add to Todd's list."

Mature coconut palms were in abundance on the island and soon the crew were climbing and twisting off coconuts. We collected seventeen water nuts and four dry nuts and loaded them in the dinghy. I also selected two sprouting nuts to humour my green thumb tendencies. On this 'shopping spree' I had brought along a wooden crate which the boys filled with sandy island soil. In the box, we planted our sprouting nuts and talked about making sure that our 'garden' did not die of thirst on this trip. We also harvested some heart of palm, enough for two days of salads. Next we went diving for conch. Until a large lemon shark chased us out of the water.

* * *

That night we sat around a campfire on *Ancestor* Island, in the lee of a palm frond hut which protected the blaze from the trade winds. The hut was a rudimentary structure, seemingly improved with new roof fronds whenever folks decided to stay here for awhile. We cooked onions and potato, and I boiled some newly discovered rice that had somehow escaped Todd's notice when he wrote our inventory list. A simple meal and we savoured every mouthful.

After supper, the boys and I thought that a ceremony was in order. I started off, standing by the fire with our water bottle in my hand. I cast mugs of water, as an offering, in all four major compass directions, blessing the land with our hopes for a healthy and unpolluted future. Then I packed my pipe and blew a puff of smoke in each direction while loudly invoking the island's name four times. This impromptu ritual was performed in a light, fun way, but we grew serious and overcome by our surroundings. Personally I sensed something mystical; something beyond my understanding, on the edge of my consciousness. Something I could not define or put into words. My bare feet became attached to this little world. I was rooted in place. It was magical. It was spiritual.

A waning moon, in the western heavens, paved a highway of light across the water to guide us back to *Ancestor*, our floating home. The lads were soon asleep and the skipper scribbled away in the moonlight and the starlight, not thinking of tomorrow.

* * *

On February twenty-sixth, *Ancestor*'s people awoke at 6:30 a.m. and hungrily devoured bowls of rolled oats moistened with tasty coconut water. Departure day. Friday again, but, we joked, not an unlucky Friday. Our bananas were no longer a threat to our ship since they'd all been eaten. Also in our favour was the ship's cat, on constant deck patrol as usual, and black enough to cause any sailor to smile. Forestay was definitely good luck.

Our route to deep water took us past the western end of Puyades Island, in a north westerly direction between the reefs. The waves breaking on both sides of us made for an exciting sail and because of them, the channel seemed narrower than it actually was. The wind held a steady Force 4 and *Ancestor* tossed her head like a thoroughbred and slid through the channel at close to seven knots. My happy crew looked back at the reefs and grinned in triumph as the deep wave pattern re-established itself and we moved away from danger. By 11:30 am, Hollandes Cays were on our port beam. Visibility was good and we proceeded on visual bearings for the remainder of the day, holding our bow at 290 degrees. Ten hours later, we raised the Manzanilla Point light, and at midnight the Farralones light was shining right where expected.

By 2:00 a.m. next morning, the wind had dropped to five knots and at 3:00 a.m. we could see the entrance to the Panama Canal. At 8:30 a.m., we were anchoring on the flats, in Limon Bay, at Cristóbal, Republic of Panama, ninety-five and a half miles from the San Blas Islands and one thousand, three hundred and three miles from Grenada. The first leg of the voyage had ended.

Cristóbal, ROP and Hilton Beverley Fraser

*O*n the flats, we were amongst other cruising boats, and sailors came by on their way ashore to say hello. There were dinghies of all shapes and sizes, occupied by folks of all shapes and sizes and a cross section of nationalities. We had been advised regarding a new routine here since there had been a few changes since last year. Patiently, Ancestor's skipper and crew waited for things to happen. Our Panama flag flapped lazily above the yellow quarantine flag, which announced our un-cleared status.

At 9:30 am, an American Admeasurer came alongside, greeted us, and immediately started measuring our hull for its tonnage calculation. He was a jovial guy who commented on the cockroaches' fine accommodation in the hold. In less than fifteen minutes he issued our Panama Canal Certificate, Number 177385. The man was still chuckling when his launch putted back to the shore.

This jolly fellow had given me directions to the Customs and Immigration offices and my boys were urging me to hurry and get us cleared-in so they could eat real food. At a restaurant, please. They more than hinted that I looked like a grubby ship rat and I should clean myself up before entering any government offices in town. Our five inch diameter mirror proved that their judgement was correct. Obediently, I shaved, washed my hair, put on clean jeans and a clean but rumpled shirt, combed out the beard and examined myself again. Ready to face officialdom, I asked my lads to launch *Full Speed Ahead*.

Clearance procedures were not too convoluted. With the signed documents in my pack, I proceeded to the Canal Authority offices and applied for our canal transit. This was also accomplished without any problems and I strolled back to the Panama Canal Yacht Club.

The PCYC is not solely a club for the idle rich, although they do cater to well-heeled resident yachtsmen, if the large vessels tied to their nice docks are any indication. But the club also does a thriving business catering to less-heeled, cruising sailors who use the club's facilities. The PCYC offers a few transient berths, a large restaurant/bar, laundry and showers, and a laid-back atmosphere for everyone to enjoy. The club also collects mail for the cruising tribe, and as I returned on this day, I was pleased to find that we did have a few envelopes waiting for us.

With a slightly guilty feeling, I ordered a much-too-cold Heineken beer, chose a table by the railing and opened my correspondence. *Todd and Brian can wait a few more minutes.* The first letter was from Hilt Fraser. He had booked a flight for Panama and he would be airborne as soon as I informed him that we had arrived in the Canal Zone. I found a telephone and made the call. Was he ever excited! I suggested that when he arrived at the international airport, he take a taxi into Panama City. Then he could catch the trans-isthmus train to Cristóbal. I gave him directions to the yacht club. "Hilt," I asked, "are you bringing your favourite guitar along?" "It's in its' case Jon and ready to go."

Back with my beer at the table, I read the rest of the mail. There was a surprise envelope from Brigid, who had sailed with us on *Ancestor* in 1974. She wanted to wish us the best of luck on this voyage. Attached to her letter were two hundred US dollars in fifties! Wow! This was a cash transfusion that would get us a substantial supply of provisions. Brigid knew me well. I am a guy who is always financially on the borderline and not brilliant enough to make sure my bank balance can support my sailing adventures.

When I rowed back to *Ancestor*, I found the crew washed and dressed in cut-offs and tee shirts and ready for shore. Even Forestay looked ready for some shore leave. I explained to her, with regret, that her passport had not been stamped and she must stay aboard and stand watch while we were away buying her treats. Todd said Forestay was not convinced, but since she had never been on land, perhaps I could fool her this time.

At the yacht club restaurant, we ordered jumbo hamburgers. I also asked the waiter if he had any greens in the kitchen, and he returned shortly saying there was some reasonably fresh lettuce. From the USA. I asked him to bring one to me. The delivered plate held a distressed-looking iceberg lettuce. I nibbled a leaf anyway and found that this was just what I needed. My dining companions groaned, embarrassed perhaps by my munching, while other guests in the restaurant pointed and grinned at me. One lady said she understood my craving and she might order some too. After hearing her say that, Todd and Brian relaxed and consumed their 'fantastic' burgers.

As usual, a number of vessels were waiting to transit the canal and we met their crews who wanted to know all about *Ancestor*. Our boat and her history fascinated them and they were astounded that she had no engine. The Admeasurer had discovered that ours was the first vessel of her design to transit the canal. We liked the honour of being the first in something.

I had to start work on our vessel and the lads were more than happy to let me get on with it. We had talked about the dangers of Colón and wandering around in the Canal Zone. Both of them promised me they'd be careful and stay in Cristóbal. I gave the okay for an exploratory trip ashore on the condition that they were to return to the club before dark. The kids disappeared out the door and I found a corner table and began listing everything that needed attention before the next leg of the voyage. Number one: the crane's iron must be replaced for sure. Number two: I needed to build a seat/bench near the tiller. Three: Anchor stowage was a problem. I sketched catheads, which would give us the ability to tie-off the anchor(s) properly while underway. Four: The rudder box had to be reinforced around the top and the tiller required repairs or alterations. The list went on, some on paper and some in my head, to be written down later when I knew exactly what I wanted.

Several hours were spent that afternoon securing the forestay, whisker stays, bob-stay and removing the dead cranse iron from the end of the bowsprit. A local man at PCYC gave me directions to his friend's place where I would find a sizeable collection of boat fittings. The man's friend had salvaged quite an inventory of nautical stuff off wrecks over the last twenty years. Maybe that guy could help me, and if not, he might redirect me to another guy who did small metal fabrications. Every port has a network of craftsmen, mechanics, chandlers, swappers. I was fortunate to have found the salvaging fellow on the first try. I dug through his enormous heap of marine fittings and bits and pieces. Ten minutes later, I struck it rich. A galvanized steel cranes iron! I grabbed it, wiped off the dirt and compared it to the old fitting. A perfect match! To make a fit for the bowsprit I would only have to remove zinc drips on the inside of the hoop. Fifteen dollars lighter, I returned to the dinghy, pleased that my search had paid off. Work could begin.

At the yacht club, I stopped to visit with other sailors who were checking out the titles on the book-trade shelf. The variety of books was super. I chose a copy of the collected poems of Pablo Naruda, a three volume set of Russian history, a worm eaten but useful pilot book for the southeast Pacific Ocean, two books about the Galapagos Islands and ten or so novels, mostly science fiction, for easy reading. I lugged all this to *Ancestor*, feeling that the world was just fine. On deck, Forestay pranced around and jumped all over me. She hooked her claws into my shirt, hoping for some tender loving care and, if I was understanding her cat language correctly, she was asking, "Where are the treats you promised?" I untangled her from my clothing so that she could sniff my books and the new iron fitting. It was her duty to inspect everything and it seemed that she found my treasures acceptable.

When the crew hollered out for a shore-boat, I rowed back to the club and loaded them aboard.

Brian and Todd could hardly wait to tell me about the pimps and hookers on every street corner in town, who made come hither eyes at them. Two young, rich, blond, North American males could mean a lucrative day's work. My boys had resisted their sexy advances. My crew preferred to spend their money on papayas, limes and guavas for our breakfast. Good lads! They had also found a hardware store with lots of marine gear for the skipper to rummage through and cat food for Forestay. As soon as she smelled the little pellets, which were most likely wheat puffs soaked with catnip, she ate a healthy portion, guzzled some water, curled up on a blanket and went to sleep, to dream, I assume, of flying fish and squid. Our meal of rice and fish did not seem half as exciting as her dinner that evening.

A few more days were spent wandering around Cristóbal and Colón, meeting cruising folk and investigating the details for our transit. We discovered that we might be able to raft up alongside a canal tugboat in the locks. This would be much easier than having to manage the long mooring lines normally required for small craft in these locks. Usually a boat has to have four lines, each three quarter inch diameter and one hundred feet in length. But the only line I could find in Cristóbal was five eighths inch diameter and as long as you wanted. I filed that tidbit of information away for future reference.

Meanwhile I installed the new cranse iron on the bowsprit and re-attached the bobstay, whisker-stays and forestay. I also designed a wooden structure to support an outboard motor - just in case. The support would have to be heavy wood, attached to the transom or the stern quarter of the hull. It would need to be removable and functional. I thought we might be able to rent a forty horsepower motor which should be adequate to give us the required six knots of speed to cross Gatun Lake. The other option and my preference, would be to get a tow into the locks and across the lake and forget about a motor. Having taken measurements and drawing sketches for an outboard bracket, I decided to wait until Hilt arrived to continue that project. Hilt would have ideas to contribute and he was very capable with tools and construction work.

Our diet had improved since we arrived in the Canal Zone. We had our favourite places to buy the best fruit, vegetables and loaves of bread. We got to know a network of sailors whom we visited, either on shore or on *Ancestor V*. Everyone gammed and shared their local knowledge while the tropical sun burned our skin to deeper shades of brown and bronze. The afternoon rains were predictable and onboard *Ancestor*, we were always ready to usher everyone into the hold when a drenching rainfall threatened. Whenever we had a crowd onboard, in a sudden squall, we retired below, formed a circle and spoke very loudly in order to hear one another above the drumming downpour pummelling our decks. The cockroaches, centipedes and crickets hid amongst the rock ballast and maintained silence while we were thus engaged.

On the first day of March, a taxi stopped in front of the yacht club and Hilt Fraser stepped out with a happy smile and his guitar case! What a surprise! There was a lot of hugging and laughing. He paid the taxi driver and dragged his sea bag out of the vehicle's trunk. Another surprise. He was wearing a white t-shirt with a blue painting of *Ancestor* on it, complete with her name and port of registry. An acquaintance of his in Sarnia had silk screened the T-shirts and Hilt had brought along an assortment of sizes. It didn't take long for us to remove our sweaty garments and don his *Ancestor V* tees. Were we cool or what? However, the most astonishing thing for me was that he was clean-shaven. What? He saw that I was confused. This man was not the hairy Hilt I knew. He had shaved his beard off for the tropics but when we had paddled together in a cross-Canada canoe trip in 1967, my good friend had sported the woolliest face I have ever seen red hair from his eyes downward. I would have to get used to this new Hilton.

It took a few trips to ferry our gang back to the boat. I conveyed Hilt, his bag and guitar first, and together we got everything safely onboard. I said, "*Ancestor V* welcomes you. Please don't step on the ship's cat."

He was silent for a long time, while his eyes scrutinized our rigging, sails, and decks - the whole ship. He turned, gave me a bear hug and said, "Thanks, Jon, this means a lot to me. I can't believe I'm actually here." I brought up the log book for him to sign-on for the voyage. He did so, with a flourish and a smile. This ceremony completed, I left Hilt to get acquainted with Forestay and I fetched the rest of the crew.

The remainder of that day was filled with talk about our voyage so far and the work to be done before venturing into the Pacific. Hilt was ready, willing and able. He made excellent suggestions about how we could accomplish each job. It was reassuring to have another seasoned sailor with us. Hilton had a lot of know-how when it came to the details of how to do things on a boat. He'd built his own twenty-five foot sloop, *Windago*, in Ontario.

While we were chatting, another sailor came rowing by to tell us that the yacht club had a space for *Ancestor*, stern-to, on the end of dock three. If we wanted to come in, we were welcome. This was good news. We immediately prepared to sail in a light, easterly breeze. Such a wind is ideal for manoeuvring. The main and jib were hoisted and the anchor was on deck. "Helm over and man the sheets." I asked Hilt to manage the anchoring. He stood at the bow, everything sorted out and ready to go. In a few minutes, we were rounding up, the anchor splashed, the sails came down and Brian rowed away with a long line to make fast to the dock. We did well and we were pleased with ourselves, partly because there was a self-appointed dock committee observing our progress; critics all. The sails were furled. The anchor line was adjusted in order to be able to pull our stern dockside easily. This way, we could disembark any time we wished. So, we hopped onto the dock to enjoy beers and friendly banter with our fellow travellers.

Several other things happened that day. We met Mary and John Hoffman who would be transiting the canal on the same date as *Ancestor*. Their vessel, Moorea, was a Columbia forty-five foot motorsailer. Last year at Aruba, we met them when we were on a very flashy fifty-two foot Van de Stadt sloop. Now we were on a very different vessel. They were happy to see us again. At the restaurant, during dinner, the Hoffman's generously volunteered to tow us into the locks and even

> DAILY NOTES AND SKETCHES *Cristobal C.Z.*
> *March 1, 1975*
>
> I hereby sign onto the Sloop Ancestor V, to sail on her continuing voyage to Hawaii & Vancouver.
> I find everything to my liking — except the skipper's cooking, and the odor of "curing" conch shells & fan coral which clutters the otherwise spacious decks.
>
> *Hilton Beverley Fraser*
> *417 Stuart St.*
> *Sarnia Ontario Canada*
>
> *Witness:*
> *[signature]*

Hilt Fraser signs on

through Gatun Lake if necessary. *Cancel the outboard motor bracket, Jon. Inspect Ancestor's towing line.*

Folks on *Departure* were looking for line handlers for their transit on the following morning. Hilt and Todd signed on for the job. Hilt could practice negotiating the canal system and that would make it easier for *Ancestor* and her crew when we made our own transit. The deal was closed with beer and smiles.

Hilt and Todd had a good time on the following day. They returned to Cristóbal on the last train that same night. Todd had obviously had a bit too much sun. Hilt, being older and wiser, looked better. Because Hilt has red hair and sensitive skin that burns easily, he always thinks about sun exposure. As soon as they were back, Hilt started playing his guitar and, like the Pied Piper, he was luring and serenading the lounging sailors on the dock and nearby boats. In the tropical night, our decks overflowed with seafarers and local folk singing their hearts out. Music creates laughter and friendships, communicates passion and compassion. The best panacea in the world. Meanwhile, Forestay stalked the crowd, attacked ankles and jumped at anything and everything swaying in the breeze. Perhaps the cat did not understand what all the fuss was about but she certainly knew how to party!

Following a late breakfast next morning, we held a conference to discuss the various jobs to be done before our departure. Hilt measured and penciled notes and made an inventory of *Ancestor*'s available tools and fittings. The skipper sorted the documents he required to arrange

At the Panama Canal Yacht Club docks

for the canal transit. On shore, Hilt began searching for materials. He enlisted Brian and Todd's help. Meantime, I had my own job. I had to locate the Panama Canal Authority office to obtain a slot assignment for our transit. Fortunately my task was easy and I was in the correct office, speaking with the right people and in less than half an hour I had the necessary document. When the crew returned, I proudly showed them our Panama Canal Ship Identification Certificate which measured four by six inches and displayed our ID number 177385. *Ancestor V* was scheduled to go on March eleventh.

Returning to the yacht club, I stopped to have a coffee with a young couple, newly arrived on a twenty-six foot sloop out of San Diego. They were as slim and hungry-looking as we were when we arrived, and I was eager to hear about their trip. In the past year, they experienced the usual frustrations; lack of wind along the west coast of Latin America, steaming hot anchorages up river estuaries, mosquitos, limited funds, and limited provisions - just to name a few of their challenges. They came through the canal early in February, and then they had taken time to do some work on their wooden-hulled boat. Having set off on light easterly winds from Cristóbal three weeks before, the couple had hoped to sail north to Florida via the Yucatán Channel. The trip was okay, except for the lack of wind and the dangerous reefs near some of the islands where they found themselves navigating without good charts. Their boat touched a reef and this caused several substantial and irreparable leaks. The bilge pump was working overtime and they decided to return to Panama for repairs. Until they did reach Panama, they were functioning in a dazed state of exhaustion, constantly struggling to pump the bilge and rationing their rapidly diminishing food supply. One day they discovered that they were completely out of provisions and the only edible food onboard was tinned cat food. You guessed right if you came to the conclusion that they started sharing with the cat. They were not catching fish and it seemed that the gods were indeed angry with them. By the time they got to Cristóbal, they had nothing to eat and they were surviving on rain water, caught in a bucket at the forward end of the main boom!

I invited them for breakfast. "Keep your leftovers for your cat," I said. The large portions of food, typical of the American standard for breakfast, arrived at the table and I watched the couple dig in. But after a few minutes, they put aside their knives and forks. They were astonished to find they could not eat everything on their plates. Shrunken stomachs were to blame, no doubt.

But they were happy and relieved to be far away from reefs, light breezes and nasty leaks. Their boat was perched on a small marine ways beside the club where they could begin to repair the damage at a leisurely pace. One garboard strake along the keel was gouged and sprung. That was the major source of their leak problem. The couple asked for a bag to save their unfinished breakfast and after a photographer snapped a picture of us together, the man declared that he'd just taken a portrait of three scarecrows. Nice guy. The Californians and I parted company.

* * *

Hilt and I got busy on our boat projects. To ensure effective anchor stowage, we cut square holes in the bulwarks up forward so that a cathead timber would fit snug to the sampson post. The four by four timber, when fitted, extended two feet outboard of the hull on each side. A hole was drilled through both the timber and the sampson post and a large galvanized bolt was used to secure the connection. Wood blocking was attached on the inside of the bulwarks to support the timber. Wood screws fixed the blocking in place. Hilt found a scrap of thin copper plate to cap the ends of the cathead timber. Primer and white paint were applied. Additional copper plate was added to the top of the cap rail on the bulwarks to prevent the jib sheets from chafing.

While rooting through our junk box, we discovered a piece of half inch copper pipe. We flattened it with a hammer, wrapped it around the top of the rudder stock and nailed it down. This additional support was necessary to prevent the rudder from breaking. Progress.

Hilt constructed a steering seat at the tiller. I went ashore and called an airline company to reserve flights for Brian and Todd for the thirteenth of March.

After a late lunch, we went ashore. At mid-day, when it was relatively safe, we walked to the Agroupolos supermarket in Colón. On this excursion, I wanted us to go as a group. I remembered on my last visit to Colón I had foolishly taken an evening stroll that resulted in a brawl at a Chinese restaurant. Not this time. Four guys were on a mission and very aware of their surroundings.

Agroupolos was an excellent market with a variety of foods and food products. Hilt was happy to find instant mashed potatoes, one of his favourite cruising staples on Windago. He gathered his spuds and I tossed twenty-five pounds of real potatoes into the basket. We bought Carnation evaporated milk, Carnation cream, a box of teabags, twelve pounds of coffee in-the-bean, sugar, honey, syrup, twenty pounds of rice, a bag of oatmeal, twenty pounds of all-purpose flour, one tin each of baking powder and baking soda, spices, canned vegetables, molasses, guavas, papayas and limes. $US 189.00 poorer, we staggered to the boat.

In Cristóbal, I purchased seven gallons of kerosene at forty cents per gallon. Our final provisioning would be done in Panama City.

The Canal Authority confirmed that we would be able to tie-up alongside a tugboat in the locks; we would not require the four mooring lines. This saved us some money, which Hilt said he would apply to the purchase of beer in Balboa. The canal transit cost for *Ancestor* was $79.00 US.

The scarecrows

Panama Canal Transit

Final preparations for our canal transit were underway. Even though we would not be moving through the locks in the traditional small boat manner, we were nevertheless required to have four line handlers aboard. Hilt, Brian and Todd made three and the vessel's captain is not considered to be a line handler. He is just a noisy character giving directions and orders. When I spread the word that we needed a recruit, we had many potential helpers. So we took aboard four more people: Jack and Brenda Wood, Australians, and Derek and Sam from the USA. Okay, I can't count. It seemed to be a cool thing to do.

On the evening of March tenth, our group came aboard, ready for action on the morrow. Party time! Other boaters came over, with their musical instruments and soon we were at full throttle, filling the warm night with the songs of many nations. Our party was not 'dry' and the decks were thronged with visitors, but in spite of this, and perhaps because they were all sailors, no one fell overboard. Food appeared, we danced on the dock and all was well with the world. I went ashore at 2100 to make a scheduled phone call to verify our transit time. The authorities told me that our pilot would board us at 0900. I was quite sober, having only had my traditional, daily, single bottle of beer.

* * *

In the morning, I roused all hands, including a few lingering guests, and reverted to my role as skipper, assisting folks onto the dock, saying good bye and planning our departure. On the big day, all transiting vessels were to be at anchor in Limon Bay, where the pilots, one per boat, large or small, would board their assigned craft. Moorea was already there and we sailed from the dock and dropped the hook within a hundred yards of her.

As we snugged down to the anchor, I was able to surprise the crew - and myself - by producing pancakes for everyone. Heaps of pancakes. On a one burner Primus stove, no less. Diners had to wait their turn since we only owned four plates but I heard no complaints. Lots of Aunt Jemima syrup splashed on deck. A large coffee pot, that somebody had loaned us, provided the crew with caffeine. It did wonders for their hangovers. I was alert and eager to start our day.

At 0900 a boat came alongside and our pilot stepped aboard, clutching a two way radio. He was a nice Panamanian man. After shaking hands, he accepted pancakes and coffee. Then we waited. Our guide received word that our fleet of small boats should be in the first lock at 1130. Hearing this, I rowed over to the *Moorea* and made fast a tow line. The north wind was waking up; a steady Force 3 breeze. I brought the dinghy aboard *Ancestor* and lashed it down on the foredeck. *Let's go!*

At 1135 we were in the first lock, tied beside a fifty foot canal tug boat. Texaco New York, a gigantic tanker, occupied most of the lock. Her transom almost touched our bowsprit. Other sailing vessels were tethered on their four lines in the centre of the lock close by. Tensions were high. The gates closed. The roaring, turbulent water mirrored our emotions. I was glad that we were attached to the tug which kept us safe until the waves abated. In no time at all, we were moving into the second lock and getting organized for the next lift. The transit was progressing well. At 1245 we entered the third lock and by 1315 we were floating on Gatun Lake.

In Limon Bay, I had suggested to the *Moorea* crew, "Once we are in the lake, and if we have a favourable wind, our boats can sail and take the shortcut away from the main channel." When the time came, since the wind had increased to a strong Force 4, *Moorea's* and *Ancestor's* sails were hoisted and we headed south for Gamboa. The pilot did not object because we were making good time. Indeed we were travelling faster than the minimum speed of six knots required by the Canal Authority.

Gatun Lake's water temperature was eighty-four degrees. We watched for crocodiles and marvelled at the bird life and the small islands and continued plowing southward through the lake, at seven knots. Our pilot entertained us with the history of the Canal's construction. At 1430, Bohio Point was on our port beam. For lunch, Hilt served a large salad complete with long, thin slices of papaya, crusty bread, and soft drinks for those who needed sugar fixes and beer for those who needed to calm down.

Moorea tows Ancestor to the locks

We arrived at Gamboa Locks at 1630 at the head of the pack! Before entering the lock and taking our position, our two boats had to wait a short while. There were no problems here or at the Pedro Miguel Locks. Though at the last lock, Miraflores, there was a delay because our tug broke a three inch diameter nylon hawser while trying to position the tanker. It was hard to believe that such a line could break, but we could see the hawser in a tangle on the tug's deck.

In Miraflores, we also sustained a bit of scuffing alongside when our bowsprit and forward starboard bulwarks connected with the tug. Our starboard whisker stay was damaged and we lost some paint on the bulwarks. That wasn't fun but thankfully, nobody was injured. As we locked-down toward the Pacific Ocean, I discussed the broken hawser with a deckhand on the tug. He said that minor accidents are not uncommon and he asked if we wanted a souvenir of the occasion. Hilt and I agreed. Seconds later, we had a two hundred pound coil of nylon rope on *Ancestor V's* deck. We laughed. Can we make fishnets and fancy shirts with this stuff out on the broad Pacific? Forestay inspected the coil, approved, and jumped inside her new cat fort. She was thereafter very possessive of her hideout. At 2145, in the darkness, we tied off on a mooring at the Balboa Yacht Club. Whoopee! The first Carriacou sloop to float on the Pacific! After the pilot left, we had a few beers before the launch came to take our line handlers and hitch hikers ashore. The wind had died, it was warm, and throughout the night giant ships maneuvered silently toward the locks. We slept on deck under a benevolent moon, pleased with life.

In the locks, Panama Canal

The Balboa Yacht Club launch makes a tour around the mooring buoys approximately every hour and when you are ready to go ashore, you simply wave and the eagle-eyed launch skipper pulls up to your vessel. I waved at 0830 next morning, holding our passports and ship's papers and I was delivered to the yacht club docks. My first order of business was to register at the BYC. The club charged two dollars a day for the mooring and an additional twenty-five dollar deposit was required from each moorage customer.

Hijack Warnings

Having been at Balboa before, I knew that the Customs, Immigration and Health offices were not close together in one location. I would be walking around for about four hours in order to complete the clear-in formalities. Thankfully, there was a line of taxis at the club entrance to dicker with. One fellow had obviously made the run often. Twenty dollars seemed a fair price considering the distances and bother involved. I jumped in and we drove away.

The clearing-in went without a hitch and by 11:00 a.m. the formalities were done.

The immigration officer was intent on warning transient sailors about hijackings in his region. This was March and already since the first of January, he had received reports concerning three missing yachts. The officer described the local hijackers' preferred strategy. The possible target vessel's crew is watched and evaluated during their stay at the yacht club moorages. The chosen victim/vessel is observed leaving Balboa. The bad guys prefer single handers but they also prey on elderly couples travelling without crew.

The Panamanian authorities interviewed one sailor who had survived such an attack. This unfortunate man and his wife were sailing southward, bound for the Galapagos. On their first evening out, the wife called her husband on deck. She pointed to a rowing dinghy ahead of them. There were no other boats in sight. The couple altered course to intercept and help the person in the dinghy who was very far from land and alone. When they reached the dinghy, they saw that the occupant was a young man of about thirty years who appeared to be dehydrated, in terrible shape and he could hardly speak. Of course, they helped him onto their boat and brought him a bottle of water immediately. Instead of thanking his rescuers, the man pulled an automatic pistol from a small bag and shot the couple. The impact of the bullet knocked the skipper overboard. Although the sailor was injured, stunned and on the verge of panicking, he struggled to keep his head above water. When the pain kicked in, the skipper understood that he had a severe shoulder wound, his boat was pulling away, eastward, under both engine and sail, his wife was nowhere to be seen and in his haste, the pirate had not tied the little tender to the yacht. The dinghy was floating nearby and somehow, the sailor managed to climb inside. Because he was a doctor, he was able to staunch the blood gushing from his wound. He shredded his shirt for bandages. A Panamanian fishing boat picked him up next day and took him to Balboa.

That doctor's vessel, a thirty-eight foot Beneteau, was found five weeks later, completely repainted, with a bogus name on both bows. The immigration officer concluded his tale by saying that hijackers kill sailors, take their boats, disguise them, make a drug run to wherever and then scuttle the vessels. I could not ascertain how the authorities found this skipper's vessel, and they were not inclined to discuss this sad event any further. Wow. Nice guys in that immigration office but their message was not a cheery one. As I filed their information away - information I hoped I would never need - I walked to the Pan American Airlines office to purchase tickets for Brian and Todd. Then I returned to the immigration office where the agent photocopied the plane tickets, stamped my revised crew list and urged me to stay safe. Todd and Brian were free to fly and Hilton Fraser was recorded as first mate of the *Ancestor V*.

The Boys Fly and We Get to Work

That afternoon, Ancestor's crew went into Panama City for more provisions. The open markets and the Supermercado were full of fresh produce. I purchased seven dozen eggs which were carefully placed into a sturdy canvas bag. Cabbages keep well on a boat in the tropics and when sliced and mixed with apple slices they provide an easily digested salad after most of the ship's fruit and vegetables have been consumed or thrown to the booby birds. Eight cabbages were plopped into our basket with only two loaves of bread since we could bake our own bread from here on. We got seven large papayas, six dozen apples, a bag of oranges, limes, lemons, and a selection of other tasty foods. While Hilt flagged down a taxi, I bought a stock of green bananas, completely ignoring the fears and superstitions lurking in the dark depths of my consciousness. Perhaps we should leave them on deck instead of hanging them in the rigging. At the club dock, we loaded our booty into the BYC launch and motored out to Ancestor. After a late lunch, Hilt went back ashore for beer and a few more personal goodies. Todd and Brian talked about their impending flight to Canada via Guatemala, Los Angeles and San Francisco. They were excited about leaving and yet sad to be saying good bye. Both of them were fine sailors and other than having to fight off the street ladies in Cristóbal, they admitted that it had been a grand trip.

That afternoon, John and Mary Hoffman dropped by. This was the helpful couple aboard Moorea who had towed us into the canal. The German skipper, Paul, of the Friendship Sloop *Albatross* showed up too. He wanted me to show him how to check his plastic sextant for parallax and index error. Many interested sailors also visited that day to explore *Ancestor* and marvel at our scheme to sail the broad Pacific with only basic equipment and without an engine. The day evolved into yet another party. Hilt was in his element, smiling while he performed a multitude of songs. With so much stomping and toe tapping, *Ancestor's* top decks took a beating.

As usual, Forestay was rushing out of her rope-coil fort to attack the dancers' feet. She avoided every attempt we made to catch her and her frisky behaviour continued for several hours until she finally retired to catch her breath. Pet owners among our guests were fascinated with our born-on-a-boat-feline who had never been ashore to sample a real cat's life. This sort of imposed quarantine might be considered to be a dismal existence for any other kitty but to Forestay, our flying fish catcher, life was thrilling. When our soirée ended, most of the guests gathered at the yacht club to continue the fun and the merriment.

With everyone else ashore, it was difficult for Hilton and me to go from full speed ahead to the quiet and stillness of our bunks. Instead, though we were both hoarse from singing, we decided to review what was yet to be accomplished in order to meet our March fifteenth departure date. We listed all the chores needing our attention. Meanwhile Todd and Brian, having finished their packing, rocked in their hammocks and enjoyed their final Panamanian night.

During one of the calmer parts of that afternoon, both Brian and Todd said they were concerned about Hilt and I and *Ancestor V*. Because they had heard about the hijackings, they believed that *Ancestor* would be fair game for pirates in the Bay of Panama. I asked, "If someone wanted to do a drug run, wouldn't they be more interested in stealing a boat with an engine rather than an old tub full of rocks and only sails for propulsion? Besides, I am sure that *Ancestor* has already been observed and evaluated by any bad guys here in Balboa and she has already been rejected. Hijackers would definitely think she is not a suitable boat for drug-running." Sensing that the boys were still unconvinced, I went on to explain how sailing works with me. "First, before going on a trip, I always travel the route in my mind. If I can picture myself arriving at my destination, everything will be fine and it always has been fine up to now. Why don't you guys try mental travelling yourselves? Follow your intuition when you do. If the destination is murky in your head or you can't quite see yourself arriving where you want to be, hit the abort button and choose somewhere else." They mulled this over. *Will they apply my methods for their Pan Am flight tomorrow?*

Next morning, March thirteenth, the boys bid the ship's cat farewell and we stepped aboard the launch at 0430. The taxi ride to the Tocumen Airport was memorable. Our driver sped like a maniac through the predawn traffic, using the car horn with wild abandon while jabbering non-stop about his passion for the sport of boxing. I wondered if he was the same driver we had used for this run last year. I could have boxed his ears to make him slow down but I resisted the temptation. Todd and I remembered our taxi ride on this very road the year before and so the ride was a bit easier for us than for Brian. We reached the terminal with time to spare. When the loudspeakers announced the departure of Flight 615, we found ourselves hugging and wiping tears away. I told the lads that I saw them arriving in Vancouver. Everything would be okay. Then they were gone, leaving Hilt and myself wandering out into the sunlight in search of another kamikaze cab driver. Our driver, this time, was passionate about politics and didn't mention boxing!

On the way back to Balboa, we stopped in Panama City at Islamorada, the Admiralty chart agents, to buy a pad of plotting sheets. There were many other tempting goodies on those shelves pulling at my purse strings but we bought only the essentials.

Aboard *Ancestor*, we were missing the boys. Their youthful, eager antics had made our lives an entertaining and dynamic picnic. Hilt played a few melancholy guitar tunes to reflect our mood but I soon gave him hell and asked for cheerier music. The afternoon rains chased us below decks but we continued to sing. Music, unfailing music, up-lifted our spirits.

Our 'to do' list was reviewed and adjusted yet again until it was realistic, considering our remaining time in port, considering how far we could stretch our finances and considering what level of enthusiasm we could sustain. The list was changed somewhat from yesterday but it was still manageable.

While Hilt was sorting material and tools, I went ashore and ran the gauntlet once more to get our outbound clearance for March 15th. The process went smoothly. I received the mandatory documents and I had a brief conversation with the same immigration officer who had first cautioned us regarding the dangers of hijackers.

"Do you have guns onboard for protection?" he inquired.

"No, we do not," I answered. "However, we will stay alert and before we sail, we will be sure to have an action plan in case we do have to defend ourselves."

"Be careful, sailor," he said, and we shook hands.

Our mood that evening was subdued. We ate our salad and poached eggs and talked about my son and Brian and about our own friendship, which had begun in 1967 on Lake Huron. The night shadows were punctuated by passing, canal-bound vessels. Every ship, whatever its size, was a dark mountain compared to *Ancestor*. Each one glided by, within a few hundred yards of us, rippling the water. I smoked my pipe. Hilt strummed his guitar. Very soon we climbed into our bunks, feeling calm, perhaps wistful, but well, and certainly sleepy.

By 6:00 a.m. we were cutting papayas and squeezing lime juice onto every slice to add a little zest to our simple breakfast.

While Hilt fed Forestay and did the morning's obligatory amount of behind-the-ears scratching, I poured our cups of coffee with honey. Ah, another day.

The minor damage we had suffered in the last lock, demanded our immediate attention. We removed an existing five-eighths diameter eyebolt from the port deck and installed it through a frame on the starboard bulwarks. The whisker stay was attached to this eyebolt and tensioned to secure the bowsprit. The turnbuckle and the shackle were wired to avoid any slacking of either device. In our miscellaneous fittings box, we discovered a half-inch diameter, galvanized eyebolt to install in the deck where we had removed the larger bolt.

The deck caulking was still in good shape but the deck itself wanted touching up. Hilt brought paint and a brush out of the hold and took care of that. In the galley, I added another coat of enamel to freshen up the cabin sole. The paint is stinky and we had to close the hatch to keep the curious cat at bay. Out on deck again, I passed a peaceful hour coating our seven dozen eggs with Vaseline. Petroleum jelly blocks the passage of air through the shell membrane, thereby eliminating the threat of rot. The eggs were nestled in paper cartons and it would be our habit to turn the containers over once a week to prevent the yolks from settling against the shell. This practice works well.

Our jobs were getting ticked off the list. We re-stowed the coconuts, still in their thick husks. Our conch shells were moved up forward where their unpleasant smell would blow away from us on our assumed downwind course to Hawaii. I climbed the mast to lubricate the halyard and topping lift blocks and to inspect the running rigging's manila rope.

A few visitors appeared, as usual, throughout the day. They did not mind us working as we chatted. One thoughtful lady brought sandwiches and green tea for our lunch and this allowed us to keep up steam with our many projects. Other sailors in port, fellow wanderers, were always extremely kind. They appreciated our little wooden ship's parties and evening sing-songs. It was common knowledge that my friend and I were departing the next day and so we hugged everyone, extended our thanks, and said our goodbyes on the eve of our departure.

My last task that day was to list all of our provisions and then check and re-stow everything. The food had to be protected from cockroaches. Those critters are a constant nuisance. We managed to partly defeat them by using sections of an old flax sail, cut carefully to fit around food bins which we secured with lengths of rope. Our sail-material-wrapping-trick created a bunch of weird looking storage lumps in the hold. I would be stretching the facts if I claimed that we were completely successful in our attempts to foil these pests. Cockroaches have not survived for eons by being dummies. At least, we were able to enjoy our meals and I suspect the cockroaches enjoyed theirs too.

The water barrel below decks was topped up with the rain water we collected during the daily downpours. A bucket attached to the boom jaws redirected rain as it ran along the boom, gaff and sail, which had been canted to give provide a positive flow. We used this system at sea as well and we were never short of fresh water.

The fresh paint on our decks and bulwarks had dried sufficiently to withstand that afternoon's two hour long deluge. By then, we had already stowed the cleaned brushes and paint tins in the hold. It was time to shower and do our laundry in the rain. Clean bodies and towels and shirts! Afterward, Hilt announced that a cool beer was required.

We went to the club that evening for a farewell visit. After we settled at a table, the waitress automatically deposited 'greenies' in front of us. As we clinked bottles and took a few well-earned swigs of beer, somebody called my name. Bill and Gill Penny, from Vancouver, were at a nearby table! We went over immediately and I introduced Hilt. I had not known that the Penny's were cruising. Their boat, *Silent Echo*, was anchored off Taboga Island and they had taken the ferry to Balboa. We laughed a lot and got caught up on the latest news. In Vancouver, the Penny's and I operated our boats in the charter trade. When Anywhere was over booked, they would take the extra guests aboard *Silent Echo* and away we would go. Our mutual friend,

Hajo Hadeler, with his ketch, *Nausika*, would get involved if we had been hired by a large group for a long weekend tour around the Gulf Islands. Wouldn't it be super, we asked one another, if Hajo suddenly showed up here? We thought about him, sipped wine and happily relived our memories of the many evenings we had spent rafted-up in small coves, while the sun set to the accompaniment of accordion, guitar, and fiddle music and of course, our favourite songs.

Bill and Gill were collecting exotic seashells to sell in ports of call along the way to defray their cruise expenses. Sadly, our evening with them was far too short. They had to catch the last boat back to Taboga. We hugged our friends and escorted them to the ferry landing.

On the way home to *Ancestor*, we came across a few fruit and vegetable stalls. Hilt and I always craved extra greens for our supper salad. There are inconveniences attached to cruising without an ice box or a refrigerator. For example, as soon as the first week has passed, there are no more salads. Fortunately we had firm cabbages, beets, onions and carrots to keep us fortified for awhile. I was not yet educated in the fine art of sprouting seeds; a skill I would learn later. Sprouts are 'live' food and we sure could have used sprouts on this trip.

Walking back to the launch, I spotted a bunch of bamboo poles sticking out of a junk pile beside the road. They were two and a half inches in diameter and six feet in length. I grabbed two of them. I had an idea.

Galapagos Bound

*O*ur *Primus stove started hissing at 6:00 a.m. on the morning of March 15th. Hilt hoisted himself onto the deck shortly thereafter and having 'pumped his bilge,' he was persuaded to sample my morning coffee. My mate must also have been well satisfied with his large bowl of oatmeal, since he added a heap of raisins and poured close to a gallon of syrup into the mixture. He mumbled, "Gamornin, skipper," and proceeded to consume the entire bowlful. Based upon this performance, Should we increase our supply of rolled oats before we leave? A hungry, healthy man has to nourish himself on a long voyage.*

The air was not moving much that morning. *Ancestor* wouldn't be sailing for awhile. Knowing that the northerly breezes begin to exert themselves in the early afternoon, we would wait for the winds to rouse themselves. Besides, it was no hardship being lazy for a few more hours. This unexpected, windless delay gave us a chance to review our

With Gill and Bill Penny, Balboa Yacht Club

provision list once more. If need be, one, or both of us, could make a fast dash to the market.

We also needed to think seriously about this pirate situation. Naturally, there had not been much talk about the hijacker threat while the lads were with us but now we felt we had to address the subject. Hilt listened carefully when I described every detail of the custom officer's account of the recent hijackings, including the account of the *pirates' modus operandi*. Hilt asked, "What can we do about avoiding contact with pirates? How do we defend ourselves?" To answer his questions, I hauled up our crate of miscellaneous bits and pieces. "Doesn't look like a weapon to me," Hilt said, eyeing the box and frowning slightly.

I dumped the contents of the crate on deck and picked up a matching set of ten inch long, square, galvanized boat nails. I handed these to Hilt and exclaimed, "Spears! With one of these nails fixed to the end of a six-foot long bamboo pole, we'll have formidable weapons." Hilt latched onto the idea immediately. We sawed the tips off the poles, leaving three inches from the new end to the first node of each shaft. Hilt drilled holes in two scraps of wood and whittled them down so that they would fit snuggly on the tips of the bamboo shafts.

This took half an hour. Then the 'spikes' were placed into the holes, the butt ends of the plugs were slid into the bamboo, and we tapped them with a hammer until they were closely fitted against the nodes. A couple of hose clamps were fastened around the business ends of the poles to hold the spikes firmly in place. Finally, we drilled small holes behind the nodes, passed thin wire through the holes around the end of the plugs, took wraps around the spikes, and twisted the wires tight. Voilà. A pair of serviceable spears. "Hilt, my friend, when you aim these at somebody, you are going to be one serious dude." We laughed and then we considered the details of how to use them in any threatening situation.

Hilt asked, "What other silly defense plans do you have?"

After a few puffs on my pipe, I replied, "I do have another idea. Yes indeed. And it is simple. And silly too." *Hmmm. Maybe we better walk through a few possible hijacking scenarios.*

I harboured the opinion that we would never get involved in a hijacking. As I explained to Todd and Brian, I was sure that the local pirates would have investigated our vessel at anchor and rejected her as a potential victim. The bad guys would know that *Ancestor* has no engine. Therefore, without wind, our boat was not much use to them. My mate agreed.

"Listen, Hilt. If we have to, we can repel a single person in a dinghy by luffing up and letting him get really close. Our spears will be hidden. First we'll just let the pirate perform his 'help-me-I'm-stranded' act. Then, when he reaches us, we will tie his dinghy alongside and tell him that he is not permitted onboard until he removes his clothes to prove he is unarmed. At this point, if he tries to pull a gun on us, he will find himself badly damaged by one - if not both - very sharp spears. And if we are any good at this hijacking stuff all, we can dump him into the water. Besides, speaking of water, we should have a full bucket ready for one of us to throw in his face, while one of us wields a spear. That should work, right?"

"Won't the guy most likely start shooting from the dinghy if he has a gun? Wouldn't our best move be to harden the sheets and sail away?"

We tossed around different scenarios and decided to play the pirate's game. We'd help him over the bulwarks and slam him to the deck while he was still off balance. Two otherwise peaceful, but suddenly desperate sailors like us should be able to dispatch one medium sized villain. If he is armed, we'll relieve him of any weapons, bind him up with our best sailor knots and let the ship's cat lick his face all the way back to Balboa to deliver him to the cops.

Having first agreed to keep dreaming up other ways to safely cross the Bay of Panama, we concluded our debate about evil mariners. For fun, I even suggested to Hilt that, while the suspected pirate/hijacker was approaching, Hilt should tune up his guitar and sing a melancholy song. That should drive any desperado away. I have no idea why my friend picked up a spear and made several unconvincing jabs at me. When the danger passed, Forestay executed a running jump and pounced on my chest!

Noon came and still no wind. Our boat was becalmed. This situation gave us an excellent excuse to have a long lunch at the yacht club restaurant. We were ready to travel and our only pressing concern - an official requirement - was to leave port today, before 1700 hours.

The first sign of wind was a few riffles on the water when we returned to *Ancestor*. Clouds were building over the mountains but for a change, there was no rain. We lashed down our spears, re-stowed the junk box and waited.

From the log:

The little transistor radio gave me a time-check broadcast WWV Boulder Colorado. Our chronometer was eight seconds fast on GMT. We are ready.

"Hey Skip!" the first mate inquired. "Have you crossed the equator before?" I replied that I had. "Well, what does it look like?"

"Kinda fuzzy and wet and it keeps moving up and down all the time."

"What do you say we have a look, Skip?"

"Well, haul ass and hoist the main while I release the mooring line. Let's go!" says me.

From the log:

Departure 1600h, Wind North Force 4, Course 180 magnetic, Main and Jib.

Leaving Balboa, *Ancestor* had a bone in her teeth. Her bow wave was a beautiful sight and her wake showed that we were holding a good course with no detectable leeway. "Wow," yelled Hilt, "we're on our way. Here we come, Galapagos." Were we excited and eager for this leg of the journey? Yes! Our enthusiasm was contagious. Forestay raced up and down the deck, jumped up the mast, and hung there, five feet above the boom jaws. Perhaps to have a better view.

Once we had all calmed down, I got into my skipper role. I adjusted the mainsail by easing off the peak halyard to spill a little wind. When the pressure felt slight on the rudder, I lashed the tiller with a lanyard to the weather rail and attached a shock chord to the lee rail. A few tweaks and our autopilot was operational. *Ancestor* steered herself like a witch. Hilt was impressed. Next. I set the taffrail log. This meant attaching the counter dial to the bracket on the taffrail and streaming the rotor out behind the boat. The recording needles were checked to make sure they were on zero. Now we could read the log and record the distance covered whenever we wished. We agreed to do this every three hours. I explained that my preference was to take the first three-hour night watch from 1800 to 2100 because I always felt that this was a critical period when one could observe weather patterns and perhaps calculate which way any squall lines were moving, if they were showing themselves. This watch was important in order to ensure that all was as it should be before sailing into the night. Hilt would be on duty from 2100 to 2400. I would take over from 2400 to 0300 and Hilt again would replace me from 0300 to 0600. During the daylight hours there would not be a watch system. Because whoever is on deck is always on the lookout for collision hazards and threatening squalls. Hilt liked the schedule. Forestay remained non-committal. She was cool with our arrangement as long as she had first dibs on any flying fish that boarded the boat and as long as she could bat around any baby squid she discovered flopping about.

At 1800, we could see Taboga Island to starboard as the wind had backed into the NNW and we managed our first gybe in the Pacific, on a beautiful night with tropic, forest-created clouds chasing the moon. A pod of dolphins water-danced around the bows. Their strong exhalations gave Forestay the creeps. The cat crouched on the cap rail to watch these aquatic dancers. Hilt couldn't stop smiling. Nor could he sleep. He played his guitar and sang a few sea shanties. We were cruising southward. At 2200, I slipped into my sleeping bag in the starboard quarter berth and dozed. Too soon the clock said 00:00. Okay. It's time for my midnight watch. Stealthily, I abandoned my bed and left the drowsy cat where she was. I brewed a pot of tea and we sipped our first lip-warmers. The log indicated that we'd travelled thirty-eight and a half miles since we sailed from Balboa. The shifting Force 3 wind made it hard to keep both sails working efficiently, so we furled the jib. The early morning light painted us onto the ocean. Together we fussed with the main until the compass needle ranged between plus/minus five degrees on our desired course. Good enough. *Ancestor* would be our teacher on our way to Hilo.

The Bay of Panama was a busy place. Thirteen ships passed us between midnight and dawn. Fortunately, none were on a collision course with our vessel. Hoping that our feeble kerosene running lights were discernible, we carried on. At daylight, hundreds of seabirds hailed us. They were having their seafood breakfasts, calling to their feathered friends, wheeling, diving, swimming, in all directions.

* * *

To invent, you need a good imagination and a pile of junk.

Thomas A. Edison. American inventor and businessman

When we and the seabirds had finished breakfast, our chat turned to fishing. I wanted to make an *Ancestor* super plug out of any useful material I could find below. In Cristóbal, I had unearthed a piece of white plastic tubing, one and one half inches in diameter by sixteen inches in length. Onboard, there were scraps of wood, wire, and a handful of fish hooks which someone had donated for spares. I sketched and described my lure for Hilt, and with his help, my project was started. Hilt scooped feathers out of the sea. Literally thousands of them floated on the surface and in short order, he had a mound of them on deck, drying in the sun. I used a hacksaw to cut the plug shape at a fifty degree angle on one end of the tube and square on the other. The overall length was five inches. Hilt whittled a wood plug to fit inside of the pipe and when the plug was inserted it was perfect. We removed the plug to drill a small hole through the centre longitudinally, where the shank of the hook would reside. The hacksaw cut a longitudinal slot in the wood down to the hole. A large hook was inserted in the wooden plug which was now re-installed with the hook protruding from the blunt end of the device. The hook itself was different from the others in our collection, because it was seven inches long. Anyway, it seemed more than satisfactory for our purposes. Lastly, we drilled tiny holes around the circumference of the blunt end of the lure and pushed feathers into the holes with glue. The feathers were positioned so that their curves bent outward from the plug. When completed, our creation resembled a feather duster with a short handle.

I was lazy that first day and I had not taken star sights that morning or even a sun line at mid-morning. A navigational update was overdue. With noon approaching, I ascertained the approximate time of the sun's meridian passage and I went through the altitude measurements. Hilt recorded times and altitudes until there was enough data to calculate the longitude. At noon on the sixteenth of March, we were at 7 degrees 26 minutes north of the equator and 79 degrees 50.2 minutes west of Greenwich. *Ancestor* had sailed ninety-three miles since leaving her anchorage. The taffrail log disagreed by three miles: a typical discrepancy when the winds are light.

Hilt played tunes to entertain us while I changed the burner on our Primus stove and hoped there were enough spare parts to keep the cooker functioning all the way to Hawaii.

More ships were spotted during the day. Fortunately, they were clear of our route. And not a pirate or hijacker in sight.

Our fishing lure, we decided, needed more feathers around the hook before it was ready. When the 'plumage' looked right, a six-foot long stainless steel leader and line were attached to the contraption.

The leader was secured to the eye of the fish hook, with a small lead sinker fastened on midway down the leader. Then came a swivel and one hundred feet of braided, black, one-eighth inch diameter line. The rope was formerly part of a fishnet we had rescued from that convenient Balboa junk pile. We secured the end of this line to a wooden cleat on the bulwarks and formed a loop six feet from the end. To this loop, I attached three feet of shock chord, pulled it tight, and tied it off to a protruding bolt-end on the bulwarks. That arrangement gave us a sag in the fishing line at the boat. The line would absorb the shock load of a striking fish, without breaking anything.

The honorary title of chief fisherman was conferred upon Hilt. His duty was to pay out the lure and line behind the boat. Since *Ancestor* was only moving at three knots, we could watch our newly created apparatus at work. With our current speed, the lure, scarcely a few feet below the ocean's surface, was pitching up and down nicely. We were shaking hands and congratulating ourselves on a job well done just as the shock chord stretched out and we had hooked our first fish! Hilt put gloves on to pull in the line while I cheered. Soon we had a four pound mackerel flapping on deck. Forestay went nuts until our home-made bonker subdued the fish. The cat was an enthusiastic hunter but she was accustomed to flying fish, not sea monsters. A shearwater, another hungry observer, had landed on the main gaff. The bird wobbled back and forth like a seasoned sailor. I wanted it to fly elsewhere without pooping on our clean white sail. This feathered hitchhiker ignored my impolite request. That mackerel was the first of many fish we would catch to augment our seagoing diet.

The wind varied between Force 3 and Force 4. Our south bound course did not need to be exact but we chose it having considered the interesting currents in the wide Bay of Panama which move northward along the coasts of Ecuador and Colombia before swirling off to the southwest in a huge, broad stream of water. Their direction was evident by *Ancestor's* leeway. We allowed the flow to carry us westward, while using the north and northwest backing winds to our best advantage. Were we wise to pretended to know what we were doing? Time would tell.

During our second night out we began to settle into a routine: Hilt hits the sack after the evening meal and the cat does night patrol. The skipper tweaks the sails and steering before settling down on his watch, with his pipe polluting the air. Every three hours, a cup of tea is brewed and served by the oncoming watch. At the beginning of a new watch, arms are jabbed to say hello. Smiles are exchanged. Information is communicated sailor to sailor, regarding steering, weather, shipping and so on. Routine is necessary. Routine is good.

We saw several ships on southerly courses on this second night, and happily, they were far from our track. Forestay, on my watch, sprang from her rope fort and tore along the deck, returning in a short time with a flying fish clamped in her mouth. She played with the luckless fish for ten minutes before dragging it to the privacy of her fort for an undisturbed meal. These night watches were uneventful except for the beauty of the Southern Cross sailing across the stage of our universe.

At first light, the sky brightened but then it darkened again and a thick haze curtained our view to the east. I cooked up a generous batch of pancakes and served them smothered in syrup with diced papaya and hot coffee. Forestay, dreaming and twitching her tail, opened one eye to check on us. Seeing that everything was as it should be, she returned to her sleep. The wind held, after veering to the northeast once more. We were okay and the self-steering was doing okay too.

I managed to get one sun line at 10:00 a.m. and a meridian passage at noon. This placed us at 05 degrees 06 minutes north, 80 degrees 08.2 minutes west. The day's run was 140 miles. We had gained approximately nineteen miles in the past twenty four hours, confirming our hunch about the current's direction and intensity. I had taken water temperatures for the previous thirty-six hours, to determine how the boat was travelling with regard to leeway and to learn more about the water's movements. Normal deep sea temperatures in this area were averaging seventy-two degrees. However, in the grip of the currents, the reading rose to seventy-five degrees, suggesting that the north setting currents pick up heat along the coast and the temperature drops when these currents lose velocity as they mingle with deeper waters.

I had trouble distinguishing between the sea and the sky during the noon sights and by 1300 the horizon had disappeared to the south and east, leaving us in dismal surroundings. I could barely see the high cirrus cloud. The gloom had devoured our visible world. To the west, it was clearer. If we had a barometer, I would have tapped the glass to find out what the atmospheric pressure was doing, but since we possessed no such instrument, I tried to stay in tune with the sky and sea, watching for erratic wave patterns which might indicate a blow coming our way. Nothing changed that afternoon and so we sailed on.

A couple of happy seaman, on the lookout for ships and hijackers and storms.

The menu for the evening meal consisted of sliced cabbage/apple salad, carrots, cucumbers, bread and tea.

Life at sea. Our routines gelled with lots of time for reading. Hilt had a couple of books on the history of the Galapagos Archipelago, its shipwrecks and survivors. He would read passages out loud and in full voice, emphasize the grim dangers that might lay ahead.

"We'll be lucky to get to those enchanted islands," I joked. "There are hijackers and pirates out there, Hilt, perhaps just over the horizon, waiting for us, fingering their gun triggers and brandishing their swords."

My book of choice these days was a volume of the collected poetry of Pablo Naruda, and although many of the poems were dark, reflecting the culture in which the author was immersed, his writing was so vivid that it was easy to sink into his world, feel his anguish, his despair, and his love. His was quite simply the best poetry I had ever read.

From the log:

Ancestor continues to steer herself. Our compass course is 180 degrees. Leeway from the current is giving us a course made good of about 195 degrees. At 1400 the sky has become ninety percent overcast. The water temperature is 75 degrees. The air temperature in the shade is 80 degrees.

The wind dropped overnight and lightning in the east made our surroundings eerie if not ominous. At 0200 ships passed us half a mile off our starboard beam. When I first saw them, I lit the starboard lantern. At first light next day, we scanned the eastern horizon and clearly saw a line separating sea and sky. This would be good for navigation but there were no stars. I was eager to test my newly acquired, four-power star scope, but up to now, either the horizon was obscured by mist or haze, or the target stars were hidden by clouds. Oh well. One day soon I would get the chance.

Throughout the night we had been serenaded by the tuneful creaking of our boom and gaff jaws. The light breezes and the sea contributed to the flapping mainsail. These were sounds we did not want to get used to yet. A bucket of seawater poured over the boom jaws helped mitigate the noise, but that solution didn't last long. At 0830 I shot the lower limb of the sun and got a check on our longitude.

The intercept was only six minutes east. This gave us a fair idea of what our assumed longitude would be for the meridian passage.

As we neared the equator, it was challenging to get reliable altitude measurements of the sun which was at an angle of about eighty-five degrees. Our noon position put us at 3 degrees 40.1 minutes north and 80 degrees 2.7 minutes west. Distance covered in the past twenty-four hours: 88 miles. We were now three hundred and twenty-one miles from Panama and we were feeling more confident about not running into hijackers this far from the coast. After a review of our track and location, we altered course to two hundred and twenty five degrees and maintained that for twenty-four hours to see if this would improve our progress. We gybed and assumed the new course, played with the sails and rudder until our boat resumed steering herself. Back to my Pablo Naruda poetry. The only interruptions that afternoon were caused by our overactive cat and some sharks who liked the shade afforded by our hull. A distant, lone whale blew, exhaled in a manner that identified the cetacean as a sperm whale. That evening, I borrowed Hilt's guitar to entertain the ocean world with sailor songs and the occasional boogie. Whatever popped into my head. Hilt and I had our own musical repertoires as well as a lot of shared, favourite ditties. Those concerts made for happy times.

* * *

It is not my intent to bore the reader with too much detail about daily life at sea. However, one small frustration during our passage to the Galapagos involved an ongoing navigational problem. Whenever I tried to obtain meridian altitude measurements with the sextant, the procedure was difficult. The sun was approaching the equator and so were we. I still used the sun for morning and afternoon position lines and I transferred this data to the plotting sheet. This information, with the occasional shot of Sirius or Antares, gave us a sufficiently accurate position.

If the sky was clear, on my night watches, I liked to steer by the stars. Hilt enjoyed this method also. Before descending to my berth I might say, "You may want to point your bow to place Venus on the starboard running backstay for two hours and then pick up Betelgeuse on the starboard spreader. That should keep her happy till my next watch." Minor adjustments needed to be made to the sails until the

Hilt in action. An everyday occurrence

boat stayed on course and resumed steering herself. The compass had no light and we rarely referred to its needle on night passages.

On the twentieth of March, we pumped the bilge and it took forty-four strokes to empty it. That does not sound very exciting. But we had to man the bilge pump by jerking the pole upward rapidly to get it primed, while at the same time keeping the entire column of water, (measuring at least six feet long) pouring, as a single aqueous unit onto the decks. Quite an exhausting and yes, maybe even an exciting endeavour!

We had departed Panama on the Ides of March and we were approaching the equator exactly at the Equinox. Good planning that. On the twenty first of March, we were nineteen miles north of the equator, trying to make landfall in the Enchanted Islands despite the light and fickle breezes. In the evening on this day, the winds turned to the southeast and weakened even more. We added the old flax staysail to the rig, snugged the sheets and let *Ancestor* sail toward the islands beyond the horizon. The current was giving us as much as twenty-four miles a day. This was very helpful in those light, uncertain winds. By noon on the twenty second, we were becalmed with our headsails furled and our mainsail tightly centered on the boat. We were now less than two hundred miles from the nearest island. We observed the sea and the current carefully, sometimes from the mast's crosstrees. Specifically, we watched for the Humboldt Current which would push us toward Hawaii.

Winged visitors greeted us daily. Mostly Frigate birds and blue-footed boobies inspected our floating island. The boobies occasionally landed on the cap rails only to be attacked by our vicious cat.

The winds eventually returned and we played each breeze carefully to creep toward land. On March twenty-fourth, at 0730, as we were eating our way through bowls of oatmeal, I nudged Hilt, pointed over the starboard bow and said "Hilt, please do the honours."

He stood up, cheered and hollered, "LAND-HO."

Our first view of Isla Genovesa, the most north-easterly of the Galapagos group, was thrilling. Nine days out of Balboa and becalmed for twenty-seven hours en route, we had still averaged one hundred and twelve miles per day. Any sailor would be well pleased. And of course, the moment we sighted land, the wind died. Totally.

Sun lines at 0830, and 1300, indicated that *Ancestor* was creeping along at two knots westerly on the current. Knowing that, we studied the water. The set was to the northwest. *Did we find the Humboldt Current or did it find us?* The south-setting currents that had guided us to the Enchanted Isles were still active. It was not easy to determine their flow precisely. We found ourselves in a vast ocean river which would be, in effect, our engine for some time to come. Our sails were furled. We drifted through an alien world, from whose pores oozed histories uncounted. The air and the sea were abundant with life. One expanse of water looked like fat boiled rice or sago pudding perhaps. Within an hour, we were viewing another life form. Imagine broom handles, vertical in the water and one fathom below the surface! These five foot long creatures were translucent. Inside their bodies, at one foot intervals, could be seen a dark nucleus. We also passed sea lions, dolphins, turtles, lizards and many unidentifiable water and amphibian creatures. All of them wonderful!

In the Galapagos

Trust your instincts to the end
Though you can render no reason.

— Ralph Waldo Emerson, American poet

Isla Genovesa was a mile off our starboard beam. Darwin Bay beckoned but we would not be exploring there. We had planned to enter the bay and anchor over night to immerse ourselves in this remote and fascinating place, but it seemed that Fate entertained other ideas.

We expected a breeze to come along soon. While becalmed, I took the opportunity to inspect the rudder fittings. Donning my mask and snorkel, I entered the water and descended. The hull looked okay. No barnacle growth yet and the rudder itself appeared to be fine as well.

Isla Genovesa in background

To test the rudder fittings, I grabbed the rudder, top and bottom, jiggled it – and almost had a heart attack. A baby dolphin swam into my arms for a rest! *Whoa, Jon, get a grip.* I hugged the dolphin tenderly until it squirmed free and hurried toward the bow. I surfaced for air and to tell Hilt what had happened. Then I hyperventilated and dove down to the same location, taking up my position at the rudder. Sure enough, there was the dolphin again, pinkish on the sides and as playful as a pup. As I hugged him and as we drifted away from the boat, something nudged my right shoulder. When I turned to investigate, I was face to face with the baby's mother. We made eye contact. The mother partially rotated onto her side to give me another gentle push with her nose. I released the baby and lightly rubbed the mother's neck. She did not resist. If I had not needed air again, we might have enjoyed quite a long conversation. From the surface, I watched my new friends leaping out of the water. They made one pass close by, almost touching me, before they turned southward. I was a changed person when I climbed on deck. Here, far from civilization and its influences, I'd had the honour of communicating with, welcoming and loving fellow beings who share this earth with all of us. I've never forgotten this emotional encounter.

* * *

Ancestor seemed committed to her course. She pointed her bow at two hundred and fifty degrees, heading for the next island to the west. My boat was too much of a lady to spin around in circles as we expected her to do. Clearly, she was on a mission.

Hilt was worried. We had no control of our ship's direction whatsoever. *Ancestor* possessed no sweep oar, and it was unlikely that one person in the dinghy could tow us. Hilt's greatest concern was that we would make landfall on Isla Marchena without wind to assist us. He mouthed the word 'disaster' and shook his head repeatedly. He and I had discussed our predicament, a discussion which I believed had gone well but Hilt remained unconvinced. I chided him for reading disaster stories about these islands. In turn, he quoted more passages, describing many of the islands' unfortunate shipwrecks; some with complete loss of life. He leafed through the pages of his book. "Hilt, you look like a Sunday parson preparing to deliver a lengthy and depressing sermon." My friend didn't smile and at that moment it was obvious to me that he was truly frightened. I said I regretted my flippancy and promised to treat the situation with the seriousness it deserved. First thing to do, therefore, was check our drift. I shot a sun line for a longitude check. Measured against the noon fix, the shot revealed that we were drifting at two and a half knots. If nothing changed in a few hours, we would fetch up along Marchena's shoreline. By my estimate, this would occur around 10:00 p.m., post meridian. Well after dark.

I agreed that our circumstances were indeed a bit darkish. Maybe we should re-analyze our problem and devise a survival plan. I spoke confidently, pulled out a sheet of paper and a pencil and scribbled some notes. Hilt liked the results and I did too. There might be wind before we reached Marchena, in which case we would hoist our sails and go either north or south to clear the land. Binoculars in hand, I climbed the mast and from that elevation, the lee shore loomed. It appeared to be a vertical cliff. We were too far off to see any details distinctly but I sensed the sea rising and falling against the cliff with a great heave. There was no evidence of rocks or reefs. Back on deck, I explained what I had seen and then I devoted my attention to the second issue; the weather dynamics along that coast. Our marine chart gave us only the basic shape of the island. The eastern shoreline jutted out boldly at Point Espejo and the coastline ran northwest and southwest from there. After we deliberated further, I came up with an idea. The water rose and fell vertically which meant there would be a corresponding movement of air. Maybe the air would develop into a wind - breeze - that would blow horizontally to the east, or north or south. We could use that air to our advantage. We talked next about the currents. The current we had been riding since Panama, had joined the Humboldt Current here and *Ancestor* was twisting and turning now in these ocean rivers which added another dynamic to our drift. What part of the island would we be 'visiting'? That question remained unanswered. Wisely, Hilt decided we should at least have a nourishing meal before dark, in case the evening's events required our energy and our strength. We ate while urging Forestay to tuck in to her leftover bonito.

After eating and before nightfall, we reviewed how to launch the life raft (thank you de Groot). We made certain that the raft's inflation line was properly secured, we filled jerry cans with potable water, tied the cans together with ten feet of line, collected food bags, which I stitched shut with twine, and then we lashed the bags together. We also filled personal survival packs with tools, fishing gear, matches and lighters, sun tan lotion and shaving gear. The spears we had made in Balboa were important items. They might make the difference between life and death if a shipwreck did occur. I cut a large section out of the old South African spinnaker sail. This material would be useful as a sun shelter or as a sail. On and on went our preparations. Until the tropic night arrived and we were suspended in an extraordinary and unfamiliar world, alone with our fears and praying for wind. Marchena Island was less than six miles distant and our boat and her crew were aiming straight for the cliffs. Even the night held its breath.

Hilt was calmer than he had been earlier that day but as the waxing moon illuminated the scene, aided by stars and planets, he became agitated once again. I stayed calm and optimistic, which many have described as my normal demeanour. Hilt said, "Jon, right here, on the east shore of this island, in 1807, the *Ann Alexander*, a whaler, was sunk by a whale. There were no survivors."

I countered by explaining what I had read. "A few burros, plus some dogs, goats and pig survived the wrecks and they are living on Marchena. If we are cast upon these shores, Hilt, we'll have the burros for transportation, dogs and cats for pets, goats for target practice and pigs for a continuous supply of bacon and ham." Hilt was not appeased, even though he knew I was attempting to raise our spirits. I cut this conversation short. It was going nowhere. We needed to be positive.

To brighten our mood, I lit a kerosene lantern and read Hilt a true story about remote Floreana Island, a seventeen hundred foot, extinct volcano; one of the Galapagos group. After the end of the First World War, the Wittmer and Ritter families settled on Floreana. Prior to leaving Germany, the Ritters had their teeth extracted and replaced by steel dentures which they wore on alternate days! Their farm was built on the west side of the island where they grew fruit and vegetables. A great number of cattle and goats, abandoned by earlier residents, inhabited the island too, guaranteeing that the Ritters always had meat.

A baroness and her lovers ventured into this seeming paradise. In short order, all the passions of a *Grand Guignol* unfolded until one day, the tragedy reached its climax. Ritter was found murdered and the baroness escaped in a boat with a select few of her lovers. Her craft was eventually discovered on a neighbouring island but no bodies were ever found. That's my kind of story!

At the conclusion of my not very cheery tale, we went to the bow to stare at Marchena. The island looked eerie, draped as it was beneath a blanket of dark clouds. Were we travelling exactly in the same direction as we had been all afternoon? Inexorably toward the cliffs? The time had come for some intense sailor talk. I lit my pipe. Hilt peeled a banana. Then he and I stood on the main hatch and tackled our dilemma head on.

Yes, we agreed, our circumstances are grim. Land is fast approaching. Yet, if *Ancestor* chooses to behave like a well-mannered lady, she will turn before we near the cliffs and before the sea drags her along the shore. Right? The current is forcing the water against the land and on impact, those crashing waves have to veer either north or south. If luck is with us, the underwater shape of the island is steep and the crashing waves will create a shove-back motion, thereby - hopefully - preventing us from slamming into the rocks. We need to be in the south or north stream of water with a good offing for safety. Hilt and I analyzed the dynamics of our boat, the shore in front of us and the powerful ocean carrying us forward.

When we had examined every aspect of our situation for over an hour, we concocted a plan: we'll get the mainsail and jib hoisted and ready. Hilt will position himself on the foredeck and I will handle the main and the tiller. Our sixteen foot bamboo pole will be placed athwartships so it won't get tangled in the rigging. As we near shore, the current, deflected from the rock face, should give us a shove and prevent us from colliding with anything. This strategy might not work if the boat surges ahead and refuses to sheer-off. We must stay keenly alert to any breeze that might develop as the water heaves against the landmass. We'll use the pole to fend us off and we'll back the sails to use whatever wind is available. We hope to reach the coastline where there are cliffs and not just a shallow, rocky bottom. The anchor will be accessible and deployed if needed.

Hilt was happy with this more detailed plan but he still had a question. "What if I stumble or trip and screw everything up? Hell Jon, it's scary!"

"You are a professional hockey player. There's no way you'd stumble. Unless I body check you really hard while we're busy saving our lives. Why don't you try some pushups to get your body primed and ready for action?" responded the ship's optimist.

"Good idea," Hilt replied, immediately stretching himself out on deck to begin his calisthenic work-out. I, on the other hand, went below to brew a pot of strong, black coffee, as strong and black as this black night, and while I was down there, I inventoried all the survival stuff which would need to be hauled to the life raft. Our dinghy was prepared for an emergency launching and its painter was lengthened and positioned so we could find and secure it to the life raft when - or if - we had to abandon ship.

Hilt counted pushups. Forestay patrolled the decks. Without warning, the moon disappeared, leaving us blind. With my other four senses, I 'looked' ahead to identify the sloughing sound of water surging against the cliffs and the pounding waterfall of waves falling back into the ocean. The currents were indiscriminate! Our crisis meant nothing to them. They were carrying us onward, into the dungeon of the night. I could feel the surface waters changing. There did appear to be some push-back from shore. I was calm and certain we would survive this perilous first encounter with Marchena Island.

At 2300 the sails were raised; the sheets were arranged and the pole was positioned within easy reach of either of us. As we strained to see the island, we were perhaps four hundred feet from the cliffs somewhere north of Point Espejo. The cloud cover was total. Heaving seas tumbled against the cliff. The depth and height of the ocean's rise and fall were difficult to judge. We were wide-eyed, anxious sailors, wrapped in complete darkness. Later, we decided that the surge rise must have been twenty feet and when the water dropped, it was an even greater distance. The water's power here was incalculable. Unsettling. Awesome. *Ancestor* was being rammed into this massive machine. Within a few minutes - or was it half an hour? - a tumult of water cranked *Ancestor* sideways to the cliff, pointing her bow northward. We were about to be dashed against the rocks.

The noises surrounding us were like those of a giant clearing his enormous throat. I had to yell, "Hilt, be prepared for a breeze. I think there's movement in the air." My friend was forward, just ahead of the mast, well braced, and clutching the bamboo pole. Time and my breathing stopped. The sensation was horrifying and yet wonderful. Would nature's power and our little shell of a ship conspire to write another tragic chapter of history for Hilt's book? Or would the gods of the sea, land and sky spare us? In a flash, my questions and the images I had conjured up vanished and I was jerked back to reality and to my action station.

We were broadside to the island, being repeatedly lifted and dropped thirty vertical feet. *Ancestor* was scarcely two boat lengths from disaster. Then I felt a definite breeze, coming from above, on the upper cliff! Wild with adrenaline, I shouted, "Hilt, back the jib!" I hauled the main boom to weather to allow the air to touch our canvas. As the boat came up on the next swell, the breeze exerted pressure on the sails and *Ancestor* advanced. Ever so slightly. We were gaining steerage! Lightly but persistently, I massaged the tiller and rudder until we finally started to turn north. We called back and forth, screaming our relief and happiness and scaring the cat so badly that she dove into her fort. Our planning had paid off. We would survive!

The breeze freshened, to only a knot or two, but that was enough to keep us sailing and easing *Ancestor* away from shore. When the wind backed into the south, we gybed smartly and pointed the bow northeast. Just moments later, the wind exhausted itself and promptly died and we found ourselves a quarter of a mile offshore and drifting on a safe, northwesterly course. Have there ever been happier sailors? I'm sure there have been, but we claimed the gold medal that night. Hilt and I hugged one another. He said, "So! What was all that anxiety and fear about? Piece of cake, I'd say." We were proud, happy guys on a happy ship and proud of my Carriacou boat too. The adrenaline rush had worn off. We were exhausted.

* * *

At 0130 we gybed on a five knot southerly breeze and adjusted our course to clear the north end of Marchena. We had wind. Fantastic! Hilt announced that he couldn't sleep for awhile. He requested the midnight watch. Fine with me. I snuggled into my bedding with my cat and we had no trouble falling asleep. Back on deck again at 0300, I was rested, waiting for the sunrise and drinking strong tea. There were countless dolphins around us. In the phosphorescence, each dolphin performed a spectacular light show for me and Forestay. Dawn must have been impatiently waiting over the horizon and when the clock read 0600, the sun leapt up, full-bodied and brilliant. It felt like we had escaped some obscure Stygian port, and were embarking re-born, on our first day, aboard a sparkling new boat, upon a new and glittering sea.

With Isla Pinta ten miles to the north east, Hilt cooked fried potatoes, onions, fried eggs, toasted the last of the Panama bread and brewed gallons of coffee for our breakfast. Pinta is an active volcano. That morning, her impressive summit, crowned with cloud, spewed strong jets of steam. I took compass bearings on Pinta and on Marchena, to port. I marked our position on the large scale chart. We had a fix. I moved the position lines forward at noon, considering our estimated drift; two and a half knots. I plotted us at 19 minutes north and 90 degrees 58 minutes west. My findings told me that we had sailed and drifted seventy five miles in the past twenty four hours. And we'd had some excitement doing it.

Hours later, I took bearings on the northern tip of Albermarle Island, sixteen miles distant. This reading was added to the navigation data-mix. Force 2 to Force 3 winds held in the south. *Ancestor* maintained her westerly course at four knots under all working sail. Until we were becalmed. Again.

Becalmed but not inactive. Our boat was suddenly being swirled around by mighty currents. There was nothing to do but furl our sails and look around in amazement. Here was the main stream of the Humboldt Current. The water temperature yesterday was eighty degrees. Today it was seventy-one. The Humboldt is an ocean river of vast proportions. We actually encountered an over-fall of water, in which the hotter water was nearly three feet higher than the existing sea level! And the sea was teeming with life. Large fish preyed on smaller ones. Sharks feasted upon bigger fish and everything else they found. A feeding frenzy. I am not exaggerating when I describe the bloody froth covering the water's surface all around us that day. We saw turtles, fish floats and even a leather shoe with no foot in it. Hundreds of birds attended this banquet. Many of them dined on tiny fish while pooping joyfully all over our decks. Hilt decided he should toss a fish lure into the sea. A wounded and bloodied shark latched on to it immediately. Even before he had swallowed our lure and chomped through the line, the shark was attacked by a second shark, who grabbed him, shook him and tore him apart. This drama played out within a few feet of our hull. I held firmly on to Forestay, who was crouched on the rail, eagerly waiting to leap into the crimson sea.

As this gruesome, real wildlife adventure unfolded, a dense fog bank was forming beyond our bow and soon we, and every other living thing in the area, was hidden beneath its dense blanket. The fog was weird. Surreal. We hastily constructed another fishing lure, using most of our remaining feathers. Meanwhile, *Ancestor* was unsure of what she should do so she spun round and round and tried to look beautiful. Although she almost made her crew seasick.

While we waited for the fog to dissipate, we talked about the previous night. Wasn't it good to be alive and well with the entire Pacific Ocean before us? Weren't the dynamics along the coast of Marchena mysterious? Not to mention frightening? Naturally, the episode was fresh in our minds but we had different versions of those harrowing events to share. Hilt brought out his book on the Galapagos Islands disasters. When he put it down to relieve himself into the Humboldt Current, I turned to the chapter about an Irish sailor who, in 1807, had been marooned on one of those islands. The man grew vegetables, which he sold occasionally to passing whalers. In 1809, he captured a vessel (a whaler?), and sailed to South America. Apparently when the vessel arrived he was the only person onboard. There's a mystery for you!

Hilt had read that story, although he preferred the yarns telling of doom, deprivation, cannibalism, murder et cetera. We joked about Hilt's fears as we drifted toward our possible doom last night. I teased, "In my opinion, it's probably lucky you haven't read the book 'Jaws' or you'd have most likely climbed the mast when we encountered those red, shark-filled waters awhile ago." Hesitantly, my companion nodded. We drank a bilge-stored beer to celebrate our good fortune.

With soothing beer in my belly, I set about dismantling our survival gear and stowing everything where it usually lived. "Consider this, Hilt," I said positively, "if we face another emergency, we will already have our survival equipment inventoried and ready to be used. We won't need to spend a lot of time worrying about what to pack and what to leave behind."

The fog eventually dissipated and in the distance, to the south, we spied a freighter going east. Our five knot southerly wind had returned. We sailed west. *Ancestor* could not steer herself in the strong current. We took turns manning the tiller, usually with a book in one hand. Since it was useless in these fast waters and unnecessary as long as we were on visual bearings, the taffrail log was neatly coiled on deck. Isla Pinta was spectacular as the sun settled into the warm ocean. No clouds hovered to steal the volcano's beauty or hide her prominent red and yellow plume of steam. And we, content and relaxed, talked late into night. Neither of us needed sleep. Instead, we wanted to revel in our surroundings. Hilt and I were grateful to all the saints or gods who were accompanying us on this great voyage.

On the morning of March 27th, the horizon was clear for star shots. I took sights of Betelgeuse, Aldebaran and Venus. The resulting fix revealed that the current was adding at least two and a half knots to our velocity over the ground. Also, we were seven miles further north than my WAG latitude. A mid-morning sun line confirmed my navigational findings to be correct. By noon, we were 44 miles north of the equator and 92 degrees 48 minutes west of Greenwich. And Hilt was unhappy.

"Jon, I've got a beef. We discussed the equator back at Balboa and my understanding was that we were going to cross it so I could photograph it and measure its width and depth, if possible. When we got within a few wee miles of it you yanked the tiller over and went west and ruined my chance to perform some important science. I'm really pissed off." He extracted a rusty, old tape measure from his pocket, reeled out the tape and waved it in front of me. "Damn it, Skipper, we are only forty-four miles north of the thing. Let's change course and do some science. Be bold, mi capitán. Show courage. Show interest. Make me happy."

Such a tirade! A mutinous sailor had confronted me, brandishing a tape measure. Something had to be done immediately to maintain order onboard. I attempted to woo him back to reality by outlining a few crucial facts. "Hilt, my friend, the Humboldt Current is very important to us. Instead of crossing the equator, we should stay in its stream as long as possible because this current morphs into the South East Equatorial Current, which will continue to propel us in the right direction. Also, according to the pilot charts, the winds near the equator, and for several hundred miles south of the equator, at this season, are so light as to be almost non-existent. It is to our advantage to edge northward to two and three degrees north latitude in order to improve our situation. Unless you want to run out of provisions and find yourself eating your flip-flops." To emphasize this last point, I showed him my flip-flops, my only footwear, and explained how nonsavory they must be. I continued my nautical lecture. "We must cross the Intertropical Convergence Zone at 130 degrees west longitude, where the doldrums narrow, according to the Admiralty Sailing Directions." I waved my copy in his face. "So, calm down mate. We'll measure your equator on our next trip, for sure."

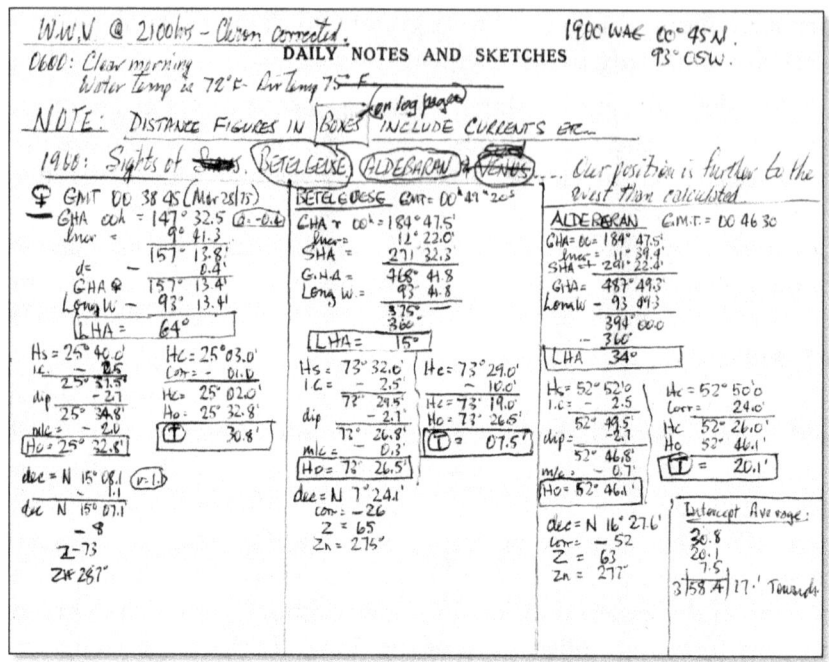

Three star sights by the messy navigator

Before he could become upset and too emotional and reject my argument, I said, "Shall we check the cricket thermometer?" That got his attention. With a flourish, Hilt sheathed his rusty tape measure and asked, "What the hell is a cricket thermometer?"

In Vancouver, last winter, I read and made notes about an interesting article. I had forgotten it until this very morning, when it appeared on top of a pile of papers. Unfortunately, I did not write down the author's name and so I must beg the reader's understanding, in advance, for literary theft. To paraphrase: "A neat trick for nature buffs is to calculate the temperature with nothing more than a tree cricket. Count the insect's chirps for seven seconds and add five to find the measurement in degrees Celsius." It so happens that temperature affects a cricket's muscles and consequently, the temperature influences how fast the bug can rub the base of its wings together to produce sound. The faster the wings move, the more the critter chirps. The warmer the temperature, the faster the cricket can move its wings. Hilt got excited and I admit, so did I. We had built-in thermometers onboard. *What the heck. Let's do it!* Full of scientific zeal, we descended to the hold. Some of our little thermometers were indeed clicking amongst the rocks. On hands and knees, Hilt approached a cricket, a soloist, who was chirping alone, some distance from the main orchestra. Hilt looked carefully at his watch and when the second hand touched twelve, he counted for the seven seconds. After a few failed attempts, he admitted defeat, because the cricket's chirps were an almost continuous sound. The temperature in the hold was approximately eighty-five degrees that day. We decided to redo the test that evening, when the air temperature would be lower. We had lots of fun and there was no mutinous talk on *Ancestor*.

We did perform the cricket thermometer experiment again at different temperatures, but we were defeated in all cases. Our conclusion: the system did not work in the heat of the tropics. Success could only be achieved with tree crickets in temperate climates. Oh well, it had been a clever diversion.

Galapagos to Hilo

According to the results of one marine scholar's calculations, if I stood on deck, which put my eyes about eight feet above sea level, the horizon would be 3.8 miles distant. I stood on deck and scoped the southern horizon. Albemarle Island was no longer visible. I tried to envision Mauna Loa as it would appear from the south east. Despite my efforts, the image was hazy; the mountain indistinguishable. I hoped the vision would clear as we approached Hawaii and that the imagined and the real would jibe.

Hawaii was still a long way off but the wind did not seem to be too concerned about that, so we relaxed and concerned ourselves with the pleasures of the onward voyage.

However, there were still chores to be done. Hilt tackled the job of stitching a canvas cover for our well-used steering bench cushions to keep them from getting washed over the side in a blow. I put a new splice in the nylon anchor rode, then re-coiled the line and lashed it to the cathead timber on deck. Then, because the sea was calm and

The mate peeling spuds

Ancestor was gliding peacefully on the bosom of the sea, I went up the mast in a bosun's chair and checked the blocks, halyards and topping lifts for wear. Everything was shipshape up there. The next task was ongoing. *Ancestor's* decks dry out from the intense heat of the sun. The deck boards shrink. In an effort to maintain the integrity of the deck and to stop the deck boards from splitting, we sloshed buckets of seawater over them every day. This helped, but rain is preferable to achieve the desired effect. The upper planks (topsides) of the hull suffered shrinkage too but we had to wait for windy days when the boat would heal over and those planks would swell. Wooden boats are great but they are full of holes.

The evening meal was memorable because I prepared it. It consisted of white sticky rice, spread thickly with butter as the base. A half fillet of bonito was laid gently on the rice bed and garnished with a few sprigs of parsley that were still partially alive. Sea salt, which I collected from a shallow tin on the foredeck, was sprinkled over the fish. The concoction was so tasty that we both wanted seconds but alas, there was no more fish. We sailed on into the night, playing with Forestay who always came alive with the setting sun. We spoke of folks back home. We wondered how they were enjoying spring in Canada. The light southerly breeze kept the sails asleep and fortunately there was no ocean swell to spill the wind on us. There was only the gentle 'scend of the sea' to add some vertical motion. A full moon lit the horizon in silver and bathed the world with a glorious light. Another perfect night to bask in the moon's glow.

Next morning I shot the lower limb of the full moon while it still had enough angle to be of any use. This gave us a longitude correction, yet the finding was puzzling because my reckoning of the current was shown to be out of whack. Later star sights that evening proved that we were also farther north than I thought we were. Oh well. At 1800, I plotted our position at 2 degrees 25 minutes north and 94 degrees 20 minutes west and I vowed to pay more attention to the current in order to gain as much speed as possible from its drift and direction. The taffrail log was virtually useless in these light winds. At two and a half knots, the rotor line angled steeply into the water astern and the rotor was not receiving enough water flow to spin properly.

On March 29th, around midmorning, the wind veered into the southwest, then further west and finally to the northwest. Our progress was negligible so we just let *Ancestor* find her own way in the confused seas. She'd sail a little to the north and then, answering the tug of the current, she would wander off in a different direction. This behaviour continued for twenty-six hours. *Ancestor* danced like a drunken sailor across the sea for more than a day.

The sun was still too high for latitude sights at noon. Sun sights were possible only in the mornings and afternoons and I relied on stars and planets for evening fixes. We were out on the broad Pacific ocean, about thirteen hundred miles from Balboa and four thousand miles from Hawaii. I reasoned that we could (would?) get accurate positions later.

On Sunday, March 30th, two interesting things happened. Number one: We decided to gybe onto another tack and in the process the mainsheet clobbered our taffrail log. As the sheet tackle swept across the stern, it smashed the counter mechanism and released the line and rotor. Without spares onboard, we no longer had a mechanical distance measurement. Number two: Our food supply was dwindling but not at an alarming rate. This was our fifteenth day at sea. Carrots, potatoes and onions, that were stowed in hammocks below decks, were in great shape: a bit of softness here and there, but no rot. We had eaten our last orange that morning but the apple box still contained some edible apples. Bananas, which were bought green in Panama, had ripened in due course and had been devoured as they ripened. They were finished in ten days. Our cabbages were still firm and essentially that was it for fresh food. Hilt drank a beer at noon every day. He still had a supply somewhere in the hold. I didn't snoop. We had a few coconuts on deck, in the husk. For snacks, we would open a nut and leave chunks of shell with the meat adhering to them strewn around, convenient for nibbling whenever we felt peckish. We still had rice, instant mashed potatoes and tins of mixed vegetables. That summed it up. My mate figured there was enough food to last another fifty days. And there was always fish. Our home-made Panama plug was awesome. Whenever flying fish soared out of the waves, predators follow them. Dorado and tuna took our lure almost every time. Forestay continued to play with - and eat - flying fish and the odd squid that landed on deck overnight. We were not starving by any measure. Number three: By that afternoon the breeze had once again steadied in the south and we were sailing westward. The bilge pump gushed about twenty gallons of water onto the deck. Hilt called out to me from the hold to come below and see something interesting. Daylight was shining through

Light breezes west of the Galapagos

some of the topsides planking! The topsides were drying out and we knew that we would have some heavy pumping to do in the future.

Hilt's guitar liked the dryness. We played the instrument daily and sang songs about the great human condition (Hilt's phrase), sailors' happy times and times of woe, and we made up our own ditties so that we could laugh at ourselves. We were both lonely for the companionship of other people. Hilton especially. Singing helped to ease the loneliness. We were certainly comfortable in one another's company but my friend had never before been out of touch with his wife and boys for such a long period. This separation, although self-imposed, was gnawing at him.

My personality is different from Hilt's. I take pleasure in being isolated and away from civilization. Friends and acquaintances have even labelled me reclusive. For me, the ocean has always been a friendly place, even if only for short amounts of time. Whenever I spend weeks or months at sea, I rarely find myself longing for the amenities of a land-based life. The ocean is alive with life forms and I have an affinity for of it. I study every aspect of the waters around me and below me. There is always something new or fascinating to discover and study. Even man-made rubbish or a ship on the horizon can be educational and fascinating.

Sound is also comforting. If one concentrates and tries to identify the varieties, source or cause of a sound, one will find that the exercise is absorbing and rewarding. In our case, out at sea, on an old wooden vessel, there was the constant sound of water being displaced by the boat, the splash of waves on the topsides, the squawk of boom and gaff jaws on the mast, the flop of a sail spilling wind, squeaking block sheaves, slapping jib sheets against the rigging or bulwarks. These become background noises. We grow attuned to them. With all the dynamics of motion created by wood, water and wind, this interaction of ship and sea becomes like a musical composition and when the tone or frequency of the music changes, the sailor is instantly alert even when he or she is asleep. Those who choose a sailor's life are generally content. And seldom lonely.

* * *

Books are another defence against loneliness at sea. I set aside Pablo Neruda's poetry and picked up the first of three volumes of Russian history that I had found on the Panama Canal Yacht Club book shelf. My mother was of Russian ancestry. I hoped to satisfy my curiosity and learn more about that nation. Maybe I could gain a better understanding of what made me tick. I already knew that I had inherited some degree of stubbornness and square-headedness from my Dutch father. What traits had I inherited from my mother and generations of her family? I read these volumes for at least three weeks and suffered a few headaches in the process.

Our recent light air conditions were rather perplexing. After studying the pilot charts together, Hilt and I decided we might get more speed by angling off to the southwest. Sheets were adjusted, sails were trimmed and off we went in search of stronger winds. Our steering needed only a slight adjustment before we were away on the new course.

That night there were rain squalls and the sky was completely overcast until after noon the next day. The rain took over the job of soaking our dry decks and the downpours filled the water barrel. Hilt filed a complaint. "Jon, there are so many leaks below decks, I've given up trying to dodge them. I dug out an old sail to cover my bed." The skipper's bunk, on the starboard quarter, was only slightly wet and did not require alterations or repairs. Besides, the deck planks swelled as we had hoped and in a few hours, Hilt's leak problem was solved.

Our dead reckoning position at noon put us at 2 degrees 25 minutes north and 98 degrees 30 minutes west. Even with the light winds, our progress was okay. Except Hilton now hoped that the course change would give him a chance to measure the dimensions of the equator after all. The southeast equatorial current, however, had other ideas. It turned us almost due west. The current was relentless. Without a strong wind, we had no control.

Our Primus stove had been ailing for awhile. Finally it became necessary to change the burner and jet, and service the air pump. With this accomplished and new fuel in the tank, the stove's performance improved somewhat but the Primus still wanted a lot of coaxing to function properly. I figured the problem was the quality of the kerosene we had purchased in Panama. Every time we cooked rice or a loaf of bread, we had to battle to get the stove working efficiently. I longed for the old deck box with the fire pit, sand, three rocks and a large bag of charcoal.

We were becalmed in the early afternoon and the following seventeen hours were spent rolling, slatting, whistling and wishing for wind. At least, the current was with us and by twelve noon next day, we'd had an admirable run of twenty-one miles.

* * *

A Low Latitude Poem

Wind
Is air
In sensible motion.
Elementary you might say,
But where Ancestor sits -
At that very place -
The planet is spinning
At approximately 1,000 miles per hour.
Yet,
Yet -
There is no air in motion.
It is non-sensible.

Shark Food

*P*recisely at sun-up, I was awakened by the cry of, "All hands on deck!"

I struggled out of my sleeping bag, jumped up on deck, and asked. "What's happening?"

"Cat overboard," yelled Hilt, as he luffed-up and pointed the bow to the east.

"Help me with the dinghy," I cried, as I untied an oar and fumbled about. In seconds, the dinghy was freed from its lashings and I flipped it over. I wedged an oar under the seats, grabbed the dinghy by the gunwales and tossed it overboard. When the dinghy landed in the water, I landed in the dinghy. This was an unrehearsed, impractical, and unwise operation, and because of this hasty launching, my body suffered a few cuts and abrasions. At the time, I felt nothing, except a sense of urgency. Because of the erratic launch, there were a few gallons of water in the dinghy but nothing to compromise the tender's stability. I stood up in the little boat, facing forward, and using the oar Bequia-fashion - a stroke on one side followed by a stroke on the other side - I made my way toward the dawn glow. Somewhere out there was the ship's cat. Probably, she had leaped to catch a sea bird and missed. Looking back over my shoulder, I could see that Hilt had hardened the sheets and was close-reaching to windward in order to keep a close eye on me. This was 'needle in the haystack' searching. Lots of ocean and one small cat to find. I didn't have any idea where to look except to eastward, so I kept scanning the ocean and praying for luck. I recall looking toward my feet in the dinghy and seeing blood mixing with the water and realizing that I was the donor. My eyes followed the red from the water to its source. There was a dripping - not pumping - gash in my thigh. *Just a scratch*. Fortunately, the sea was fairly calm. I could paddle easily and at the same time search for our wee beastie, although I was becoming weary and disheartened. Until I saw a shape in the water moving to the north east. Energized, I altered course and came up on a small wave and there before me was the fin of a shark. The shark was circling around something, and seconds later I caught sight of a little nose poking above the water and a furry body hanging straight down. Forestay was about to become a meal! I hurried closer and stabbed at the shark with my oar. This upset the big fish. He made several runs away and back to the scene until he decided to ram his head into the side of the dinghy - which did not capsize - but my fate was uncertain for a few seconds. I hung on to the gunwales to stabilize the boat. As soon as the dinghy quit teetering and bouncing, I reached over the side and plucked one cat from the ocean. The pitiful thing was like a wet rag. I placed her on the back seat. Thankfully, the shark had given up the fight so I was able to sit down and examine Forestay. She was definitely alive but shivering which indicated possible hypothermia. I pressed her against the warmth of my body, applied a few gentle squeezes to see if she would vomit and then I replaced her on the seat. We slowly paddled home. Hilt had done a good job holding his station so the return trip to *Ancestor* was brief and uneventful.

Onboard, I washed myself with fresh water and bandaged my scratches. The damage was nothing to be concerned about and the discolouration caused by the bruises and the swelling were quite colourful. *Ancestor* resumed her course, steering herself and we were once again a crew of three. Hilt appointed himself Forestay's nurse and in a few hours our feline crew member was back to normal and curled up in the safety of her rope fort. Understandably, she had no interest in prowling the open decks. Not for awhile, anyway. The entire rescue operation had taken only twenty minutes but for me, it seemed much longer. Hilt said he took a photo of me, standing stark naked in the dinghy with a single oar, intent on a valiant rescue mission. In hindsight, in our opinion, the whole operation was a fun adventure, now that Forestay was snoozing safely onboard.

Chatting during an early brunch, we agreed that if it hadn't been for the shark's fin slicing the calm water, we would not have located the cat. I also agreed that it was very silly of me to attack the shark with an oar. This led to musings about how a person behaves in dangerous situations; how a person reacts like any other animal when a life is at stake. At the thought of what I had just done, I shivered for a moment.

Onward, Ever Onward

*T*he sky cleared with the coming of the new day and I was able to get two sun lines, which when plotted, showed that we were thirteen miles further west than we had estimated. Good news! Hilt rewarded me with a cool, noontime beer. Both of us were proud of *Ancestor*. She had covered sixty-eight miles in the past twenty four hours.

That afternoon a pod of six, east bound, sperm whales, entertained us. They were within half a mile of our boat. As we saluted them, Hilt and I debated the currently popular opinion that places sperm whales on the endangered species list. Hilt reckoned that if these great beasts were on a slightly different course, we might have become the endangered species instead of them. I nodded pensively. *Don't whales have finely tuned senses to ensure both their safety and ours?*

On April fourth, following my daily inspection of the masthead gear, with the help of binoculars, I suggested that we fashion a new sail. In the hold, we had one of S/V *Silverstreak's* old spinnakers. Without further discussion, this was spread on deck, looking as if it was begging to be resurrected. The decision was made to use only the top portion of the spinnaker, mainly because the lower section had been removed at Marchena Island. Today, we hoped to make a triangular raffee from the upper part of the sail. Out came needles, thread and wax, and after trimming away the excess material, the bottom edge of cloth was rolled and stitched as tightly as possible. That task consumed the remaining daylight hours. By noon the next day, we were able to sew grommets into the bottom corners of our raffee. The result of our handiwork was weird looking but serviceable.

The wind, by this time, had settled into the southeast at a steady eight to ten knots. We attached half inch manila sheet ropes to the bottom corners of the raffee and enlisted the leeward boom topping-lift to hoist the sail to the masthead. Up it went, very spiffy, with its blue, green and white coloured panels. The sheets were trimmed. We proud sailmakers stood astern to admire our creation. *Ancestor* liked the new wind-catcher and her speed increased noticeably. Wind velocity is greater as the distance above the water increases. Our boat would slide down a trough, the main and jib would respond to the lower pressure, while the raffee stayed full and taut, pulling us steadily along. We used this helper-sail for many days and were pleased to find that it was able to withstand gusts up to fifteen knots without blowing out. When the sail did eventually self-destruct, it did so with class. Four of the vertical seams tore simultaneously and that was the end of our triangular work horse. Stitching the thin nylon sail cloth with a palm and needle was out of the question. The deceased sail was dried and stowed below. Maybe the material could be useful for some other purpose in the future.

While on the subject of needle work and making things, I recall Hilt crawling out of the hatch one morning with a determined expression on his face. "Hey, Skip, is it okay with you if I make myself a vest with strips of this old flax sail cloth?"

"Hell, yes," I replied. "I might even try my hand at making a hat. My hair is getting thinner every day and my only *chapeau* blew overboard last night." A new project was born and hours were spent seaming and stitching while *Ancestor* roared westward.

As is common with most red-haired humans, my mate has sensitive skin. He also has a large patch of scarring on his back where he had undergone radiation treatments for a cancerous growth sometime in the past. His arms did not seem to be overly sensitive and his legs seemed to be immune to burning, so he concentrated on protecting his upper body. He used an old shirt for a pattern and then cut the twelve ounce flax cloth into panels. A few days later the shirt was finished and he looked dapper. My hat was not so stylish. I intended it to resemble a Greek fisherman's cap, with a rigid peak, grommets on the vertical sides for ventilation, and a top of larger dimensions than the head piece itself. On paper, my design looked good and the pattern pieces seemed okay when I cut them out, but I believe that my attempt as a milliner did not meet the requirements of any Greek fisherman's cap. Disappointingly, the final product did not look very much like a "fisherman's hat." Oh well, that cap kept the sun and rain off my scalp even though it was slightly wonky. I added a chin strap which held the thing in place through thin and thick weather. My efforts however, did inspire Hilt to try his hand at the head gear making business and a few days later he was wearing his own unique version of a sailor's hat. On the inside band of our 'masterpieces,' we wrote the ship's name, and our latitude and longitude.

Enough about hats! Routine chores at sea: invert the egg cartons every five or six days. Move the water from the barrel in the hold to the galley. Check all perishable food items. Pump the bilge if necessary. Feed the cat when she has not received her nightly quota of flying fish. Clean her sand box. Maintain the kerosene stove and running lights and fill them with fuel and trim their wicks. Wet the decks regularly in order to keep them tight. None of these tasks were strenuous but they were important, nevertheless.

With regard to water, we were using about one and a half gallons per day for cooking and beverages and slightly more when we had showers. If a rain squall arrived during the day, we would strip down, rinse ourselves all over as fast as possible with the first blast of heavenly water, then apply soap and hastily rinse again. When doing laundry, we used the same procedure as for body washing, only we didn't get as wet. Sleeping bags were washed whenever we could afford using that amount of water; they become very smelly, very quickly, in the tropics.

* * *

On April fourth, twenty-one days out of Panama, the chronometer decided to have a rest from timekeeping and Forestay decided she would bring me a gift. I was awakened by an unwelcome object in my sleeping bag; something wet, slimy and chilly. Forestay was very considerate in presenting me with this token of her esteem but she had slipped the fish and herself deftly in beside me and there she proceeded to bat the critter around to demonstrate how one should prepare such a fine meal. I responded ungratefully, by grabbing the fish and the cat and throwing them up on deck, all the while cursing loudly. Hilt found this hilarious.

Although, our defunct chronometer was not a humorous or laughing matter. We removed both the front and back covers to inspect its inner workings. There was no moisture or corrosion evident and the spring was intact and not over-tightened. Hilt was more interested in repairing the device than I was. I left him to it while I went off to check out his ten dollar 'Diver Dan' wrist watch. I checked its accuracy with the WWVH shortwave Universal Coordinated Time signal. 'Diver Dan' was a few minutes fast. From now on, the plan, each morning, would be to correct the watch before the morning sights and once more before any afternoon or evening sights. Hilt couldn't get the chronometer working so 'Diver Dan' became our official timepiece. I did not have a wristwatch because an unfortunate accident had caused it to be given to Neptune. As a result of that mishap, we were very careful not to damage or lose Hilt's watch. Without the chronometer, a few conversations about navigation were essential. In a nutshell, (seashell?) I assured Hilt that, thanks to 'Diver Dan's' crucial role, our navigation would be accurate and our safe travels would continue. This made my friend smile.

On the sixth of April, we were 2,006 nautical miles from Panama and in total, 3,235 miles from Grenada. *Ancestor* had made one hundred and twelve miles in the last twenty-four hours. Hilt's watch was ticking to its own drummer and the drummer must have been a bit tipsy because occasionally the time would read five seconds fast per hour and the next check would show it to be three seconds slow. I had to readjust 'Diver Dan' before each group of sights.

Shortly after we plotted the noon position that day, nine humpbacks paid us a call. The nearest whale was almost same length as *Ancestor*. He or she passed within fifteen feet of us, exhaled just upwind, and sprayed our port side liberally. We were much impressed with the odour. That whale had a bad case of halitosis! Forestay went nuts, running up and down the cap rail and hissing her challenge to this strange, huge flying fish! Late in the afternoon, there was a heavy rain shower and by 2000, we were becalmed, with all sails slatting gently in the stillness.

* * **

Between the sixth and twelfth of April, we continued to sail westward on light southerly breezes. Hilt played his entire musical repertoire. When the concert was over, he passed the guitar to me for a few of the songs that I liked to sing. As we moved further and further out into the Pacific, I noticed that Hilt's tunes pushed the boundaries of sadness, heartache and melancholy. I preferred to play jollier music. I like happy poetry and happy songs and when a boogie beat pops into my head, I hit the strings and let loose. I hoped my music would lift my friend's spirits.

With respect to reading, as I have described earlier, there were plenty of good titles aboard. At this stage of the trip, after many years, I was re-reading Tolstoy's Anna Karenina. I appreciated the story even more the second time. Hilt had books about hockey, a sport which was a big part of his world until he was lured to Panama by his passion for sailing. His tales about sailing disasters in the Galapagos Islands were now stowed elsewhere to stay dry. We did re-live the Isla Marchena incident occasionally and we recalled more details about that near disaster every time the subject arose. When I felt that I was ready for other-worldly stories, I would dig out a science fiction title and plunge into that for awhile. I love 'hard' science fiction, written by scientists who have some understanding of physics, and who have vivid imaginations. Such authors can invent a plausible future for our part of the universe. My all-time favourite sci-fi novel is *The Last Question* by Isaac Asimov.

In our present, local universe, we had our routines, which I have already listed, for day and night. But periodically, these regular activities are interrupted or postponed. For instance, there was the occasion when the weather topping lift parted at the crosstrees. The half inch line had chafed through from the constant motion of the boom, mast and hoist-block, working in conjunction, but not always in concert. Anyway, in this case I spent several hours putting a long splice in the broken line before I noticed that it was too rough to get up the mast to reeve it through the block. That job had to wait for another day, and even then it proved to be a chore. We had ratlines up the starboard lower shrouds and these are not difficult to climb if one always positions only one foot on a particular ratline at one time. At the crosstrees (spreaders), while the vessel is going through her normal motions, I can watch the mast move about five inches laterally each time *Ancestor* rolls through a sea. When this movement is added to the swaying of the shrouds, with a human balanced on the ratlines, the dynamics are interesting. Suffice to say that work up there is challenging. If the sea had been calm, I might have used a bosun's chair, but in this situation, the chair would not have worked to our advantage.

One day, at mid-morning, we encountered at least a hundred tuna. And we counted eight sharks accompanying them and gulls and frigate birds who wheeled through the air waiting for the next round of feeding. We were some 2,200 miles from the Galapagos, the nearest land, and we wondered why the near-pelagic frigate birds and gulls were way out here. I told Hilt about the sailor's lore which explains that sea birds contain the souls of dead sailors and living sailors must always welcome them. There were no dolphins associated with this hunting group that day but we did see dolphins often. They were our constant companions. Our friends.

Hilt, the timekeeper, with a stricken look on his face, informed me on April tenth that his wrist watch had stopped! *Woe is me.* But I put on a brave face and said, "Take off his trousers and you are sure to find what's gone wrong. Diver Dan is an expensive timepiece and he might only be having a short nap or something." This malfunction could have presented a major problem for us but we were spared further anxiety when Hilt realized that Dan's battery simply needed re-seating. He moved the battery around carefully to ensure it was contacting properly, and much to our joint relief, Dan started ticking, in sync with time, and ready for rating once again.

I got sights of Venus and Betelgeuse that night to confirm our latitude. *Ancestor* was sailing at nearly two hundred and seventy degrees, although she was wavering slightly from her course due to the current. We were content to let her continue on her journey.

Our first month at sea was celebrated in mid-April. Balboa was 2,401 miles behind and Hilo was 3,100 miles ahead. Our estimated date of arrival at Hilo was May 18th, and we were still a happy ship.

Because of the constant port tack we had maintained for weeks, heeled to starboard, our topside paint had accumulated a garden of green weed along that side of the boat. This did not impede our ability to sail, but it was fun to study the growth. The grass was approximately three feet in length, delicately stranded and very decorative. Over the port side, there were tiny barnacles growing on the bottom paint. Barnacles would definitely slow us down when they grew to maturity. We checked our scrapers and scouring pads to make sure we had the proper tools to remove these pesky hitch hikers. Whenever we were becalmed, I would go over the side and remove the mini-barnacles. All I needed was a coarse scouring pad. Hilt was always on watch when I was assigned 'barnacle brigade,' which became another one of our routine jobs. He kept an eye peeled for sharks and he passed me the tools I needed. Only once did I have to leave the water because of sharks. They had swum close several times, attracted by the action of the scraping, the smell of barnacles and the guy making all the fuss. When the sharks swam to within ten feet, I tossed our tools on deck and clambered aboard. Barnacles are not concerned with the velocity of a boat through the water; they attached themselves to a hull no matter how fast or slow a vessel is moving. But we could not scrub them away while the boat was underway and this gave the barnacles the advantage. And *Ancestor's* speed suffered.

On one of my scraping excursions, I swam away from the hull for a little exercise and when I returned to about four feet from the boat, I paused, treaded water, and watched. I had never before seen these sea creatures feeding. Amazing! The whole side of *Ancestor's* hull was alive! Mouths were open and many small, bluish-green tentacles extended from the shells. The tentacles were waving and dancing, seeming to follow a beat or rhythm. I didn't have the heart to attack them with my scraper.

My crustacean-threatening antics must have awakened the wind. The light southerlies roused themselves. We were rocking and rolling.

There were strange currents here. The Southeast Equatorial Current was fairly steady but it was modified by narrow-banded counter-currents which disturbed the surface waters and caused *Ancestor* to shear around. Some of these east-setting currents were only a few hundred yards across. I measured the water temperature and the average reading was eighty-one degrees. The temperature in the Southeast Equatorial Current averaged seventy-five degrees. That confused us.

There were other interesting events happening too. One bright and sunny morning, my reading was interrupted by a shout from Hilt. "Hey, Skip, look south. You're not going to believe this." He was right. An area of water south of us, measuring approximately 200 yards by 1,000 yards, was completely occupied by dolphins moving eastward at a fast pace. The largest pod we had ever seen. The mammals were leaping and blowing in typical dolphins' style. We estimated there were more than a thousand of them. Although we waved and shouted hello, they were obviously on a mission. Undeterred, they dove and swam away. I recorded this sighting in the log book so I could reference the coordinates at some future date. Hilt figured the pod was in a hurry to get to a conference in the Galapagos Islands and this is why they didn't stop to put on a fancy aquatic show for us.

We were nearing rain squall territory. The Tropical Convergence Zone was giving us far more water than we needed to fill the water containers, or for bathing or for our laundry. Now and then, the winds would die completely while grey clouds advanced low on the horizon.

When a squall hit, when the tempest tormented us with pounding tons of water, we would drop the peak halyard a little and perhaps ease the mainsheet to spill the wind. During such disturbances, Hilt remained in the hold, strumming his guitar. I would stand on the galley ladder, hanging on, and with only my head sticking out of the hatch, I could keep a watchful eye on the drama. Forestay, being a cat and much wiser, would disappear into my bunk bag, for some shut-eye.

Whenever the squalls wearied of knocking us about, we would reset our sails and compare our impressions on how nice, or disagreeable, the latest storm had been. Following a blow, the winds were slow to rally and when they did, they were usually light south easterlies.

Such weather encouraged us to be creative. We tried to be innovative with the sail plan. I recall once we brought the cumbersome storm trysail on deck, hoisted it to the masthead by the clew and secured the tack to the deck. I confess it was a weird arrangement and because of its heavy canvas and because of the heavy bolt ropes, the trysail was useless. The idea and our efforts entertained us for awhile but other than that, nothing was accomplished.

Celestial navigation was better now than it had been for some time, because the sun's declination had increased to ten degrees north. We were able to perform meridian passage sights again. Even in overcast conditions, there always seemed to be enough cloud breaks to take shots of the moon, stars, or planets.

Though recently, Hilt was voicing some skepticism. His doubts and anxiety focused on navigation yet he seemed disinclined to take over that task himself. He trusted me and he had confidence in the instruments but he was feeling vaguely bewildered and disquieted. When he slept, he had nightmares about never seeing land again. After he admitted this, we addressed his concerns often. I was probably a little flippant during these exchanges. A few weeks later it dawned on me; Hilton's recurring dream was a problem. We decided to solve it by tackling the topic of navigation head on. He wanted me to talk in detail about how I learned the art of navigation and about how I found it easy to perform the routine tasks involved. We had this same conversation several times before reaching Hawaii.

By the twentieth of April, the shifting wind backed into the southeast and settled down to a nice Force 4. *Ancestor's* speed exceeded six knots again. Which made us happy. Our daily runs climbed. In succession, we sailed one hundred and twenty and then one hundred and thirty-six, nautical mile days. This was more like it.

A male orca dropped by to say hello to *Ancestor* the day the trade winds settled down. He stayed alongside for a full hour, frequently within five feet of us. Several times the orca dove under the hull only to leap out of the water on the opposite side. The encounter was exhilarating and we were sad to see the large dolphin leave us and take off toward the east.

Nimbostratus clouds dumped rain on us occasionally that night and between these showers, the clouds would separate, letting the waxing, three quarter moon perform its magic. At one point, as the clouds parted, Hilt came up to relieve the watch and there was an enormous white rainbow. The first we had seen on this trip. A WOW event!

In forty days of travel, we estimated that we had consumed two gallons of kerosene and this included kerosene for the stove to bake bread twice a week. Each loaf needed forty minutes baking time, which is a handy thing to know.

In order to keep *Ancestor* steering herself and to keep her tracking in the constant southeast trades, we had to let the mainsail full out and sheet-in the jib close to the boat's centreline. Even with the changing currents, *Ancestor* wanted to steer herself.

On April 23rd the sky was hidden behind ninety percent cloud cover and a strange haze, both caused by the currents and the currents' differing temperatures. The foreboding sky made me glad that we had no barometer to consult. That might have been too scary. During the night, we passed due south of Vancouver, some 2,790 miles away.

Two days later we set 'Diver Dan' back one hour when we passed into a new time zone. Progress! At 1230, Hilt pointed out a ship, 'hull-down' on the horizon. Only the superstructure of the vessel was visible. Gradually, the image of the oncoming vessel grew larger through our binoculars' lenses. I believed it to be a Japanese fishing boat. Having seen no other traffic for a month, this was exciting. My fingers itched for a VHF radio to hail our neighbours but that was a futile wish. The ship must have spotted us too, however there was no sign from her to confirm our suspicions. We watched her and held our westward course. An hour after the first sighting, the fishing boat turned east. She passed within a few miles of our port side. By 2100 *Ancestor* was again alone and becalmed.

In the morning Hilt and a four foot long whitetip shark woke me up. Hilton was experimenting with new fishing tackle - a rusty old hook with a slice of salami sausage for bait. I came on watch at 0600. After an exhausting struggle with the fish, he brought it alongside. He was trying to gaff it. Half asleep, I mumbled, "Hilt, don't you think it's silly to bring a shark on deck? Besides, that whitetip's too large for Forestay to eat!" My protestations proved unnecessary when the shark chomped through Hilt's hook and swam away.

I was relieved but Hilt was upset. He said, "We could have had a man-eating shark party!"

Ancestor drifted on that calm sea for most of the day until a light southerly breeze came along in the early evening. We started moving once more. The afternoon had been exceptional for viewing marine life. Ten dorado - mahi mahi - cruising in the shadow of our hull, were ignoring a 'herd' of rapidly swimming trout-like fish. The fish, whose name we did not know, swarmed and darted in every direction around our vessel. What were they doing? Whatever their motives, these 'trout' were definitely entertaining. A whitetip followed in our wake also, just cruising and evidently not hungry. Yet. A small school of six to eight inch long silver fish took up position forward of the bow but they became lunch for a small pod of dolphins. Sea jellies floated about as well, in various sizes and shapes, including one group that were as big as automobile tires! Their bodies were divided into six-inch sections and each section contained a dark nucleus. Hilt, Forestay and I were not the only ones appreciating this varied and incredible menagerie. Flocks of petrels and shearwaters hovered above the current stream, watching and waiting, to reap the bounty of the sea.

On this date we ran out of sugar and powdered milk.

Another morning, a pair of humpbacks decided to match our speed through the water. The whales, one on each side of our bow and fifteen feet from the hull, kept pace long enough to thoroughly frustrate the ship's cat and fill the rest of the crew with awe and a sense of helplessness. By chasing us, they were displaying a behaviour that I had not seen or even heard of before. Normally you only see humpbacks at a distance, when they surface to blow or do their great, barnacle-scrubbing flops. We were thrilled to see them at close range. Were they acting out of character? Just for us? Who knows?

The current in this region was amazing. Everywhere there were huge swirls and eddies and massive upwellings of the sub-surface waters. For me, it was good sport to dip a bucket of this clear water for temperature checks with my wet thermometer. After three tests at daybreak, the average reading was seventy-nine degrees: very warm. When I similarly checked the upwelling water, the maximum reading indicated a temperature of seventy-five degrees.

Morning and noon sun sights established *Ancestor's* position as 02 degrees 44 minutes north, 128 degrees 50 minutes west. Therefore, having consumed a plateful of mahi mahi fillets, we engaged in a serious discussion. The time had come to alter our course, drive toward the north east trades and find the wind equator.

Wearing Ship

"Okay Hilt, we've got a problem. For the last thirty days, for 2,356 nautical miles, we've been on a port tack. Except for the cat rescue, we haven't had to touch the tiller. That's a pretty good run. The question now is – do you remember how to gybe the ship?"

A long silence ensued before Hilt answered, "Well Skip, I think we should have a beer and maybe together we can figure it out." Minutes later, my friend emerged from the hold with Budweiser beers, passed a can to me, sat down on the deck and said, "First of all, what the hell is gybing anyway?"

"Well," I said, sipping my cool beverage, "it's where we point the bow toward a different direction and let the wind come across the stern. We carefully hand the mainsail through the eye of the wind and let the sail go to the other side of the boat. Simple as that. In the old days, it was called wearing ship. It'll be easy, mate."

"Hmmm. I'm not sure about that manoeuvre, Skip. Sounds kind of weird to me. Can't we do something less strenuous and achieve the same result?"

"No way man. We have to go traditional on this one or that big old albatross up there will report us to the Grand Sailor, and then we'll be in big trouble." This was fun but when Hilt decided that we, including the ship's cat, ought to vote on it, I put my bare foot down on the deck with a thump and said, "No way mate. You know that Forestay wants to go to the Philippines. And she knows there will be lots of flying fish for snacks but you and I would most likely starve before we got there. That's it. We wear ship. Now. No votes. Finish your beer and let's do this together." We clicked beer cans, drained the contents, stowed the cans and did our thing.

I unlashed the tiller. Hilt readied the mainsheet. I hauled the tiller to weather, expecting an immediate response from the rudder, only to find that our small rudder, and the amount of fouling on the hull, made *Ancestor* very sluggish. She didn't want to wear around!

At this point, Hilt trimmed the mainsheet while I put *Ancestor* on a broad reach to gather speed. Then we tried the manoeuvre again, all the while laughing and swearing like maniac sailors.

We needed three tries to wear her around on to a starboard tack. Finally we succeeded, trimmed the main and jib sheets and settled her on a course of 300 degrees and aimed for the northeast trade winds; our ticket to Hawaii.

The fouling on the hull was worse than we thought. When I had last scraped fledging barnacles, the hull didn't look too bad. Obviously, the barnacles' rate of growth had since accelerated and this was worrisome. On my mental list, I shifted the 'foul hull' entry to the number one position and I hoped there would be more calm days so that I could alleviate our barnacle problem.

That afternoon we saw the same fishing vessel again. Twice. The men onboard were busy working. Several hours later, we came upon one of their large floats with a radar reflector attached. The float line on the fishermen's gill net stretched far out to the west. Again, the crew did not show any interest in our little ship and they displayed no flag on their transom. Neither Hilt nor I could identify the vessel's nationality.

April 28th was a Cream of Wheat morning. Carnation Sweetened Condensed Milk and crisp bannock lathered with strawberry jam and black, honey-sweetened coffee rounded out the breakfast. The skies were dark, the air was muggy, and once more, I was glad that *Ancestor* did not have a barometer. Though the sky was overcast, we managed to find enough breaks in the cloud cover to shoot the sun several times before noon and around 1400. The results were adjusted to calculate and plot our noon position. Our numbers showed a day's run of ninety-nine miles. We were happy with this and also pleased that *Ancestor* continued to insist on steering herself toward Hilo.

Rain showers arrived in the afternoon; a good time to do laundry. We soaked the clothes, applied soap and scrubbed them on the rough lumber of the hatch cover and then the rain stopped. No rinse cycle! By mid-morning of the next day, it showered enough to finish the job.

For the remainder of that day and into the night, we were treated with grand lightning displays. Thankfully, there was not much thunder although at times, we definitely felt too illuminated. I would have put my sunglasses on for protection if they had not blown over the side weeks ago. I practiced squinting or, during the worst flashes, I squeezed my eyelids tightly shut.

Darkness dropped its soggy blanket on us that night. Seven flying fish, from a single squadron, glanced off the mainsail and crashed onto deck. Forestay went crazy. I managed to catch four of these little flyers and toss them back into the ocean before the cat got wise to my rescue operation.

With a southeast wind, in heavy rain showers, we sailed into the centre of the Tropical Convergence Zone. Forty-five days out of Balboa, *Ancestor* was at 5 degrees north and 129 degrees, 53 minutes west. By 1600, she was becalmed and drifting eastward on the equatorial counter current. We furled all sails to enjoy the ride on this black and determined ocean river. The rough seas were caused by the southeast swell joining the counter current. Knowing there was nothing we could do about our situation, we just held on and waited. And waited. Hilt and I took the opportunity to collect water off of the mainsail and top up the water containers. No one onboard would need to worry about suffering from dehydration.

Ancestor's hull had not yet had the chance to tighten-up after our long spell of constant, hot, dry weather and now we had to pump the bilge daily to keep Hilt's bunk dry.

We entered a night of dense cloud, rain and calm seas. We would stay below, stay snug, rest and relax in what I referred to as 'Hilt's kingdom.' The lantern's glow brightened our hideaway. We made ourselves comfortable with old sails and bedding. Earlier that day, I had cooked up a batch of soup using most of our remaining vegetables. With the pot wedged securely between us and with chunks of bread dipped into the mixture, Hilt and I praised the delicious flavours of those old veggies, knowing there would be no more fresh vegetables for a long while. After the meal, I sat under the hatch cover, which was slightly ajar, and smoked my evening pipe. Meanwhile, my friend was busy tuning his guitar, preparing for the evening concert.

That night was unusual down there in the hold, in the middle of a confused Pacific Ocean. Our songs alternated between sorrow and happiness. When Hilt decided to take a break, he gave me the guitar. I don't understand what happened but I was not in the mood for my usual ballads and shanties. I began plucking the strings in time with the rhythmic roll of the boat, trying to imitate both the sounds *Ancestor* produced and the pitching and rolling of the sea. At some point, I think my music was echoing the voices of our floating world. This experience was strange and fascinating.

On the morning of May 1st, the rain stopped and there were ample breaks in the cloud cover for a few sun sights. In the past twenty four hours, *Ancestor* had covered thirty-two miles on an eastward course. When the rain ceased and since we were becalmed, it made sense to take advantage of the warm, calm day to air our bedding and mattresses. By mid-afternoon, a light, persistent breeze came out of the east. Up went our sails. A course was set for 325 degrees. Hilt went forward, faced northeast and whistled for wind in true West Indian fashion. There remained only about 1,850 miles to Hilo and the poor guy was running out of beer! By midnight, Hilt's whistling yielded the desired effect. The wind obediently backed into the northeast and settled down to a steady Force 4. Here were the northeast trades to carry us toward a safe harbour!

At daylight, the usual routine rigging checks were done and then both of us scanned the ocean's magnificent panorama. Hilt pointed to the north where a sailfish was leaping approximately one hundred yards from the boat. What was it was chasing? We couldn't tell but we were thrilled.

Less inspiring was the massive expanse of garbage we encountered on the edge of the Northeast Equatorial Current: glass fish floats, fish nets, plastic egg cartons, empty tins which should have been punctured to let them sink. Gone was the joy of sighting sailfish. Soon though, we were clear of the mess and plowing through a pristine ocean once again. *Ancestor* had the bit in her teeth and she wanted to run.

From the log:

0015h Forestay is having a six inch squid for a midnight snack.

0300h Winds northeast, Force 5, squalls.

0600h 100 percent cloud cover. Mainsail eased off to get us through 30 kt gusts.

0730h Pumped bilge, ~ 42 gallons. She is working hard in heavy seas. In galley, spilled pancake batter beneath stove. Woe is me.

Tramping in the tradewinds

1100 to 1145h   Aloft to masthead to replace jib halyard which had broken. Heavy work.

1200h   3 sun lines put us at 9 degrees north and 130 degrees 22 minutes west. 7 weeks out of Balboa today. Hilo is only 1550 miles away!

1300h   Altered course to 290 degrees magnetic.

* * *

Ancestor pushed through the waves in a Force 5 until noon on the 4th of May. Then the winds eased off slightly. Our fouled hull was causing a lot of drag. Nonetheless, we were averaging 5 kts.

From the log:
ACCIDENT REPORT

Hilt, while off watch in early hours of the morning, was viciously attacked by a lantern, leaving him with a gash on this left eyebrow. Skipper cleans the wound and applies a band-aid. Bloody mess!

* * *

We had been monitoring our remaining provisions and we were still okay in the flour and rice department. The flour was in a sack and in order to keep it from becoming a solid blob, someone had to shake the bag frequently. Because the steady pitching and rolling of the hull induces the fine powder to settle, one of us had to monitor the bag. Otherwise, the cook is left with hard flour which is difficult to use.

I was the ship's baker on this trip. For me, this task was not a burden but a pleasure. However, you might not agree if you ever have the chance to sample the results of my endeavours! Earlier in the voyage, my bread was bread: yeasted bread. Anyhow, as we continued our voyage, I didn't have much fun, or success, getting my dough to rise in the tropical heat, despite the fact that I usually double-kneaded the sponge. I got lazy. I reverted to making quick bread: bannock, in my terminology. As already mentioned in this story, I had accumulated some knowledge, skill, and imagination, concerning the making of bannock and I had created my own version of this very old, traditional recipe. So! In these chapters, bread is henceforth referred to as bannock.

Our ship's oven was a twelve inch diameter aluminum pot, formerly a pressure cooker, inside of which I placed an inverted, smaller-dimension tin plate, for the bannock pan to sit upon.

The lid of the old pressure cooker had lost its sealing ring ages ago. Consequently, the lid tended to sit a bit lopsided on the top of the pot. Without a proper seal, I no longer possessed a pressure cooker but a plain old pot. Therein heat could be contained. Fine with me.

If I was being lazy, or if the weather was not cooperating, I used a liberally grease-smeared frying pan instead. This worked but the resulting bannock was not as appealing to the crew as the baker's pot bread. Besides, before mixing my ingredients, I had to sieve the flour through a piece of screen to remove the weevils; the flour bag's permanent residents. And as much as I like protein in my diet - and the weevils would have added protein - I preferred to get rid of the beasts.

* * *

While *Ancestor* continued to rush toward Hawaii, over the bounding main, we were experiencing a bit of extra chafe on our rigging. The sails were okay though various other difficulties did come along to make our daily lives entertaining. When I heard a noise up forward, in the early hours one morning, I went to investigate. The starboard after shroud deadeye lanyard had chafed through. We could have suffered a dismasting! I quickly un-shipped the tiller to let *Ancestor* luff up. Next I grabbed a twelve foot piece of polypropylene rope and hurried forward in the predawn dark. Fortunately, the moon provided sufficient light for me to locate the damage and repair the lanyard. I used the broken line to secure the shroud and keep it fairly well positioned. Then I tied a large knot in the end of the replacement lanyard and fed it through the deadeye holes until the shroud was firmly reattached. Slippery polypropylene is hard to use but I persevered and managed to make the knots tight. I hadn't bothered to call Hilt for assistance, mainly because he was a little under the weather and I was on a nine hour watch. All is well that ends well.

The next hour was spent contemplating *night*. On the moon, one night lasts 336 hours. On the earth, at our latitude, night thrives for about twelve hours. I decided that I preferred Earth's nights.

At 0245 the weather topping lift chafed through at the crosstrees and all was not well! Luckily, this breakage did not affect the integrity of the rig. I set to work, recovered the rope and spent the sixty minutes doing a long splice in it. I managed to lose one of our two gaff hooks over the side while trying to retrieve the topping lift from the water. I was not having a great day!

Although he was not looking to be in his best form, my friend joined me on deck at sunrise, ready to help. Hilt hand steered for the ten or fifteen minutes it took for me to go up the mast and re-rig the topping lift. I used a twist shackle to install the block to the mast, in order to give the block more flexibility. Hopefully this would reduce the chafing and save rope. And effort.

With the noon plot on the chart, we carefully scaled the distance. *Ancestor* had covered 149 miles in the past twenty-four hours. Her best day so far.

The trade winds continued to blow us on our way and despite having a fouled bottom, our speed mostly exceeded six knots next day. While we liked this fast pace, neither of us was keen on the amount of bilge pumping we had to do. Every six hours, the bilge was pumped dry.

There were other interesting things happening aboard. *Ancestor's* rudder stock had developed a vertical crack. Repairs would be made as we bombed-along. First, a hole was drilled through the stock and two four inch spikes were driven through the wood to clinch the ends of the rudder stock where they protruded. A piece of half inch diameter copper tubing from our junk pile was flattened with a hammer to form a metal strap. The strap was fitted around the circumference of the rudder stock, directly below the tiller and nailed in place with copper nails. The initial crack may not have been critical but our concern was that it might propagate under the strain of heavy, rough seas. This repair was in addition to the copper strapping we had already done.

Noon to noon, between May 5th and 6th, we made 152 miles; our new record. Hilt wanted to celebrate with a cool beer but apparently he had run out. So we whooped and hollered instead. Forestay poked her head out of her 'fort' to see what all the fuss was about. Unimpressed, she returned to her peaceful shelter. Smart cat!

Towards evening, Hilt's head appeared through the hatch. He said, "Surprise, Skip. Two potatoes and an onion!" This bonanza was unearthed while he was organizing the food hammocks, which were suspended from deck beams below. Surprisingly, upon inspection, the vegetables were in excellent condition. How had we missed them until now? Rather than scratching our heads in wonderment, we planned the menu for our evening meal: steamed rice, fried slices of spud, sliced onion, browned to perfection, and mahi mahi steaks. Rice is nice but potato is sometimes perfect. A satisfying supper.

Evening approached. Hilt and I serenaded the heavens for awhile. When he went below for a nap, I experimented with sounds on his guitar. I found pitches and chords which imitated the creaking hull and the swishing of the sea along *Ancestor's* waterline. One minor chord mimicked sail and wind sounds. I was still at it when Hilt returned hours later.

Because of this clear night and its sparkling stars, I didn't want to crawl into my sleeping bag. On deck, there was one, almost dry place that afforded some protection from the salt spray. I lay there and conversed with Hilt. Forestay, nestled on my chest, purred loudly enough to be heard above the ship's sounds. Our conversation was mainly about canoeing and sailing, wilderness and urban crowds. How would we ever cope with being on land again? What did Hawaiian women look like? How long should we stay in Hilo before heading to Canada? Friendly chatter. Eventually, Hilt suggests it was my watch again. I stood, shook myself and said, "Okay mate, I'm ready. You make the tea."

By 12:00 p.m. the next day, Hilo was only 920 miles away. *Ancestor* was holding the trade wind and Hilt and I were proud of our progress.

This afternoon, an easterly wave pattern caught my attention because it did not conform to the northeast wind. And when there were converging wave trains, the seas rose to sixteen feet. The wave height was okay but I was focused on tropical depressions. Without the proper instrument onboard, there was no way for us to know what the barometric pressure would indicate. I reviewed the old Buys Ballot's law. The law calculates the distance and direction of a moving storm and includes safety tips on how to navigate while keeping the vessel in the correct quadrant of the system and thereby avoiding the worst of the weather. All of this was moot. If there was a big blow, we would have to negotiate a peace treaty with the gods of the sea and air, head southward and hang on. The WWVH broadcast, I was relieved to recall, mentioned nothing about a cyclonic system in the North Pacific.

The easterly swell diminished the following morning, a sea change that also diminished our apprehensions. Hilt ate rolled oats for breakfast, while I had bannock and the last fried egg. We had miscalculated the number of eggs needed for this leg of the voyage. *Ancestor's* provisioner should have bought a dozen more. Jokingly, I accused Hilt and Hilt accused me about the speed at which our eggs had been consumed. Which man had eaten the most? Neither of us was willing to take the blame for this unanticipated lack of eggs so early in the voyage. Then we discussed our remaining provision and it was unanimously agreed that we would not starve before reaching Hilo. If we continued to catch fish.

By noon, we were at 15 degrees north and 141 degrees fifty minutes west: 123 miles in the past twenty-four hours. The course was changed to 290 degrees, our sails were adjusted and *Ancestor* was thanked for her perfect steering. It was a fine afternoon to visit the dolphins, who seemed to enjoy the companionship of our vessel. Or did they perhaps enjoy the small fishes - soon to become their lunch - schooling in the shade of our hull?

In the Dumps

> *We had become, with the approach of night, once more aware of loneliness and time – those two companions without whom no journey can yield anything.*
>
> Lawrence Durrell, in Bitter Lemons

Hilt was in the dumps. Not clearly understanding what problems he might be having, I asked him about his mood and after a long hesitation, he said, "I want to know what I am doing here? Don't get me wrong, Jon. I'm very happy to be onboard with you. But I feel out of place. Maybe I should be on land, where humans are supposed to be. I dream about gardening, being in the company of my fellow humans, hugging trees, going to parties where the beer flows and musical instruments twang and there's lots of laughter. Everything's always the same out here. I even dreamt that we were lost and would never find Hawaii!" When Hilt checked the chart, the daily track should have put him at ease and erased any doubts he might have regarding our position. But my friend was confused and that made him feel 'dumpy'.

I listened to him with compassion. He was confiding in me by putting his mental cards face-up on the chart table. He held nothing back. Both of us had to come to grips with his anxiety. What followed was a lengthy talk in which we tried to analyze what was causing his 'dumps'. I did not share his feelings of loneliness but I did admit to having had similar emotions - momentary phases - on previous trips. I teased him about what I thought was his major problem. He was out of beer. He grinned, but not for long. I needed to change the topic and cheer him up.

"Hey mon, how much weight have you lost since we left?"

"Wow," he said. "Wait here. Go nowhere. Let's figure that out." With these instructions, he dropped down the hatch, rummaged around in his kit bag and when he came back on deck, Hilt was wearing a pair of long pants, the very trousers he was wearing on his arrival in Panama. Hilton stood sideways, gave me a full body profile, and rotated one hand inside the waistband to demonstrate how fit he was. His pants were at least five inches too big! What a laugh we had! I also commented on his muscle tone, which had been nonexistent when he signed on. Suddenly my friend was joyful, out of the 'dumps' and happily strumming his guitar. We both howled at the magnificent and magical world. May tenth. Two months out of Balboa. Going strong.

Ancestor's hull had tightened up nicely and as a result, pumping the bilge was not such a tedious and exhausting chore. These days consisted of less heavy work and more relaxed sailing. A proper balance in our lives.

Toward sunset, a flock of bosun birds filled the skies above us. Their long, yellow tails marked glide paths around our rigging. One lone albatross cruised the air currents, reminding us that we were still in the pelagic world, even though land was approaching.

* * *

DEEP SEA SYNDROME

Don't sing me a song about repairs to the heads,
About lines of position and hammocks for beds,
About storms, gales and cyclones that rough up the sea,
Of your first perfect landfall – or islands alee.

But tell me of mountains and valleys and streams,
And green vegetation – the stuff of my dreams.
Please pleasure my mind with yarns of the land,
About solid pine forests – how regal they stand.

For I tell you right now that I'm done with the sea,
When we sail into Hilo I'm bound to be free.
She can lie there and stay there, 'til her chains turn to rust,
'Til the roaches all starve and her hull you can't trust.

When her paint peels and crumbles and she's full of dry rot,
I'll be up on the mountain, tilling my plot
And planning my cottage (fireplace eight feet wide),

Far away from the trade winds, the salt and the tide.

But hold – what's this happening? The sun touches the sea,
A perfect day's ending and my spirit's still free.
I must have been dreaming and a little depressed;
I'll stick to the ocean. You can have all the rest.

* * *

My body was very smelly. Rank! I took a sea water temperature measurement: sixty nine degrees. That would do for a bath. I poured buckets of cool sea water over me, lathered up with green sea soap, rinsed once with a second bucketful, rinsed myself a third time with fresh water, toweled myself off and voilà. Good as new. Funny thing how the cat shied away and hid from all that splashing on deck whenever we bathed. Forestay was probably remembering her recent salty, sharky swim.

Ancestor was ploughing through the ocean furrows, dragging barnacles on her belly and shedding long tendrils of sea grass. In the deep night, mermaids fluoresced in watery curtains of emerald green. They danced among the whales and mesmerized the deck-watch throughout the deep night.

While I checked the time signal from WWVH on our shortwave radio, on the evening of May eleventh, I accidentally rotated the dial to an AM channel. Surprisingly, I picked up Radio KIVN Hawaii, broadcasting a clear signal and flooding us with Hawaiian music: steel guitars and happy, uplifting voices! Just right for the sailors on the *Ancestor*. Hilt bounded onto the deck. He laughed, reached for the radio and began dancing his version of a Hula. I didn't spoil his merriment, even though we were down to our last set of batteries. I was sure we'd find the Big Island even without celestial navigation. Let the good times roll.

KCCM, Hawaii entertained us the next evening. Their sound was solid Hawaii and we revelled in the music.

The ocean current was definitely setting to the west: 270 degrees. I recorded this information and we adjusted our course to compensate for the current's new direction. Ever since we passed through the doldrums belt days before, the current had been moving steadily southwest.

At dawn, on May 13th, while I was on the bowsprit checking fittings, the jib snapped and knocked my special sailing hat off my head! After lamenting its loss, I went to the hold and chose a scrap of flax sail cloth, went astern and immediately started making another hat. A man has to be properly attired when he arrives in Hawaii. According to sailing lore, Hilt reminded me, losing a hat overboard is an unhappy omen, foretelling that the voyage will be a long one!

"Thanks mate," I said, "but I consider the loss to be simple bad luck and another bit of sailor lore is that bad luck can be dispelled by having the person responsible turn around three times, then spit or fart." Accordingly I proceeded to spit over the side. Farts were not forthcoming.

The winds, which had been steady in both direction and force since the first of the month, had changed to light easterlies. Our speed was reduced to about three and a half knots. Hilt was simultaneously trying to whistle up more wind and teach the cat how to dance. The lesson was an up-hill battle for my friend. Forestay kept wiggling from his embrace. Oh well. My mate's cheerful antics made us laugh.

* * *

From the log:

Wind back up to Force 4. Thirty percent cloud cover. Water temperature 69, air temperature is 69 degrees as well. How come there is no fog? Noon position: 18 degrees 23 minutes north, 149 degrees 55 minutes west. 310 miles to Hilo.

Making ~ 7 degrees leeway. Course adjusted to 290 M. 6,490 miles from Balboa. Avg. day run is now up to 93 miles.

Provisions: 5 lbs. rice, 10 tea bags, 4 tins mixed veggies. 5 cups of flour, 1 shot of rum, 3 spoons of baking powder.

No more of the following: cheese, margarine, crackers, biscuits, cream of wheat, oatmeal, raisins, pipe tobacco, beer, potatoes, onions, fruit.

* * *

By daybreak, there was still persistent cloud cover, the northeast wind had increased to Force 4 and Hilt was claiming that my bannock these days was lacking almost everything except dough. Obviously he was being picky. He gets that way when he runs out of beer. Having updated our noon position, I noted that the sun was now south of us and the declination angle was easy enough to manage for meridian passage sights.

The current was now setting toward the northwest. The wind was veering east. This made our situation more interesting. *Ancestor's* jib had just undergone a seam repair and when we were resetting it, with both of us still on the foredeck, we gybed! Hilt ran aft. He managed to control the mainsail but he suffered rope burns and scratches on his right arm and rib cage. A lumpy sea, and a changing current, had caught us off guard. This was our first accidental gybe. Hilt was injured and in need of a shot of rum - so he said. To relieve his pain, medicine had to be dispensed. Soon I heard the distinct sounds of slurping and sighing coming from the aft deck. When Hilt was feeling better, we talked about how *Ancestor's* shallow keel and an unbalanced sail plan can influence our motion in light winds.

We reviewed our accidental gybe and rather than criticizing *Ancestor* for sloppy steering, we gave ourselves hell. Neither of us wanted to piss our boat off. In my opinion, in this situation, we needed a square sail, a sail we did not have onboard. Nor did we have the material to make one; another moot point.

From the log:

Hilton B. Fraser, this date, has performed hair surgery on the skipper. If I had a mirror (which has been lost) it would be fun to see my new self. For some reason - vanity? - Hilt would not let me return the haircut favour.

Since crossing the doldrums, Hilt had stopped shaving. He was now well on the way to becoming the bearded voyageur I had paddled with back in Canada.

At 1830, we used the radio to take bearings on the loudest Hawaiian station. We were on course, hoping to make long broad reaches to get the best performance out of the boat and to avoid silly gybes. By 1500, the wind had turned east and dropped to eight knots, further hindering our progress. The diminished winds did make it easier for *Ancestor* to steer on her own.

About a mile away on a southerly course, at 0300 the next day, we sighted a ship displaying her range lights and the red port light. Because there was no danger of a collision, we held our course and speculated on whether or not they could see us on their radar.

Polaris appeared at 0500 and our horizon was clear to the north. I took sights and updated our latitude. We were 19 degrees 00.4 minutes north. Added to the noon sights, our position was confirmed at one hundred and forty miles from Hilo. Slowly but surely we were getting there. Our excitement was building as we slogged and pushed our barnacle-bottomed boat toward Hawaii. Our conversations were obsessively focused on the richness and flavours of salad and Chinese food and cool beer. What will it be like to walk on solid ground again? We were anxiously waiting for our first sight of land.

Hilt cooked an excellent breakfast on Saturday, May18th, which consisted of rice and a tin of mixed vegetables. We ate the mixture with chopsticks, all the while dreaming about the variety of delicacies we would soon taste in Hawaii. After a series of thunderous burps, Hilt scoured the horizon for the Big Island. Nothing. He murmured something about being lost and then he went below 'to have a snooze to settle his intestines.' Alone on deck, I amused myself by imagining Mauna Loa looming into our world.

1020. Not yet noon. I shook my friend awake. "You're needed on deck."

Hilt emerged from the hold and asked, "What can I do?"

"Mate, I need your help. Look around and do the honours."

Hilt turned slowly, faced the bow and after a few seconds, he shouted, "Land ho!" and broke into the grandest smile I had seen in two months. We hugged each other and performed a series of exultant landfall dances. Our celebrations definitely confused the cat, who couldn't keep up with our fancy footwork. "Hey Skip, I'm so happy, I want to kiss you on the cheek." As he approached, arms outstretched, I sprang to my feet and ran full tilt toward the fore deck with Hilt in hot pursuit. After a number of laps around the deck, he gave up the chase and dropped down the hatch. He returned with a tin of beer in each hand! "I hid these so that we could celebrate when, or if, we made landfall." We sipped and clinked those aluminium cans together. I admit that beer went down very well.

From the log:

1200h Unable to get sun sights due to heavy rain squalls.

1330h Complete overcast, cannot get sights, cannot see Hawaii. Took radio bearings on KPUA Hilo. Looks okay.

1430h Jib halyard breaks at masthead. Hove-to under mainsail.

1515h Finished repairs at masthead. Installed a one inch wooden cheek block and a three quarter inch diameter sisal halyard. Skookum. Also re-rove the flag halyard on the way down.

1800h Complete overcast to north and west. WAG=20 miles east of Kamukahi Point. Approximately 30 miles from Hilo.

1900h Kamukahi Point light bearing 240 magnetic.

1930 Becalmed. Furled main. Sheeted-in jib. Set main-trysail.

2200 Rolling rail to rail. Very rough. It was a great landfall though!

* * *

Around 0300 the next morning we encountered a gillnetter. She was showing a 360 degree white light and a 360 degree red light from her masthead. Because we had no steerage, we drifted past her course sideways. *Ancestor* came within 200 yards of her net but our shouted hellos and alohas got no response.

Intermittent, light puffs of wind prompted us to set the mainsail at daybreak and move northwest along the coast. By 0830 we were again becalmed.

Hilt was frustrated and I was impatient. The nearest point of land was only six miles distant. Hilo was thirteen miles away and all we could do was bob around in a huge wind vacuum, created by the towering volcano.

Midafternoon. I hoisted the Q and American flags from the starboard spreader and our Grenadian ensign on the after rail. We were ready for town. That night, we had a gourmet feast of fried mahi mahi fillets on a bed of rice. Forestay had spent most of the day on the port rail, peering at the strange sight of the Big Island and continually sniffing the air for clues as to what lay ahead. When we were making supper, she rubbed against Hilt's leg until she received her portion of the fish. She had not caught a squid or a flying fish for thirty hours and since there was none of her favourite food flopping across the deck, she was willing to lower her standards.

By 1700 we were drifting northward past Leleiwi Point and by the time the island had swallowed the sun, *Ancestor* was one mile off. Conditions here could be tricky. I expected some back eddying around the point and that caused concern. *Ancestor* could get swept ashore if we were caught in such waters. Thankfully, we had been fortunate on our approach to Hawaii. When we passed east of the most southeasterly point of the island, we had enough offing to ensure a northward drift. We avoided the southwest setting current that was sure to be at the Leleiwi Point. Hilt played his guitar and we sang our way into Hilo Bay that night with all hands on watch.

Before daylight next morning I was reminiscing. We were like an old windjammer, banging and slatting and waiting for wind. Or a tow. Hilt suggested that we could launch *Full Speed Ahead* at dawn and he would row us into the harbour. Good idea. I had also considered towing ourselves in, until I remembered the foul state of our hull. Well-fed crewmen in a couple of long dinghies, pulling in unison, might actually be able to haul *Ancestor* but one of us could not do the job alone, in our six foot, Sabot-style dinghy, even if said dinghy did have a cool name.

At last, as the sun etched the eastern horizon, a light Force 3 easterly breeze carried us into the bay where the wind died yet again and we resumed our windjammer-like behaviour three miles from the harbour. The local radio station was promising five to fifteen knot east winds. I optimistically started gathering and checking our necessary documents for Customs and Immigration clearance.

Not too many hours later, just as we were finishing our breakfast of mahi mahi scraps mixed with rice, a fishing vessel, the *Malahini*, altered course and motored over to visit us. Her skipper asked if we were having engine trouble and if we were, he offered to help. We recounted our adventures to the *Malahini's* crew who were now spanning their starboard rail and gaping at us. We explained our predicament and I admitted that it would be fantastic if they could take one of us ashore to buy food. Could we put *Full Speed Ahead* and her oars aboard the fishing boat? Then we could hide the dinghy on shore until one of us rowed back with provisions. (I drooled at the thought of a nice head of lettuce).

Malahini's skipper listened attentively, nodded, and went to the stern of his vessel. He picked up a coil of three quarter inch rope and tossed it over to us and said, "Aloha and welcome to Hawaii, sailors. We'll give you a tow to the anchorage. It's only three miles away." And so, at 0945, on the morning of May 19th, 1975, we let go the anchor and *Ancestor* came to rest in six fathoms of water.

'Statistics'

Balboa to Hilo - 5,625 nautical miles

Travel time - 64 days

Becalmed - 152 hours total (6.8 days)

Average day's travel - 88 miles, (including calms)

Fresh water consumed - 56 gallons

Provisions remaining - 2 pounds white rice and 2 tins of assorted vegetables

* * *

Hilt and Forestay helped me launch *Full Speed Ahead* so that I could go ashore and attend to our obligatory arrival business. Nearing the beach, I studied the wave patterns and decided to make a high speed approach in order to deposit the dinghy and myself in Hawaii. I barely managed to step out of the boat and grab the bow before the next big roller shoved the dinghy farther up onto the sand. *Jon, it's been over two months since you've been ashore and you're walking on terra firma. Could be tricky. Exercise caution.*

I was right about the walking thing. With one hand on the dinghy, I stood up straight and let go of the gunwale. Wow! The earth wobbled underfoot. I managed a few determined, staggering and stumbling steps and set forth. Anyone watching me might have enjoyed a laugh at the expense of 'a drunken sailor'. Once I had mastered the walking-on-land procedure, I went back to the dinghy, retrieved the document case (hand-made of ten ounce canvas) and directed my footsteps toward the Customs and Immigration office. The land odours were almost overpowering. They forced me to stop and breathe long and deep. Such a sweet, tropical, Hawaiian perfume! Unintentionally, I also inhaled the scent of my own body, which was rather exotic, though unlikely to please anyone. *Hmmm.*

Having been to Hilo before and knowing the location of the Customs and Immigration building, I proceeded with cautious steps. The people I encountered responded to my hearty greetings with smiles and waves. The elation of my arrival and my intense emotions must have shown on my face. I could have rushed over and hugged everyone I met but I controlled myself. Humans truly are social animals. Even deep sea travellers. Despite my fragile frame of mind, I resolutely walked to the offices and made my way inside.

Bureaucratic and Air Conditioner Shock

*E*ntering the air-conditioned room was like entering a refrigerator full of uniformed officials. Bewildered, I paused on the threshold. Whoa. Remain calm and be cool. The cool part was easy considering the temperature, which had to be forty below zero - Fahrenheit or Celsius. I stayed my course straight to the counter, where a very serious individual eyeballed me. "Yes?" he asked. "Can I help you?"

"Yes," I replied. "I am the captain of the sailing vessel *Ancestor V*. We have just arrived in port and we are anchored off the beach in Hilo Bay. There are two of us onboard, both Canadian citizens and our last port was Balboa, Republic of Panama." I placed our passports, clearance documents, crew list, cargo manifest and the ship's registration on the counter. The guy glared at me. I was perplexed but not for long.

"Mister, I don't care who the hell you are. You have disregarded the Port of Hilo maritime regulations and you better have some explanations for me. I need answers or you'll find your boat in quarantine and maybe under seizure."

It took a few moments to grasp what he was saying. I could not understand what, if anything, I had done wrong. Everyone else in the room crowded around to hear what was happening. "First of all." he ranted, "You did not call us on either 2182 kHz or on channel 16 VHF as is required by law. Therefore we were unaware of your approach. Next, you have anchored in a bay which is a designated no-anchor zone. Now start talking."

My initial response was, "I'm sorry. We don't have a single-sideband or a VHF radio on the boat." I described the vessel in detail and I described our voyage from Grenada, through Panama and the Galapagos, our sixty-four days at sea, and how good it was to be in Hawaii. I added a few tidbits about our current provision list and

At anchor in Hilo Bay. Radio Bay in background

how I hoped we could resolve this misunderstanding amicably so my crewman and I could spend some money in Hilo.

As I made my lengthy speech to this extremely stern-faced individual, another fellow, the immigration officer, started sorting through our documents. He took them to a photocopier and pushed the necessary buttons. Nearby, a very attractive lady was staring at my clothing with an amused smile while I grovelled to appease Mr. Big. Half an hour later, thankfully, everything was sorted out. My antagonistic customs guy relaxed a little although he laid down the law in no uncertain terms. I acted very contrite and humble. In summary, his indisputable comments basically reminded me that, as a mariner, it was my responsibility to understand the requirements and regulations of any country I wanted to enter. Furthermore I should shape up and 'get with the program.' Naturally, I said that I agreed with every word he uttered and from this time on I would educate myself.

The gentleman representing the Department of Agriculture informed me that he would be coming onboard when *Ancestor* was anchored in Radio Bay. But for now, he was satisfied with what he had heard. I left the office exhausted, as if I had completed some sort of marathon. Although I was not physically weary, my mind had been shrunken and squeezed in a bureaucratic wringer.

I returned to the beach. The spring that had been in my step upon arrival had morphed into a sad, sand shuffle. I was not the happiest sailor in town. We had to move to Radio Bay as soon as possible. When Mr. Big told me that *Ancestor* must move to a different anchorage, I almost blew it when I confessed that my boat had no engine and we would only be able to sail into Radio Bay when there was an adequate breeze. The expression on the customs officer's face was startling: apoplectic. He could scarcely comprehend what I was saying.

When I returned to the dinghy, there were two smiling Hawaiian families preparing a picnic. They waved me over. One man asked, "Are you off that old sailin' ship out there?" I said I was and then we sat down together, sipped cold beer and talked about my voyage. They were astounded. They couldn't get over my sixty-four day trip from Panama. I told them about our lack of provisions. Aghast, they urged, "Go get your mate. And hurry! He might be starved to death by now. Here's a beer for him." This was the Hawaii I knew and as I walked toward *Full Speed Ahead*, I was restored. My full-stride, happy-stepping gait was back!

Just Hang Loose

*H*ilt and Forestay greeted me with alohas. After I boarded, I asked them both to read the documents. Hilt gratefully accepted the paperwork and a cold beer. He examined our in-bound clearance papers and the passports stamped with three month visas. I did not bother narrating the full story of my meeting with officialdom. That dramatic tale could wait. Instead, I lowered and untied the Q flag from the halyard. We were now legal to go ashore and party!

Hilt had cleaned himself up well considering he had no mirror. I tidied myself and we inspected one another and made corrections here and there. We were beautiful guys and we were heading ashore to find good food. Poor Forestay had never been on land in her short life and I felt guilty about leaving her behind on anchor watch. When dealing with the customs man, I dared not mention the cat. Forestay's presence might have acted as the tipping point and caused a major bureaucratic eruption and my blood would flow like lava from a volcano when the customs man murdered me on the spot. Our main concern here and now was to have fun and that is what we intended to do.

On the beach, the picnicking Hawaiians strolled toward us. I was chuckling silently to myself about the little exhibition they were about to witness when Hilton took his first unsuspecting steps ashore. *A movie camera would be appropriate.* I advised, "Hilt, we'll time our landing to make use of a wave that will shove our dinghy up on the sand. You be ready and as soon as the boat touches land, jump out on one side and I'll jump out on the other side. We'll show these folks how seasoned sailors do this stuff." My friend nodded. We chose a strong wave. Hilt leapt out first, hanging onto the gunwale. I jumped out on the opposite side. "Well done, mate," I said. "Now grab the painter and pull her up the beach." The drunken sailor show began. Hilton took two steps and fell flat on his back! Puzzled, he stood up and searched the sand for whatever he might have tripped on. Nothing there. He continued up the beach, slewed sideways, off course, staggered and fell again; this time on his right side! I couldn't speak because I was killing myself with laughter and pointing at him.

Hilt at last understood. He grabbed *Full Speed Ahead* to steady himself while he yelled, "You bastard! You set me up. I'll get even." and other similarly harmless threats. A few minutes went by before he was confident enough to walk over and shake hands with the thirteen members of our welcoming committee. A man gave him a can of icy beer. I declined the offer. I remembered how difficult it had been to get the first cold one down since I had not ingested anything icy cold since Balboa and my body wisely said, "No thank you."

Little did I realize that, having met these kind people, the news of our arrival would travel like a gusty trade wind and spread throughout the city. This would be proven over many days whenever the local folks waved and welcomed us with their gentle alohas.

We parted from our new friends and headed for Radio Bay to telephone our loved ones and let them know where we were and how we were. Hilton was particularly excited and anxious. As I mentioned earlier, prior to this trip, he had never been out of contact with his wife for more than a week. In twenty minutes, we were at the inner harbour.

Foul hull at Hilo

Crew ready for shore leave

Radio Bay is not large. Rather, it could be described as snug. The bay's entrance is on its northwest corner. A long, man-made breakwater juts out from the southern shore to form the main dock. Freighters can moor on the breakwater's seaward side and inside the breakwater, the U.S. Coast Guard has moorage for the *Cape Small*, their patrol craft. Along the southern shore, running east to west, is a concrete seawall, and to the east, the landmass stretches north for a few hundred yards to a spit of the land which extends to the west, forming the north side of the harbour. Near the centre of the inner and protected harbour, small crafts drop anchor and stern tie to the seawall, Mediterranean style. The south shore is occupied by dozens of shipping containers, mostly eight by twenty feet in size and positioned back from the water. This is the island home of Matson Lines. The area between the seawall and the container heap is attractively arranged with laundry and shower buildings, picnic tables, and the intervening spaces are filled in with sod. Telephones are available so we dug into our pockets for coins to make our calls.

Hilt spent a long time on the phone. While he was thus employed, and after I had completed my own conversation, I explored the seawall and spoke with a number of sailors. It was enlightening to talk with these long distance travellers about their passages to Hilo from every point of the compass. Although these mariners were strangers, I knew we would soon become acquainted when we sailed in and joined the crowd.

Wandering around the seawall, I could see that I didn't need to worry. There was sufficient room in the harbour for *Ancestor*. We would have ample space to manoeuvre when we came in.

* * *

Getting into the city from Radio Bay took forty five minutes. We were careful. We needed to retrieve our 'walking-on-land-muscle-memories' from long-term storage. Hilt wanted to stop and chat to everyone who waved or greeted us. The poor man had been starved for company, as much as his body had been starved for real food.

In Hilo, Hilt decided that we should have a beer before our celebratory arrival meal and even though I was not craving any beverage below air temperature, I agreed. We turned onto Keawe Street and entered the Village Tavern. The air-conditioned reek of stale beer and cigarette smoke assailed my nostrils. Rock music bashed my eardrums. I was tempted to leave but Hilt bellied-up to the bar and ordered pints of draft.

There were six people at the bar, all nursing chilled drinks and looking us over. The bartender said, "So, you're new here. Where you from?" This was good for openers and Hilton was more than eager to launch into the tale of our trip to Hilo. He took his own sweet time, sparing no details and there were lots of 'far-out!' and 'no-way!' to be heard. The bartender promptly came out from behind the bar, shook our hands, and announced that our beer was on the house!

My mate continued his sailing sag awhile I leisurely checked out the other drinkers in the tavern. One lady, who looked familiar, sidled up to me, held out her hand and introduced herself. "Hello," she oozed. "I saw you at the Customs and Immigration office this morning and I liked your performance." She said that Mr. Big fumed for quite awhile after I left. "It would be my pleasure, sailor, to have you over to my place for a quiet meal sometime." She actually called me 'sailor'. I thanked her for the invitation and swiftly changed the subject. I wanted to know why she was at the bar at this time of day instead of working somewhere. "It's my half day off," she answered. "I always stop here for a drink on the way home."

Our conversation turned to Hilt's and my attire. Evidently, our clothing was rather different. *Ancestor V*'s T-shirts were simple and labelled us as different alright but I didn't think there was anything else special about our apparel, compared to, say, any other men on the streets. Hilt was wearing short trousers (shorts I had bought in Grenada but had never worn) because his long pants were ten times too large for him since he had lost so much weight. I wore very scuffed and patched blue jeans, which happened to be the only trousers I owned. It turned out that our old, flax, sail cloth, complete-with-chin-strap hats were the main focus of the bar crowd's attention. Our lids were considered unique. Off they came. Everyone asked to try them on. My one and only beer was warm enough to drink during the hat modelling fun. Hilt was on his second pint and going full steam ahead. We had a jolly time with this gang.

My smiley secretary, whose name I had already forgotten, was acting way too familiar and my craving for a delicious salad could no longer be ignored. I persuaded Hilt to down his brew and join me in search of the Chinese restaurant some acquaintances had mentioned.

While we were finishing our drinks, a very attractive lady cozied up to Hilt. "Hi there, Hilton. Welcome to Hilo. My name is Bruce." Her announcement quashed the chatter in our vicinity of the bar. All eyes were glued on Hilt. Bruce nearly fooled me too. His physique and demeanour were entirely female but his voice, although he had likely tried to feminize his speech, gave him away. My friend was frozen in time, either because he was speechless or because he was composing a polite response. Who knew? No one took a breath. The 'lady' snuggled even closer to my mate. Hilton faced his admirer, set down his beer and gave Bruce an affectionate hug! *Good old Hilt knows how to handle himself in any situation. He must be a sailor.*

I approved of Bruce's flirtations for several reasons. One, Bruce had supplied me with some juicy teasing topics to use on Hilt later, and two, Hilt swiftly downed the remainder of his beer and bid goodbye to our pals. My stomach was growling. Real food was necessary and the sooner the better. I had questioned my ability to get Hilt underway again. He has a capacity for beer that I will never possess and the idea of leaving him behind on our maiden voyage ashore was awful. Now we were leaving, to the accompaniment of many tavern patrons' boisterous and enthusiastic farewells. Ms. Secretary gave me her phone number. I thanked her and said that I would call. A little white lie but her advances made me feel good. *Was it the smell of my salty, unwashed body that had charmed her, or was it my skinny, undernourished profile? Hmm.*

Good Job

*H*ilt's swagger increased after our refreshments but I was setting a smoother course. Maybe that was just my ego inflating and a slight, drunken buzz kicking in. The Chinese café was exactly where it was supposed to be and we were excitedly anticipating a meal that was not limited to rice and fish fried up in *Ancestor's* galley.

The cafés midafternoon lunch crowd consisted of four individuals who were shovelling enormous amounts of food into their mouths. I nearly gagged at the sight and quickly distracted myself by asking Hilt where he preferred to sit. The room was massive compared to *Ancestor's* close quarters. I suppose we looked ridiculous as we fussed to find a suitable perch in that huge place. When we did sit down, a waitress flopped menus on the table and asked, "You want coffee?"

Before Hilt could respond, I said, "No, please bring a pot of jasmine tea." The pot was delivered. When we read the multi-paged, multi-choice menu, we were soon bogged down and struggling with indecision. *Let's have a bit of magic here.* I motioned for the waitress to return to our table. She reappeared, clutching an order pad and a pencil. "Is it possible," I said, "to speak to the cook before we order?" My question baffled her but she regained her composure, spun around and made a bee-line for the kitchen, most likely having ascertained that we were wandering nut-cases. (She would have been correct).

Out of the kitchen came an aproned Chinese man who seemed unruffled by my request. He came to our table and nodded hello. Hilt looked at me expectantly. Before I could open my mouth, the cook said, "You men are sailors." It was a statement. "In China, many of my uncles and cousins are sailors. That is why I am able to identify you so easy." With that declaration, he sat at the end of Hilt's seat and said, "Tell me a story."

Our story was easy to relate. I did not embellish or otherwise add any more facts than were necessary to bring *Ancestor* from Grenada to Hilo. He listened and then asked about our boat. I told him about where *Ancestor's* design originated and how the design had ended up in the West Indies. I described how these boats are sailed and the trade they were used for in the eastern Caribbean. The cook smiled. He was not the inscrutable oriental now. He asked, "How do you catch fish?" and "How much food on your ship now?" I told him about our remaining and much diminished provisions. He laughed and explained, "Now I understand why you are in my restaurant and why you want to speak to me." This happy conversation was the prelude to what was to be a fantastic meal.

I said, "We are not accustomed to having such a wide selection of food. It's hard to choose what to order. My body is dying for vegetables and some meat instead of fish. A small salad would be perfect and afterward, if you could cook small portions of your favourite dishes, we would enjoy that very much."

Our cook agreed that small portions would be best for a pair of half-starved sailors. Smiling broadly, he stood and beckoned his waitress to follow him to the kitchen. Seconds later, bottles of Tsingtao appeared in front of us. Icy droplets of water rolled onto the place mats. That beer looked inviting but a cold drink did not appeal to me. Hilt, of course, definitely approved. He swallowed half of his in a single gulp. *Man! How can he do that? We are so different, he and I.*

Steamed rice was served, along with cup-sized bowls of broth with wontons floating in each. We drank the heavenly soup. Next came a platter of fresh romaine lettuce, raw broccoli and thin slices of raw cabbage. Sighing with pleasure and thrusting our chopsticks repeatedly into the pile of green and purple vegetables, we made quick work of the salad. Our host returned with shots of a clear beverage, a palate-cleanser, with an alcoholic kick. He did not reveal its name but we guessed it was a type of Chinese schnapps. Minutes later he brought boneless chicken, rabbit and pork, with a superb side dish of black bean sauce. Now the rice bowls came into play. We picked up pieces of meat, dipped them in the sauce, added rice, smacked our lips and ate this wonderful selection of delicacies. When this feast had been devoured, we were stuffed and completely satisfied.

Our savior and favourite cook, Sam, came again to our table to ask if we wanted anything more. "No thank you," I answered. "We are pleasantly full and could not eat another morsel." We shook hands and bowed and I thanked him again, profusely, for the perfect meal.

"Your black bean sauce is the best I have ever tasted. Where did you purchase it?"

"Did not buy. I make it here."

We spent another half hour with Sam, conversing and drinking fresh Kona coffee together. Sam then reached into a pocket and gave us fortune cookies. "These cookies are not a Chinese custom. They are a western idea. Open them and read me your fortunes. This is a special occasion and I liked preparing food for hungry sailors. Nothing is sure in this world," he said, "but sometimes magic happens to make the world a better place."

We extracted the white slips of paper from the cookies. My fortune promised, "You will travel far and meet people you will not forget." Hilt's foretold, "You will have a happy life and sing many songs." Sam was impressed. I asked if he would share his fortune with us. He shook his head. "My culture has many superstitions. At this time of the year, I would be foolish to take a chance." We rose from the table and went over to the cash register, where Sam picked up our bill with too many numbers on it and silently tore it to shreds. "For you sailors, no charge." We were astonished. Our host came outside with us. "Before you go, let me try on your hats." I wished we had brought the camera.

I explained that *Ancestor* would be sailing into Radio Bay next morning if there was a breeze. We offered to show Sam the boat and he assured us he would come.

* * *

Hilton and I hiked back along the shoreline, our digestive systems working overtime. Hilt did not even suggest stopping at a tavern and he did not even react when I teased that Bruce might be waiting for him at The Village Tavern. We were packing papayas, avocados, limes, bread, oatmeal, coffee, sugar, honey.

We were also carrying an assortment of cat food for Forestay. The ship's cat was a pretty important member of the crew. Forestay was unlike most cats I had known. She did not display the haughtiness or aloofness one usually has to endure around these little beasts. Certainly our cat never seemed to hover on the edge of our group like some felines. She participated in all kinds of activity. During sail changes, she would rush at the mast, jump and dig into the spar with healthy claws, and when the sail change was completed, she would land on deck and race us to the tiller and the sheets. Hilt and I felt badly about abandoning our puss when we went ashore for our arrival celebration. Now we planned to make up for our neglect by providing a meal fit for a queen cat.

Full Speed Ahead was waiting, hidden near shore. Rowing out to *Ancestor*, we marvelled at the tendrils of light green, long grass hanging off the topsides. We could also see that the barnacle growth on the underwater hull was almost continuous. How did we ever make it to Hilo? 'Clean the hull' was moved to the top of the to-do list, just under the line 'Finish clearing customs'. There would be a lot of work for us in the coming days!

We came alongside to a chorus of meows. Forestay granted permission for us to come aboard. Immediately, I opened tins of cat food and arranged them on deck for her inspection. What a sailor! She went to the first tin, sniffed and gobbled up the contents! Whoever coined the phrase 'Variety is the spice of life.' should have been aboard. For *Ancestor's* crew, today the saying was 'Food is the spice of life'. After the cat's feast, while Hilt and Forestay had an evening wrestling match, I loaded my pipe with fresh tobacco and puffed delicate smoke rings, exactly as my father had done a million times to entertain his son. Night was falling in our part of the world and I missed being able to see the horizon for this daily event. Not that I cursed that great shield volcano bearing west of the bay but I pondered the way we humans perceive our world when embraced by new landscapes. The time had come for Hilt and me to rehash our first day in Hawaii and sing under the stars. It would have been soothing to hear someone else strumming a lone ukulele on shore.

When we spread out our sleeping bags, I told Hilt about my challenging morning at the Customs and Immigration office. He listened, chuckled at the most ridiculous parts of my story and asked, "Will the agriculture inspection be a problem tomorrow?"

"No," I said. "Compared to the other folks in that office, the agriculture fellow seems to be pretty low key. Should be an easy process." Our whispered conservation ended. We drifted off to sleep after a very eventful day.

* * *

In the morning, the dawn sky was the colour of pewter; varying shades of dull and thick grey. The gloomy colours were dispersed by the sun's arrival. Birdsong and land-scents competed with the traffic noises as people hurried off to their work.

Forestay abandoned her perch on the rail, where she had been inhaling the blended odours of trees, flowers and vehicle exhausts. She was now in search of her morning tin of whatever. Her eating habits were curious. Could she be a malnourished cat? Did she have tapeworms? Hilt and I concurred. Why worry? She's just another member of the crew who is more than eager for a change of diet now that we are at anchor.

The air grew warm quickly and with the rise in temperature a breeze was stirring. I climbed the mast to inhale the air at a higher elevation. Up there, it was possible to identify a pattern in the wind that was not discernible on deck. Conditions were okay for a short cruise and so we busied ourselves with preparations for the sail into Radio Bay. A short time later, the anchor was resting on the cathead, the mainsail and staysail were hoisted and we started our big day-trip. We had tied several lengths of rope together to give us a line long enough to reach shore from our bow anchor position in the bay. *Ancestor* roused herself, and notwithstanding the heavy growth on her hull, forged ahead like the noble vessel she was, no longer a captive in Caribbean waters but a world wanderer.

The breeze held. At the centre of the bay, Hilt climbed into the dinghy with one end of the shore line. The other end was attached to *Ancestor's* stern. Hilton carefully flaked down the rope and as I dropped the bow anchor, he began to row for shore. My anchoring was sloppy but I did not care a lot about style at that moment. Having put out plenty of scope, I hurried to the helm, sheeted in the main and nosed the boat toward the seawall. *Ancestor* advanced at half a knot with enough way to carry her in. We gybed and when her bow was pointed at the middle of the bay, I dropped the mainsail and let go the staysail halyard. All this didn't take very long. Hilt was at the seawall. He handed our line to some cruising folks who had gathered there for the entertainment we were providing. I went forward, recovered the slack of the anchor rode and as our newly appointed dock crew pulled from shore, I adjusted the anchor line to control *Ancestor's* movements. In minutes, she was in place with two short stern lines attached from her quarter points to the seawall where more than twenty sailors were commenting, *"Well done guys."* and *"Wow!"* and *"Where the hell are you from?* and *"What kind of boat is that?"*

Hilt stepped back aboard to help me furl the sails and tidy the deck. We arranged the stern lines so that when we were aboard, there was a gap of about eight feet to the seawall. To go ashore we could haul on one line or both until we were able to step onto the seawall. Then we would release the lines allowing *Ancestor* to return to her 'off-shore' position. 0800. Our day-trip was over.

Cat? What Cat?

*I*explained to our volunteer shore party that we had to clear with the Department of Agriculture before we were truly permitted to enter Hawaii and therefore we did not have much time for chatting. I overheard a few 'Oh ohs,' and worried about what that meant. Hilt shrugged his shoulders and went below to tidy everything up for the inspection. Forestay yawned and climbed into her rope fort for a morning nap. I phoned the office and I was told to remain onboard with my crew. The officials would be with us presently.

Two gentlemen arrived at the seawall, clad in highly polished black shoes, creased trousers, and briefcases. The agriculture officer was accompanied by the customs officer. Greetings were exchanged. I pulled our stern to the seawall and invited them aboard. No handshakes but no glowers either. After introducing Hilt, I invited the men to proceed. The agriculture officer removed a number of forms from his briefcase. These appeared to be checklists. The fellow started to fill in the blanks on his papers. Questions, using his list as a guide, were posed first, followed by a thorough inspection of my boat to verify my information. In his opinion, the only sticking point seemed to be whether our remaining few pounds of rice were acceptable and he circled this item on his form. Meanwhile, the customs officer roamed around the boat examining everything. He acted as if he was genuinely interested in our vessel. He asked Hilt a few questions. Hilt, being the friendliest human on the planet, responded with smiles and answers that seemed to satisfy his guest. Fine, so far.

The agriculture inspector completed his check list. Then he asked me more questions: "Do you have any souvenirs consisting of animal hides taken from endangered species?" "Is there any livestock on this vessel?" My replies were consistently negative and in a few moments he closed his folder, walked to the main hatch, peered below and lowered himself into the hold. I could hear him moving sails about and pushing things around but he had no comments or questions so I was feeling confident. Basically, we had nothing to declare. How could he find anything that was against the agricultural allowances for

Hawaii? Before long the man was back on deck and descending the ladder into the galley-bunk-chart-room. Again, no comments were uttered or heard. Within ten minutes, he rejoined us on deck, asked me to sign the document, stowed his papers inside his briefcase with a snap, and sat down on the starboard rail astern. He would not be concerned about the foreign rice, he explained, if it was cooked and consumed only on the boat.

Hilt made a pot of coffee and the four of us relaxed. The customs officer, whom I had thought was angry with me because of my ignorance concerning marine protocols, spoke quite pleasantly and inquired about our onward trip. Great!

Without warning, just when all seemed right with the world and we were enjoying a good conversation and delicious coffee, Forestay leapt from her fort and attacked my leg below the knee! "YOU HAVE AN UNDECLARED CAT ONBOARD!" exclaimed the customs officer. His colleague grunted and shook his head sadly. I groaned.

Hilt said, "What cat? Oh! *That* cat,"

Shocked and bordering on catatonic, I happened to glance behind our 'guests'. There were at least twenty people watching *Ancestor's* drama unfold. I heard unsympathetic giggles, outright laughter and many, mumbled 'Oh ohs.'

Before the customs guy could launch into a tirade, I found my voice. "Hell!" I said. "I forgot about the cat. I've never had a pet on a boat before. I just didn't think about her." My excuse sounded lame. Even to me. *Is this what is known as deep shit?*

After the official's ranting subsided and his body language became less alarming, we managed to find a way out of our dilemma. I signed a document acknowledging that, if our cat was found on land in Hawaii, it would be captured and killed. I also signed a bond for $3,500 US that would have to be paid upon Forestay's demise. Hilt said not a word. He cuddled the cat and moved away from the two men. But it was over. These bureaucrat had discovered a problem and they dealt with it. I just wanted these dudes off my boat. As fast as possible. I had once more been found wanting. I was an 'idiot Canadian sailor', according to a certain person, who also claimed that we were lucky that he had not ordered us to leave port immediately. To use Hilt's term, I was feeling dumpy. I hardly noticed when the men went ashore.

Someone on shore tossed two cans of beer to us. As I thanked him, I tried to clear my head and shake off this unpleasantness. I'm the kind of guy who never feels shitty. Many of my acquaintances would say my problem is that I am too optimistic and frivolous about almost everything in my life.

Still cuddling the cat, Hilt came over and hugged me. "Hell, Skip, don't take this too seriously."

I took a sip of beer. Hilt's advice helped me to recall, from years ago, one of Brendan Gill's favourite sayings, which expresses an attitude and philosophy of life that I share with him completely. I raised my bottle, spread my arms wide, and when the gang on the dock quietened down, I said, "Not a shred of evidence exists in favour of the idea that life is serious."

Everyone applauded and suddenly we were all laughing and talking about the inspection. I had come back to life and once again *Ancestor* was a happy ship.

* * *

Now that we were officially cleared into Hawaii, we were legally able to go ashore and meet this supportive crowd of sailors whom we had not yet had the chance to visit. Forestay re-entered her fortress and we left the boat. I was content to let Hilt act as our spokesman. He explained who *Ancestor* was, where she came from and where she was headed. Noon arrived before folks remembered that they had other things to do. My friend and I went back onboard to organize ourselves for the remainder of our stay.

We made a plan. Well – sort of a plan, based on what tasks needed to be done in Hawaii: scrape the hull, check and replace tired blocks, patch sails and so on. I explained to Hilt that we should depart Hilo on or about the fourth of June. This date should make it possible to avoid the heavy gales in the north eastern Pacific. That gave us two weeks here. We would have to re-provision for a four to five week trip, have lots of parties, make lots of music and have a lot of fun. We shook on it. Hilt said, "No problem with that, Skip."

I noticed several guys from the Coast Guard cutter, *Cape Small*, strolling in our direction on the seawall. A muscular, well-groomed German Shepherd dog, the ship's mascot, was with them. We invited *Cape Small's* crew members aboard, sans dog, and we spent an interesting hour or so learning about their Hawaiian duty. They were joyful, joking fellows. Hilt had found soul-mates.

Hilt went ashore with his new friends for a tour of the cutter. I went to the cabin, for a little solitude, away from prying eyes of the people passing by in a steady stream. Our work plan looked to be achievable. The 'financials', however, were another story. I would have to have a talk with Hilt to see if we could put aside enough money to provision the boat, before getting carried away with other spending. Hilo offered lots of local food, both fruits and vegetables. Bread was inexpensive. The danger lay in our plan to 'party' which could turn out to be costly if we got carried away or if we ignored our priorities.

That afternoon I had a visit from our friend Sam, the Chinese cook, and his wife. I invited them aboard. They scrutinized the boat and spoke quietly together in Mandarin. I let them tour the hold and the galley on their own while I boiled water and made a pot of jasmine green tea. Forestay was alert whenever we had guests and this occasion was no exception. She perched on the counter top in the galley, nudging me to do this and that, while meowing constantly to comment on everything. Sam and his wife were finishing their tour when I brought the tea and mugs on deck. The cook asked if he might take pictures and I said, "Yes, take all the pictures you like and then I can take a nice shot of you both." They were pleased. We had some tea.

"This cat is sailor too?" asked Sam. They were delighted to hear Forestay's story. Sam said, "Very good to have cat on ship and if you need food, is good to eat!" He then described his best Chinese recipe for cat.

Following tea, Sam pulled an envelope of black and white photos from his bag to show me the various craft on the Yangtze. Two were owned and operated by his cousins. In his youth, Sam had spent time on both boats. He drew my attention to the long sweep oars (yulohs) used to scull boats when they were without wind. Even when he was a child, Sam said, he could scull his cousin's forty foot sampan at a speed of one knot, if there was no opposing wind or current. The cook suggested that I make one of these oars and he would show me how to use it. That was a grand idea and I almost made a yuloh. Unfortunately my intentions slipped through the cracks and we departed Hilo without the oar.

After a few hours of happy-time on *Ancestor*, Sam and his wife left. In parting, Sam said, "I do not own restaurant but I am cook. Please come to visit again before you go to Vancouver." I promised to do so.

It had been quite a day and it continued to be busy as the afternoon hours turned into evening hours. A pair of Hawaiian men, whom we had met on the beach when we first landed, came over to investigate *Ancestor*. They offered some fantastic advice. Having examined our barnacle - encrusted hull, one of them asked, "What are you going to do about those?"

"I'd hate like hell to scrape them off my boat with sharp metal tools because the hull planking is pitch-pine and very soft. I haven't really figured out what to do."

The second fellow said, "Take your boat to fresh water and anchor for a day or two. The barnacles will die. That's when they're really easy to remove." I ruminated on this for awhile, trying to picture myself getting *Ancestor* high enough up a stream to be above the tide. Was it possible? They saw my confusion.

Speaker number one explained. "A very short distance from here there's a powerful, sub-sea, fresh water spring that comes to the surface. You only have to take your boat there, anchor and wait for Mother Nature to do the rest." Now I was excited. Knowing we did not have an engine, they offered to tow us to the spring with their launch when it was convenient for us. I could hardly believe our luck. I thanked them warmly. As the men turned to go, one of them gave me a slip of paper with a telephone number, saying that I should phone whenever we want to do the fresh water trick. I hadn't even asked their names!

After dark, Hilt showed up with his pals. They came aboard with several cases of beer and predictably, Hilt found his guitar and the evening's entertainment got underway. *Ancestor's* commodious deck became crowded with cruising sailors. A fellow from Tennessee arrived with a flute, a lady with a ukulele, a guy from Kentucky with a banjo. Our impromptu band included bongo drums, castanets, a mouth harp, two harmonicas and more instruments that I can't remember. This was a BIG jam session and tremendously exciting for a Hilton and me who had been isolated from the rest of humanity for the past couple of months.

Hilt, the self-appointed host guitar-picker, led the group. He was amazing to watch. He sat on the rail and with his feet, drummed the beat on the deck. My friend was in Hawaiian heaven. Feeling the vibe too, I passed drinks around. I had already consumed a beer earlier and did not want another but finally I opened a bottle, took a sip, and placed it on deck. Apparently this was the proper thing to do. Heads nodded in approval. I went with the flow.

Until I noticed that one of Hilt's buddies had a fat joint tucked above his right ear. I caught his attention by stepping to within six inches of his face. "Is that a joint? And if so, why the hell did you bring it aboard my boat?"

I must have spoken rather loudly because the music stopped and everyone was watching the confrontation. The guy stood and focused his eyes on mine while he stretched to his full height and snarled, "It's none of your goddam business if I have a bit of 'Jane' in my possession." He sneered and looked at his audience. I concentrated on remaining calm. He was a big man. A full six inches taller than me. Instinctively, I knew he was a scrapper but in my current frame of mind, I managed to keep my cool and show no fear. I said, "For your information, it is my business if you bring pot onto my vessel. In the United States of America, there happens to be a zero tolerance law. If the authorities find dope on my vessel, *Ancestor* will be confiscated and her crew will go to prison. You bet it is my business. Now get that joint out of here and take yourself with it. You are not welcome." No one moved. It was a stand-off.

He continued to look me in the eye, doing his best to stare me down. The big man laughed and said, "I ain't going nowhere, Mister Captain, sir. What are you going to do about it?" I had been in difficult situations before and I had learned how to defend myself. I had cocked my right arm slightly behind my torso and I promptly showed this bully exactly what I was going to do about it by leaning my left shoulder against his right shoulder, pivoting and giving him a powerful jab to the solar plexus: a one-punch fight. The bulwarks caught him below the knees and the force of my right-hand punch drove him into the water.

His friends jumped over the side to help their mate. I asked the crowd to stay quiet so we could hear what was happening. What a mess! A twelve foot Zodiac dinghy arrived in the splash-zone and many hands struggled to pull the floundering swimmer into the boat. His size made the task difficult. The entire incident upset me. I regretted the fact that someone had brought dope on my boat in the first place and I also regretted my behaviour. I should have asked the man's friends to deal with him. But the guy's attitude annoyed me. He was not only belligerent, he also posed a threat to *Ancestor*. Maybe I did need a beer.

Hilt handed me the guitar and said, "Hey Skip, sing us a song." I sat on the rail, opposite the Kentucky banjo player, smiled at him, I said, "This will be in A," and I launched into "Oh Lonesome Me." The music was like a balm, soothing everyone. The melody brought us back to our cheerful, tropical reality.

Next day, I was lethargic. Not because of a hangover, since I only had my usual one beer the night before. I blamed my mood on the events of the past few days. Admittedly, my one-punch performance didn't help either. *Oh well, It's nothing that a good cup of coffee and a nice papaya won't cure.* Most of our friends had returned to their boats before dawn but a half dozen party-goers remained sprawled on deck like rag dolls, or spent musicians, or fun-loving sailors. Hilt was not below decks. He must have wandered off with his new pals. He would show up soon.

I take great delight in slicing papayas in half, scooping out the seeds and squirting lime juice on the flesh. The smell of freshly brewed coffee woke up the lingerers. My guests rubbed their eyes, gathered themselves together and gratefully accepted breakfast. Peace was restored onboard in an hour when the merry-makers left and the skipper and his cat could laze on deck alone and that was fine with both of us.

The day's first visitor was a Macadamia nut farmer who lived on the slopes of Mauna Loa. I invited Jim Smith aboard. He and I enjoyed a friendly conversation. *Ancestor* fascinated him. Yet again, I was busy giving a full account of our travels. When Jim was leaving, he asked if I liked macadamia nuts.

"I certainly do, but I can hardly ever afford to buy them."

"My last crop was good. I'll bring you a sample next time I'm in town."

Before lunch, our helpful Hawaiian boatmen came by to say that they could tow us to the fresh water springs at 10:00 a.m. tomorrow. Excellent news! I would be ready.

Hilt returned looking rested and pleased and raving about last night's party. "Skipper, this is living!" His early, dawn adventures were not mentioned and I didn't press him on the subject. The possibility of *Ancestor* having a clean hull was exciting enough and he promised to be ready to cast off tomorrow morning.

Today there was still shopping to do. But first, our list of provisions must be reviewed and tweaked until it made sense. Eventually, with our revisions completed, we ventured into town.

At Sam's restaurant (I forget the name of the place), Hilt ordered war wonton and I had a plate of black bean chicken. We were gaining weight and that was healthy. Sam joined us briefly but his busy kitchen soon called him away. Following this satisfying repast, we strolled through town, window shopping. In a small market, we bought guavas, papayas, limes, a fresh bunch of gai lan, a basil plant and a large ginger root.

Fearless Forestay

We returned to Radio Bay by mid-afternoon. Our trip to town had been worthwhile for the exercise, the lunch, and the loads of food on our backs. Twice, locals, who obviously knew all about us, stopped to smile and talk and in both cases, they offered to buy our hats. Handmade sailor hats were popular, it seemed, although we couldn't understand why. "Maybe we should settle here and become hat manufacturers," said the entrepreneurial first mate.

"Okay, Hilt, we can set up shop on *Ancestor*. Each day we can display our newly completed bonnets and folks can point out what they like and we'll sell them for cash money."

Onboard, we found our shipmate a bit edgy. She did not greet us the way she always did after we had been away. Forestay was definitely out of sorts. Following a few feeble meows, the cat jumped onto the furled mainsail and squatted there, hunched and twitchy. We unloaded our provisions and stowed them in the galley hammocks. On deck, Hilt offered me a beer and my body told me, "Yes, beer would be just the right beverage after our long, hot walk."

Hilt and I stood facing aft, the main boom between us. We were perfectly positioned to witness an amazing event. A scraping sound was coming from the mainsail near the mast. Gripping our beers, we turned just in time to see Forestay, a flashing blur between us, running past at full speed. The boom, in the gallows housing, was slightly upswept at the stern. Forestay launched her streamlined body in a beautiful arcing flight that cleared the gap between boom and seawall. She landed on shore, rolled several times and came to a stop. The cat was on land for the first time in her life! Anxiously, she stood there, surrounded by all that endless space and those exotic smells. She sniffed furiously, trying to get her bearings and then she bolted for the double-high shipping containers which filled most of the beach area. Both Hilt and I cheered, but then we looked at each other. Dread replaced our appreciation of Forestay's magnificent leap. "Shit!" I bellowed.

"This could cost me three thousand, five hundred dollars and the life of our shipmate if she is caught!" Frantically, we pulled *Ancestor's* stern up to the seawall so we could leap off and pursue our feline fugitive. At the same time, we heard the Coast Guard's mascot barking loudly. He was nearby when the cat hurled herself landward and now, in a frenzy, he was speeding toward the container pile, yowling and growling. Dust flew everywhere. Relentlessly, the dog pursued the cat around the huge containers. Forestay was fast but the German Shepherd was narrowing the gap.

The chase ended rather abruptly when Forestay recognized her floating home and made a bee line for it. We jumped aside as she jumped from the seawall, landed on deck, and skidded for twelve feet before screeching to a halt. The Shepherd stopped on the verge, growled once, recognized Hilt, panted, and wagged his tail.

I examined our favourite cat, checking her for damage, but I could find no wounds of any kind. "Wow," I said, "not even a splinter!" Hilt came over and offered our athletic puss a sip of beer. Forestay got a whiff of it and licked her lips and partook of the foamy beverage. What a show.

We all needed a drink!

* * *

By early evening Hilt had gone off with his friend Bob Hilby from the *Cape Small*, assuring me, before he departed, that he would be onboard and sober for the move to fresh water the next morning. I invited a young, happy, and enthusiastic couple off a twenty-eight foot Herreshoff sloop to join me for a meal. He was Dutch and she was Japanese Hawaiian. They had a rabbit on their boat named Spare Provisions. The Herreshoff's next port of call would be Tahiti and her crew wanted to talk about the best routes to that Polynesian island. The couple brought a bottle of Chardonnay and a chicken which I cooked for the three of us. I lightly steamed basil leaves and soaked them in a small amount of balsamic vinegar and olive oil. This heady mixture was spooned over the fried pieces of chicken, with rice and steamed gai lan on the side. In my opinion, the dinner was fantastic and by the way they tucked in, there was no doubt that everyone appreciated my recipe. To wash it all down, we sipped their refreshingly cool wine.

Later, as we traded tales and as the full night blanketed the bay, we heard people singing lustily. Three men were staggering along the seawall, arm in arm.

Oh no no no, I don't smoke it no more,

Tired of waking up on de floor.

No tank you please, it just make me sneeze.

Make it too hard to find de door.

Hilt and his friends were back.

* * *

Ancestor was towed next morning to the underwater spring where we anchored in six fathoms and put a stern line ashore to hold our position over the up-surging fresh water. This hull cleaning process was fascinating. We said things like, "Take that you barnacles!" and "This is totally amazing!" The water temperature here was five degrees colder than the ocean. To us, it felt frigid. Perhaps we should draw straws to choose who would dive in tomorrow to check on the barnacle-adhesion. Until then, there were other things to attend to. After confirming that *Ancestor* was firmly stationed and secure, we rowed ashore, Hilt to meet a family who wanted to give him a tour of the volcano, and I to the customs building to update the bureaucrats on *Ancestor's* movements. The short customs meeting went okay but the officials were not amused, claiming I had ignored proper protocol: I should have consulted them prior to moving my boat from the harbour. Once again I was accused of bending the rules. These gentlemen educated me further, in a rather gruff manner, repeating the regulations and handing me a copy of their 'What Mariners Need to Know' manual. In the background, my secretary friend giggled into her sleeve and gave me a big wink. All was well.

On the boat once more, I settled into a relaxed vigil. We were anchored close to the shore, which was covered in large deciduous trees, species which were mostly unknown to me. I added to my mental list: Ask locals to identify flora. There were no insects other than bees and I was able to chill out completely and concentrate on my tan, even though it did not need much work.

The sun slid behind the mountain for an evening nap, though later, of course, the day-star would vanish for its nightly, twelve-hour, deep sleep. When Hilt came back from his tour, he told me about his deep respect for Madame Pelée, the goddess of the volcano. My mate decided to install a small effigy of this deity on the boat. Finding the appropriate figure would be his challenge on the morrow.

Birdsong and a gently sighing easterly breeze combined so that we found ourselves whispering. The tropical twilight was perfect. Often, the natural world is too delicate to disturb. Our human noises were out of balance with the beauty around us. Even Forestay seemed to share our opinion. Her purrs were gentle. She wasn't bouncing about as she is wont to do when the evening's coolness deposes the bright, sun-lit day. We three quietly found our nests and fell asleep in paradise.

* * *

I dove into the shockingly cold water on the following morning, plastic scraper in hand, to test the adhesion of our barnacles to the hull. The critters were looser and much easier to remove than they had been before their fresh water soaking. Hilt and I opted to stay here for another twenty-four hours and let the stream perform its magic. We decided to do our barnacle scraping tomorrow in the warm waters of Radio Bay.

My shipmate had planned a full day on land. I had no problem with that. During his absence, I could do a few switch-out jobs. When Hilton rowed ashore and disappeared into the trees. I remained onboard, smoked my pipe and consulted our to-do list. There were not a lot of items on the page. I scratched out those tasks we had completed and I prioritized the remaining chores which still had to be done. As soon as Forestay gave the go-ahead, I got to work.

Lunch was stir-fried rice with vegetable scraps left over from yesterday's supper. Following this repast, Forestay helped with the washing up by licking my plate and the wok. Silly cat thought she was a scullery maid. With lunch out of the way, I was inclined to find my hammock and rest for a few moments. Having persuaded myself that a little leisure time might be pleasant, I climbed into the swinging bunk to determine if I was right or not. Half an hour later I awoke, convinced that yes, this had been the proper way to finish my lunch break. Then I heard a splash and turned to investigate.

Hawaiian Mermaid

Someone was swimming from the beach toward the boat, with one hand in the air gripping a plastic parcel. Whoever it was, the individual was not wearing swim fins, because he/she was moving very slowly. Amused, I waited for the person to get closer so that I might identify him/her. While waiting, I tied a boat fender horizontally along the hull six inches above the water. This would permit my unidentified visitor to climb aboard without coming in contact with the barnacles. "Good stuff," I said to myself and when I looked up, I was astonished, and pleased to see my smiling secretary, sans costume, in the cold fresh water. The water temperature was making her gasp. I helped my guest clamber up the makeshift ladder and I laughed. "Wow! I've caught a real Hawaiian mermaid. The first one I've ever seen."

Stepping on deck, she laughed and said, "If I had a tail, I'd slap your face, mister." After she dropped her clothes bag, I gave her a towel. She shivered and nodded gratefully. Her arrival had been unexpected and the thought of welcoming a real live, totally naked mermaid aboard was having an effect on me. She dried herself off while I pumped the Primus to boil water. Soon we were sitting on the rail, sipping hot tea and grinning at one another.

My swimming secretary asked if we were alone and I assured her that we were, with the exception of the cat, of course. She had seen *Ancestor* from the shore but she wanted to come aboard and have a closer look. Hence, this mermaid swam over for a visit. Apparently it was also important to her to not be seen by anyone else. So here we were, on a hot and sunny afternoon. After a few sips, she asked, "Can you give me the tour?"

"Certainly Ms. Mermaid. This way please." I escorted her to the main hatch which had a removable hatch cover twenty-five inches square. "This is the ship's hold where we store water, provisions, sails, et cetera and this is also where the mate sleeps. His bunk is on the starboard side. We can investigate this part of the boat first, if you like." She was only wearing a towel and I was impressed by the way she lowered herself into the hold without disturbing the towel. *Mermaids are cool.*

I followed her through the hatch but when my feet were on the floor timbers and my arms were still at the outer hatch level, I heard her say, "Stop right there, sailor. You cannot show me your boat very well, dressed in those old jeans." A tug at my belt buckle. A pull on my zipper. A downward tug on both pant legs and the mermaid's husky voice invited, "Okay, you can come below now."

We examined beams, timbers, ballast rock, sails and all else from a number of different positions. Three hours later this portion of the tour came to an end and I suggested a can of beer and a serving of excellent Hawaiian sunshine for a change of scene. She agreed. On deck, we examined one another for bruises. I found hand cream to spread on those scuff marks which had mysteriously appeared on our arms and thighs. My mermaid said, "That was a rough tour, mister sailor, and one would hope you are not always that unkind to your guests."

"Yes, it was difficult," I admitted. "I will need to soften my routine if I hope to have repeat customers."

The remaining idyllic hours were passed in idle chat. Ms. Mermaid was engaged to be married when her fiancé returned from mainland USA but she was wavering in her resolve. Would it be wise to wait for a year or so, until she was sure of herself? If she had any doubts, I suggested, maybe she should keep the brakes on and see what happens. I also mentioned casually, that I did most everything in my life based on intuition, on hunches, and for me this approach had proven to be an excellent way to live so far.

The sun melded with the mountain while we explored the galley/sleeping area and the confines of my quarter berth. Until today, I had thought my bed was a tight fit for one individual but *Ancestor's* skipper was astounded to discover that his bunk actually suited two people, if they were compatible and unencumbered by pajamas or other clothing.

At last, the lady announced that she must return to the world. While she dressed, I swam ashore and rowed the dinghy to the boat for transportation. Too soon I was on my own, back aboard and recovering from the surprise and pleasure of my Hawaiian mermaid's visit.

Barnacle Crew

Five volunteers and I made up the barnacle crew. Our gear consisted of swim fins, snorkels and face masks and our tools were three inch wide, plastic spatulas. Thus equipped, we slipped into the warm waters of Radio Bay to remove our unwanted guests from the hull.

It was gratifying to peel the barnacles and weeds from the wood with a minimum of effort. In less than an hour, Hilt was serving beers on deck. When the water had cleared around the hull, I dove again to inspect the planking, and search for loose caulking and bad fasteners. Finding no problems, I inspected the rudder and its fittings before climbing aboard for a celebratory beer. *Ancestor* looked more like her old self.

With a clean hull, I longed to be back at sea. I thought *Ancestor* was restive too. I know we humans tend to project our personalities onto inanimate objects. We anthropomorphize, referring to a boat or a ship as 'she'. We sense her concerns. We become best friends with her. And when the time comes to sell our vessel, we weep over the finality of the sale transaction. I am certainly no different in this regard and here I was, communing with this wonderful, West Indian hull, trying to take her pulse, as it were, in order to determine whether or not she was eager to romp on the high seas with me again. I abandoned my musings to rejoin the friendly, happy crowd aboard. The scraping volunteers received accolades from *Ancestor's* crew, while they waved bottles of beer in one hand and plastic spatulas in the other. At some point, it was declared that there was to be a music jam on the H28 that night and all were welcome. Hilt gave a lusty cheer and strummed a few tunes. Everything was normal in the harbour.

Before lunch, I headed to Hilo for a stroll and to purchase more fresh food. Hilt and I were putting on weight. Hilton's gain was mostly around his waist whereas my additional weight seemed to be generally all over my body. I felt healthy and my bones and muscles and lungs appreciated the walk, especially when I was carrying a full pack of food back to Radio Bay.

Hilt had made many friends and he liked to spend most of his shore time visiting and exploring the countryside. Hilton is a gregarious man who can handle large quantities of beer, which I cannot. In many ways, we were different but despite our idiosyncrasies, we shared a love of boats and the sea. This made us a team.

At the restaurant, I greeted Sam and ordered wonton soup. When the cook had a moment to spare, he asked me, "When is *Ancestor* sailing? I want to be there when you leave."

"The day after tomorrow. With any luck, we will clear the harbour by 8:00 a.m." This departure date was in accordance with the plan Hilt and I had made when we arrived and I thought it wise to stick to it. Our schedule gave us a target to work towards. I believed we could easily accomplish everything and be away on June 4th.

Sam said, "I'll be there." and he rushed back to his kitchen.

Hiking back to Radio Bay, my thoughts about Hilt's health and well-being were dark and upsetting. That he was having a good time with his new friends was not in dispute although in my opinion at least, his health was deteriorating. Being 'blasted' every night for over a week would be pretty hard on anyone's constitution and in my estimation, my friend was unwell. Every morning he was slow and lethargic. There were dark rings under his eyes. I doubted that partying was his normal way of life and I expected that what was happening here was anomalous behaviour. Anyway, we had better head out to sea as soon as possible.

On *Ancestor*, I stowed the food I had lugged from town. Some was for our immediate consumption but most was for our ongoing travel. I couldn't help but worry. Could we afford to provision the boat for this forty day crossing? Hilt was generous with his money but his funds were limited. The state of our finances troubled me often. Maybe there was a silver lining to the gloomy cloud I was visualizing. I optimistically hoped that all would be well and so I pushed my concerns to the back of the mind and I focused on being organized and prepared to cast off on the 4th.

Just Have Fun

Dusk draped dark curtains over the bay. Sailors and their instruments materialized and drifted toward H28, the action-boat. Party time! Hilt had returned early from his carousing and was one of the first to board the Herreshoff. I followed him soon after. The ship's mascot, a medium-sized white rabbit, was hopping about, evading the party-goers' scuffling feet. I went to sit in the cockpit near the main hatch but there were rabbit turds everywhere! Oops. Our hosts didn't have time to clean up after Spare Provisions. The poop was not fresh so I simply brushed off the seat with the side of my hand, sat down and accepted a beer from the hostess. I amused myself by watching other guests who were also looking for places to sit. They scowled at the bunny, scorned her droppings, hesitated, muttered, and finally resigned themselves to wiping away the mess to make a clean sitting space. Hilt initiated the musical proceedings with a medley of sing along tunes. A flute accompanied him and a variety of instruments chimed in, creating a jolly, party mood.

Around 3:00 a.m. in the morning, the festivities abated. Folks wandered off until there were only six of us remaining. Someone decided that from now on, a departing guest must first compose a new ditty and perform it for the hosts and their friends. If the tune produced enough laughter from the audience, the singer had the freedom to leave. Good fun! One by one the songsters indulged in their moment of glory by hooting out their compositions. Hilt's offering was about *Ancestor's* silly, foul-pipe-smoking skipper. When it was my turn, I plunked an A-chord using a sort of calypso beat and when the muse nudged me, I added a chorus about how one should always hang loose in Hawaii. The first verse was about arriving in Hilo Bay with no wind. The next verses were about Hilt and his girl friends on the island. I loved the tune which had jumped into the guitar and everyone roared about Hilton's adventures.

Here are the lyrics:

We arrived in Hilo harbour in the month of May,
And that's where we decided we would have to stay,
We hoisted up the main and put the jib to use,
But that's when they decided they would just hang loose.

Chorus
Just hang loose, just have fun,
Sippin' on a drink or lying in the sun,
No need to fight it. What's the use?
When you're in Hawaii you should hang loose,

We went to Village Tavern on Keawe Street,
And met a little lady who was oh so sweet,
She sauntered up to Hilton and said, "Hi, I'm Bruce,"
And that's when he decided he would just hang loose.

Chorus
Hilton found himself a naughty hula girl,
Took her down the beach for a little whirl,
His wife was not excited. She said, "What's the use?"
I think she knew that Hilton would just hang loose.

* * *

Before I left, my H28 hostess asked, "What is your favourite kind of cake?"

No need to think. "Chocolate."

She smiled her lovely Polynesian smile and said, "I thought it would be chocolate."

On *Ancestor*, after a much needed rest, I awoke to shafts of golden sunlight glimmering through the trees on the eastern border of the bay. *Last day in port. We need provisions and we're going to be busy.* I hustled around making coffee and slicing up a juicy papaya for breakfast. Hilt had not yet popped out of the hold. I had a quiet time alone. For a few minutes anyway.

"Good morning, *Ancestor*. Could I have a word with you?" called a stranger standing on the seawall. He introduced himself after he climbed onboard and we shook hands. The fellow accepted a cup of coffee. When we were comfortable, he asked "Do you want to sell that Hang Loose song you performed last night?"

Caught off guard, I hesitated before answering. "Well, I don't know if I can even remember how it went." The man drank his java and suggested that I write the song down so we could review it. I found paper and a pencil and spent fifteen minutes doing just that. Once the words were sorted and organized, I borrowed Hilt's guitar to find the beat and tune again. At this point, the gentleman asked politely if he could record my rendition on his cassette recorder. "Sure. Why not?" said I.

When I had finished singing, he dug into his backpack, pulled out a clip-board holding a stack of paper, thumbed through the pile to find the right pages, and explained, "This is an agreement. A combined contract/waiver document. I am willing to pay you $200.00 US for *Hang Loose*. By signing below, you relinquish any rights to this piece of music. You will receive no royalties if the song is recorded. Lastly, your name may not be mentioned as the writer/originator."

I signed the form enthusiastically and he immediately gave me four, crisp fifty dollar bills. A handshake sealed the deal and that was that. He had me sing the song once more while he drained his coffee cup and then he simply left. I was elated. *We can provision Ancestor! I do not have to ask Hilt for money!* Yesterday I had been so worried but I'd had a hunch that somehow, everything would work out. Maybe this chance encounter was not magic but it was magical enough for me. *Wow! Two hundred bucks! Provisions for the next leg of our voyage!*

When Hilt poked his head out of the hatch, I told him of our good fortune. He nodded sleepily and returned to his bunk. *Oh well. It only takes one person to do the provisioning. I'm out of here.*

Several days ago, a man had said I could use his small pick-up truck and now I contacted the owner, who lived near the bay. His offer was still valid. So! Off I went. Key in the ignition. Gearbox in neutral. Turn the key and listen to the rumbling under the hood!

Having travelled at an average speed of five knots for the past few months, I seemed to be breaking the speed limit as I roared down the road at 25 mph. I checked the speedometer frequently to make sure that I wasn't speeding. The ride was exhilarating. I could grin and laugh at myself without reservation because I was alone and as free as the breeze. *Simple things for simple minds, Jon.*

In town, I found a supermarket and loaded a shopping cart with four dozen Budweiser beers for Hilt and one dozen Heineken for me. Next was Forestay's cat food. I did not dare to forget these items. A mutinous crew could not be tolerated. Referring to my list, I rolled my cart methodically down every aisle to grab Hilt's instant mashed potatoes, hot sauces, mustard, spices, powdered milk, Carnation canned milk and Carnation Sweetened Condensed Milk, baking powder, baking soda, flour, sea salt, pasta, cocoa, coffee, tea, rice, oatmeal, raisins, dried mango chunks, sugar, honey, strawberry jam, orange marmalade, five loaves of bread, whole potatoes, onions, yams, sunflower seeds, butter, cheese, olive oil, balsamic vinegar, a bottle of dark rum, a small jug of Grand Marnier. I was doing well but my wallet was getting slimmer.

At a general store, I bought a five inch diameter mirror, a pair of cotton drill pants for myself, plus socks, a long-sleeved shirt and a pair of work gloves. A funky hardware store, barely noticeable from the main drag, had Primus stove burners, jet cleaners and the other paraphernalia we needed to keep the cooker percolating. I bought plenty of spare stove parts. When my purchases were heaped in the truck, I had a pipe and re-read the provision list.

My final stop was for fruit. Under a fruit stall's twelve by twelve foot tarpaulin canopy, I bought fifteen, red flesh papayas, twelve mangos, 20 guavas just plucked off the tree, fifty fresh limes, a dozen avocados from Maui and a dozen apples from the mainland. In the neighbouring stall I acquired a stalk of bananas and some home-grown leaf tobacco. Life was good, the truck was loaded and I was off to Radio Bay.

I backed the pick-up to the edge of the seawall where Hilt and his coast guard pals were just leaving the boat. In case Hilt had not remembered about our good fortune with the Hang Loose song, I retold the story and described my shopping spree.

"Hey first mate, I hope you have a blast tonight, because we will be setting sail in the morning."

Hilt pulled me aside. "Skip, can't we wait a few days? Wait for wind? We're having too good a time here. We can't leave yet."

I knew changing his mind would not be easy. I reiterated our sailing route and I patiently listed all the reasons why tomorrow was opportune for leaving the islands. I even pulled rank a little which did not aid in keeping our discussion on an even keel. My final words were, "Hey Hilt, when we reach Victoria, we can party some more. And by the way, we have five dozen beers, so there'll be no shortages on this leg of the trip."

When Hilton and the lads were gone, I transferred the provisions from the vehicle to the boat and then I stowed everything. With this job done, I surveyed the ship and inspected every detail until I was satisfied that *Ancestor* was ready for sea.

The skipper of the S.V. *Cypriana*, whose home port was Honolulu, came along and asked if we were definitely outbound on the morrow.

"Yes, we are set to go and we hope to cast off at 0800."

"I'll be up early,' he replied. "If there is no wind, I can tow you out to where you should feel a breeze." I appreciated his kindness and I promised to give him a call if we needed help.

When I took the pick-up truck back to the owner, I also took our passports and ship's documents with me. Conveniently, the truck owner's home and the Customs and Immigration offices were close together. I informed the officials that *Ancestor V* would be sailing at 8:00 a.m. tomorrow and I requested out-bound clearance for Victoria, British Columbia. I thought there were smirks on a few of the office employees' faces when I said this yet I was both surprised and relieved to find that there were no problems in getting clearance. *These guys will be happy to see the aft end of Ancestor and her crew.*

Because Ms. Mermaid was not in the office that day, I did not have a chance to say farewell. I hoped that she would show up before our departure to say good-bye.

Just before leaving the Customs and Immigration office, I reached over the counter and shook hands with the officials and I thanked them for their kindness. In turn, they wished us a safe voyage.

The evening light faded. I cooked rice, prepared a salad and grilled a piece of my newly purchased mahi mahi. I ate slowly to savour the food, especially the lettuce and arugula, which I knew we would be missing in the near future. Folks came to talk and say 'bon voyage' and I had a visit from Jim Smith, the farmer from Pahoa. Knowing we were leaving, he had brought us a fifty pound sack of macadamia nuts in the shell as a farewell gift! "Here you are, Skip," he said, chucking the bag at me across ten feet of water. I was astonished. Macadamia nuts are very expensive anywhere and to receive a sackful was amazing. I accompanied him to his car to thank him again. We hugged. "Think of me once in awhile, Jon. I would most likely sell my farm if I could go on a voyage like yours. I'm jealous but very happy for you and your crew." He drove around the corner and disappeared.

Later, after my last pipe of the day, while I was adjusting the hammock for a cozy sleep, I heard, "Hey sailor, come here and say goodbye." My favourite Hawaiian mermaid! I was quick to pull *Ancestor's* stern close enough to the seawall so I could jump off and greet her. She approached and sniffed at me, explaining that she wanted to store my scent as a memory of the best day she had ever had on a boat. I didn't touch her or move. I just waited while she finished sniffing, although I did laugh a little because this was a unique situation. Then she kissed my lips lightly and gave me a small packet, bound with blue string. The lady made me promise I wouldn't open her gift until Hawaii was over the horizon. I thanked her and tucked the packet in my jeans pocket. I did not even know her name, and somehow I intuited that I never would, even though she knew who I was from Hilo newspaper articles and also from the customs documents she had to process. Not fair! But our encounter was magic. My wonderful mermaid granted me one last kiss before she walked away. I was happy.

0400. Hilt returned from his gallivanting. He needed my assistance getting to his bunk without mishap. My friend had never returned this late before. This alone convinced me that tonight should be his last night in Hilo. I was worried that my friend might kill himself if he tried to keep pace with his young friends. In all the time I had known Hilt, he had never refused a drink. He had an infinite capacity for grog and joy. If his drinking was allowed to continue for a few more days, I feared he might wind up in the hospital. I resolved to stick to my sailing schedule and let the chips fall where they may.

Tow Job, Shanghaied Crew and Travel

Polaris,
Our guiding star
To new adventures.
Keep it on your bow
Then on your left shoulder.
Later – watch for the Aurora in the vault
And maple leaves floating on the sea.

Sailing day. The sun's first rays cut through the trees while I untied my hammock from the rigging, rolled up my sleeping bag and anticipated a strong, hot jolt of coffee. And unexpectedly, just as I was enjoying that first cup of the day, Sam hailed me from shore. He waved for me to pull the boat in. I invited him aboard and he accepted a mug of freshly brewed caffeine. I apologized because Hilt was still asleep and not feeling very well this morning. As Sam could see however, Forestay was busy patrolling the decks to make sure we were ready to travel. The cook only had a few minutes before he must hurry off to the restaurant. We stepped ashore. Could I wait a moment while he fetched something from the car? He returned with a jar of his black bean sauce. I thanked him profusely. Sam said, "When you have black bean fish, you think of Sam." With that he hastened away and sped off into the early morning light.

I stowed Sam's bean sauce in the galley and climbed back on deck to discover another visitor. "This is for you, Jon. One chocolate cake to go!" exclaimed the jovial hostess from the H28. I leaped ashore to receive her gift and to give her a warm hug. Behind her, to my astonishment, there were even more people gathering. The Hawaiians, whom Hilton and I had met on the beach when we first arrived in Hilo Bay, had also come to say good-bye. They gave me guavas, limes, papayas and avocados! Wow! And I had been worried about provisioning *Ancestor*! The Hawaiians boarded, went forward and started tying lush, green fronds onto the rigging. One man said this was an island tradition. Whenever a friend or family member goes on a long voyage, it is customary to decorate the departing vessel. These fronds keep the boat and her crew safe and well until they reach their destination. (Some of this greenery survived in the rigging all the way to Victoria). I was overwhelmed by their thoughtfulness. We had done nothing more than befriend these generous folk and I now understood that such friendliness sustained them and their way of life. I opened the hatch, hoping Hilt would join us. To my dismay, he was totally out of the circuit.

Before the Hawaiians left, they danced a hula on deck, accompanied by a ukulele and a choir of gentle voices. Their song lamented our leave-taking and the melody made me weep. The music ended. They stepped ashore. Everyone hugged me and thanked me for visiting them in Hilo. I had never experienced such an emotional send off before and I thought that I might never enjoy one like it ever again. In hindsight, I was glad that my mate was asleep or I believe he may have persuaded me to stay forever in this island paradise.

Cypriana's engine fired up; a sure sign that we were committed to our departure. I calmed down. Although there was no wind, it was time to go. I cast off astern and started to overhaul the anchor rode. The sailors in the bay were shouting, "Farewell!" I waved and thanked them for the good times we had shared. Soon the anchor was lashed to the catheads and the *Cypriana* tossed me her towline. I fed the line through a hawse pipe, made it fast to the sampson post and let *Cypriana* take up the slack. *Ancestor* came to life and regally pointed her bow towards the open sea. Her home.

A quick look at Hilt's Diver Dan watch confirmed that we had left our anchorage exactly as planned, at 8:00 a.m. *Cypriana* motored steadily at five knots, the perfect speed for this operation. Later I saw ripples on the otherwise flat water. Gradually, the breeze was increasing. I hoisted the main and staysail and signalled for *Cypriana* to stop the tow. he decelerated and I released the rope, which was briskly overhauled by the tow boat's crew. *Cypriana* turned back toward Radio Bay.

We were on our own and even though the winds were not cooperating yet, we were moving forward. Course 360 degrees magnetic. Hilt was asleep, in sharp contrast to Forestay, who was super active, careening around the decks until she finally pounced onto my lap where she panted and waited for an affectionate scratch under the chin.

My mate awoke at 1400. Perhaps because *Ancestor* was rolling and pitching a lot.

I expected Hilt to make a scene when he emerged from the hold and I was not disappointed. With his arms through the hatch, he squinted to leeward before he swivelled his head toward the south. His facial expression was hard to read. I watched him in silence until he said, "Goddam it, Skipper, what are we doing out here?" He was genuinely puzzled.

"Hilt, my friend, we are bound for Victoria, having departed Radio Bay at 0800 and we are now off and running, or drifting, northward. Forestay and the skipper are happy. I know you have a hangover but that will wear off and as soon as you get a good meal under your belt, you'll be happy too."

There was an uncomfortable pause and then he said, "Skipper, you bastard, you shanghaied me. We talked about this. I thought we'd decided to stay a few more days." Hilton hastily crawled out onto the deck and made for the lee rail, over which he retched and gagged for five minutes. Appearing to be exhausted and uncoordinated, he stumbled back to the hatch, where he stopped and waited while I finished explaining why we were leaving on the scheduled date.

"Regarding the charge of shanghaiing you, it is my understanding that shanghaiing refers to the practice of kidnapping people by drugging them or tricking them aboard an outward bound vessel. In this case, you drugged yourself. On alcohol. Furthermore, you came aboard willingly."

With his head hanging on his chest, he considered my words for some time. Finally, he grunted and went below, leaving me to speculate on how this drama would play out. I was apprehensive. Hilt was one of my best friends and I did not want our relationship to end because of his drinking spree at Hilo. Sailing northward, I ate a light meal of salad and avocados, washed down with fresh water. *This could be a long watch.*

By sundown *Ancestor* was again becalmed. I furled her sails and settled down for a bumpy night by wedging my sleeping bag and some pillows against the bulwarks where I could burrow into the bedding. A kerosene lantern hung from the rigging to alert any oncoming vessel that might approach during the night. Hopefully, the light would encourage ships to avoid us. Hilo's higher buildings and the airport beacon were visible but the rest of the waterfront was over the horizon. Mauna Loa was massive. The volcano seemed very close. I puffed my pipe, studied the stars and chuckled at Forestay's antics. She was prowling and attacking shadows wherever they appeared. The ship's cat played contentedly and I sensed that she was, unlike Hilt, happy to be underway once again.

Light but welcome winds woke me. I hoisted the mainsail and the jib and tacked north. When the breezes fell asleep, I did too. On this first night, bound for Canada, *Ancestor* rocked and rolled. In the night I heard a solitary porpoise puffing alongside. Was she old, and having lost some of her faculties, did she seek us out for companionship? At sunrise, she was still with us.

While the sun began illuminating the new day, I stuck my head through the hatch. *Is Hilt awake? The air below is foul.* I moved the hatch cover aside to ventilate his sleeping quarters. "Hey, first mate, could you handle a bowl of oatmeal and dry toast?" Rip van Winkle roused himself, rolled over, opened his eyes and responded affirmatively. Pleased, I went to the galley to cook a pot of porridge. *An appetite is a healthy sign!* I stirred the oats with my spurtle, a utensil I had carved out of a chunk of local Hawaiian wood that I had found by accident on the road into Hilo. I was proud of my spurtle. It made me smile.

Hilt came on deck, grasped a shroud and valiantly tried to fill the ocean with used beer. "Wow! What a bladder!" I commented, while he continued to pee nonstop. Afterward, he came aft, scanned the horizon and plumped himself down on the steering bench. I passed him a coffee from below, where I was preparing a stack of toast and a large bowl of oatmeal. I would eat my portion straight out of the pot. I refrained from making any frivolous comments although I expected him to start berating me. He was probably very upset that we were no longer in Hilo. But the scolding didn't happen.

"Hey Skip, have you seen my hat? The sun will be burning my head to a cinder if I don't cover it soon." I dropped into the hold and found the hat, all the while thinking that it could have easily been lost during Hilt's wanderings ashore. With his head safely covered and a second cup of coffee on the go, Hilton looked me in the eye and said, "I don't quite know how to say this, Skip. I guess I went sort of nuts in Hilo. Maybe it was the long period of solitude that made me react the way I did – Anyway, thanks for getting us out of Dodge. You were right to do what you thought was necessary."

Before he could say anything else, I said, "Mate, don't apologize. You had a grand time and I only wish I had been able to fit into your groove. If I ever have to shanghai you again, I'll club you over the head and drag you aboard by your toes." His warm, firm handshake was fantastic.

"Skip," Hilt said shyly, "if the shoe is ever on the other foot, so to speak, I'll do the same for you."

By the time the sun reached its zenith, the temperature reached eighty degrees in the shade. I took visual bearings on discernible land masses by sighting over the ship's compass. Our 12:00 p.m. position was 20 degrees 07 north, 155 degrees 02 west: thirty miles north of Hilo.

Hilt resumed standing watches that afternoon while we worked the light, fluky winds. Tack, tack, tack. We tacked more in the last twenty-four hours than we had from Panama to Hawaii. By nightfall, the wind was easing to a northeaster and the returning trade wind was appreciated. *Ancestor* insisted on steering herself. Hilt and I let her. The first flying fish crashed on deck soon after the sun had settled into her nighttime sea-hammock. Forestay was delighted. She took full advantage of every poor beast who became a toy and then a meal.

After a supper of salad and avocados, we talked about safety. Whenever we set sail, it was my habit to discuss all the possible hazards that may occur on the boat. We agreed to use our handmade safety harnesses if we deemed that equipment necessary. We agreed to always move slowly and cautiously to execute sail changes or reef the mainsail. Anything at deck level is a danger to life and limb, even Forestay. We also agreed to pick up any two-legged or four-legged shipmates who fell overboard. It was a profitable conversation and in my opinion, everyone going offshore should adopt a similar routine. If a crew discusses and rehearses what to do in any difficult or life threatening event - ahead of time - that sailing team will not hesitate when a perilous situation occurs. The crew will react correctly, to the best of their ability, in order to cope with challenging circumstances. Confusion and panic are avoided. No one need wait for instructions. Instead, prepared sailors know what to do to try and avert disaster.

That night we traded watches regularly. The wind held. Rain showers dampened the decks. In the morning there was no sign of land and we revelled in the excitement of being at sea again. Despite the lazy winds, we covered eighty-five miles, on course, by noon. I managed several sun sights in the morning hours and I accomplished a meridian passage shot at midday. *Ancestor's* hull was clean and she surged forth like a sea witch.

My mate and I sat together on the deck that night. Neither of us was tired or in need of anything. Hilt was showing signs of a full recovery. He even seemed to be satisfied with a single beer at suppertime. Content and with a full stomach, he slowly lost himself in thought. Not wishing to disturb him, I played a number of quiet tunes on his guitar. After dark, he rallied and said, "Hey Jon, light your pipe and listen to my latest idea."

When pipe smoke was billowing around me, I said, "Okay mate, I'm all ears."

"Jon," he asked, "what are you going to do with *Ancestor* when we get to Vancouver?"

"Well, that is easy, Hilt. I will have to sell her after I pay the import tax." I puffed my pipe and raised my eyebrows, to indicate that he should continue.

"That's what I thought," Hilton said enthusiastically. "I have a proposition I'd like you to consider. I dream of buying *Ancestor* when we get to the coast. The ballast would have to be removed, the mast, rigging and bowsprit would have to come down and be secured on deck. I'd arrange to have her shipped to Sarnia."

His idea caught me by surprise. I could never have conceived of such a plan. "So, what would you do with her on Lake Huron?"

"I've noticed how people everywhere react when they see this ship! Folks in my neck of the woods would be tripping over each other to get a chance to board a West Indian smuggler's vessel in Sarnia, Ontario! I would organize day-sail charters. Our American neighbours would be very interested. I'll bet I could make a hell of a business." We were silent while Hilt scratched Forestay's ears and our brains whirled and visualized the possibilities of such a scheme.

"Hmmm," said I.

Evidently, Hilt had spoken with his wife, Barbara. She was not averse to the plan. More silence. *Ancestor* steered us north on that perfect night. "How much would you want for her, Jon?"

"In order to recoup the expenses of this trip and make a few dollars, I was going to ask ten thousand dollars, Canadian."

"I expected that kind of a price and it seems reasonable to me."

We both started daydreaming about making landfall in Vancouver and Hilton trucking *Ancestor* off to Ontario. For me, it was troubling to envision my vessel being hauled ignominiously across the country and deposited on a lake. No dignity. No class. On the other hand, I did have to sell her and here was a fair proposal.

"Hilt, let's talk about this some more at leisure. If you haven't changed your mind by the time we get to British Columbia, the deal is on." We shook on it and since this was Hilt's watch, I bid him a good night and went below to inspect my sleeping bag for flying fish or squid before crawling in for my three 'off' hours.

At midnight, I relieved my friend. We drank tea while he reported our course, speed, wind direction and the set of the sails.

The night cooled down. So I did not get overheated while I primed the bilge pump (twenty-three strokes) and emptied the bilge. *Smart lad.* Beneath the star-lit heavens, the Force 3 trade winds remained fairly constant. Polaris was almost twenty-three degrees above the horizon here: a useful position for future latitude checks. Unfortunately, we had moved northward and at approximately ninety degrees, the sun's declination was of no use for noon hour latitude updates. I puffed my pipe and cuddled Forestay until Hilt reappeared.

* * *

Keeping watch can stress a sailor's eyes. A fellow once explained to me that it is good for the retina to experience direct sunlight. Such exposure, if carefully practiced, is said to make one's eyesight more acute.

I blinked at the rising sun for a few minutes and then massaged the eyes with the palms of my hands. It seemed to wake me up properly for sure.

With my vision refreshed, my mind pursued another topic and I recalled a small gift from a Hilo mermaid. I found her packet, untied the blue string and opened it. The package contained a condom in a sealed envelope and above the mermaid's telephone number, on the wrapping paper, were written a few lines: "Hey sailor – thanks for a wonderful time. Stay safe. Give me a call." There was no name.

* * *

For the next few days, we endured erratic winds which changed hourly from north east to south to southwest. These conditions produced unsettled seas that tossed us about, spilling wind from our sails and chafing our running gear. We persevered, trying to control the grumpiness that lurked behind our mental barricades. Hilt and I took turns hand-steering in order to maintain a respectable course and we joked about this unfortunate situation. We actually had to sail *Ancestor* instead of just sitting happily and letting her control the ride. Despite these challenges, we covered sixty to seventy-five miles a day. We had no reason to complain.

There was plenty of sea life around to distract us. Dolphins greeted us daily and spouting whales were sighted often. We dubbed a pair of visiting yellowfins 'resident tuna'. They were thrilling to watch while they patrolled three fathoms below in the shade of our hull. Occasionally the fish would disappear, no doubt to go to the nearest sushi bar for a snack. They would return unexpectedly and resume tagging along with *Ancestor*. The yellowfins stayed with us for nine days and we were disappointed when they moved on.

The westerly setting current and the light winds combined to set us to the west. We were losing ground, so to speak, and we grumbled occasionally about this inconvenience. Even though we knew that the wind and water would affect us this way and we knew we had to cross the trade wind belt before finding the northwest winds that would help us to the coast. Based on what I could remember, I believed we were in a transition zone where the wind should veer to the south. There was no choice but to wait patiently for Mother Nature to oblige us.

A steady Force 3 blew into our sails when the wind did eventually co-operate and settle in the south. Our vessel was put on a starboard tack to minimize the drift from the current but not too far to the east of north, where the dreaded North Pacific High lurked. That region of calms develops in the north pacific summer. The North Pacific High (NPH) is a curse for any engineless sailboat.

Ancestor was steering herself again and we made satisfactory progress: 707 miles, 8 days from Hilo. We were doing fine.

Nearing the shipping lane which connects Panama and the Philippines, we became extremely cautious. Hilt and I were not surprised when we encountered three ships and dissected their great circle course. Two of them were ore carriers or bulk freighters on a westerly heading. The third, east bound, was a tanker. We could see her full length catwalk extending between her aft superstructure and her bow. Before dark and because we were definitely not alone out here, we trimmed our running light wicks and made sure that the lanterns' tanks were full of kerosene.

From the log:

0200h, ship bearing two and half points off the starboard bow. Ancestor is the burdened vessel. Lit and installed starboard running light. Passed astern of ship with half mile clearance. Back on 360 degrees. WWVH reports that centre of high-pressure area is located 37 north, 145 west. Lined bow with Polaris and recorded that there is no evident deviation on true north. Note: 15 degrees variation here. The old compass is developing a bubble.

The centre of high pressure was approximately 150 miles from our location. Its proximity did not worry us because the centre tends to drift constantly. By tomorrow, this large weather system could be right on top of us or it could be hundreds of miles to the south. These winds do not normally die off altogether, but they can be fickle. Sailors try to dodge the central zone. Our intention, after a lengthy discussion, was to get as much northing as possible before angling toward the Strait of Juan de Fuca.

At dawn, there was eighty percent cloud cover and the wind had backed to south east, at Force 4. *Excellent!*

Hilt informed me that today was Sunday, the fifteenth, Father's Day. Were our sons thinking of us as we were thinking of them? In the afternoon, Hilt fiddled with the radio dials and we were soon listening to CKDA Victoria! When it faded, he readjusted the dial and found Sea Fun, Vancouver. That channel was lost too but we decided to search for a clear radio station every day. Hilt said he could fill in the silent spots with his own tunes if need be.

Monday the sixteenth of June was memorable. A chill hung in the air and I had to don my trousers! My ragged, cut-off jeans were folded and stowed as we bantered about the wildlife onboard. Would the cockroaches, crickets and centipedes survive the cold weather of the North Pacific? Hilt thought they would, considering the insulation provided by the hull timbers. I disagreed. Surely they would die off by the time we reached Victoria. A wager was made, hands shaken and because there were no casinos or poker chips out here, the lucky winner would be rewarded with a shot of hot rum. We also placed bets on *Ancestor's* daily run, the noon to noon distance she covered. Our guesses were recorded and when the navigation update was done, we eagerly checked our estimates. The one closest to the actual mileage got bragging rights, while the loser was responsible for preparing lunch. Forestay did not participate. She was much more interested in gorging on flying fish and squid.

On the subject of squid, there was a six inch squirming specimen on deck next morning. "Hey man," I asked Hilt, "would you like fresh bonito for breakfast?" When he said yes, I got busy with our fishing tackle, basically, a three inch hook, knotted onto a length of monofilament fishing line without weights. The hapless squid was fixed to the hook. Over the side went our bait and I paid out the line carefully, checking first to confirm that its bitter end was secured to the boat. When the hook was twenty-five feet aft, we had an immediate hit. I struggled to hold on and bring in our catch. In five minutes, a dark bonito was flopping at our feet and Hilton and I were cheering. "Will that be fresh enough for you sir?" I asked.

As I was skinning the fish, we noticed two Black-footed albatross behind us, gliding a hundred feet above the water. "We got visitors," said Hilt, and Forestay, who had been totally preoccupied with the bonito, diverted her gaze, spotted the seabirds and jumped up on the taffrail to hiss at our airborne friends. When they were flying within fifty feet of our stern rail, I tossed chunks of fish skin over the side. The big birds landed and made a commotion while swallowing their free breakfast. "Well," said Hilt, "I bet we've made friends forever with these guys." In fact, he was not far wrong. The albatross followed us for hundreds of miles. They became confident enough to land on the aft deck and beg for handouts. The small cat would stalk these legendary avians every time we caught a fish.

Two weeks out. To commemorate this milestone, the winds determined that we needed a rest. They died off and began to perform their fickle manoeuvres. For thirty hours, the breezes danced around every point of the compass, causing the crew some consternation while forcing *Ancestor* to joust with the winds to stay on course. Rough sailing! We tacked frequently and when the breeze did calm down and settle in the easterly quadrant, we were exuberant. Then came fog and cool temperatures in the low sixties. We shivered and scrambled for warmer clothing. The tropics had spoiled us and now we had to adapt and become tough Canadians again. The sea water temperature was only fifty-eight degrees! "Look out you cockroaches and crickets," I stuttered through my chattering teeth. "I hope you brought parkas and toques for this trip." No clicking replies came from the hold. Would our mute, downstairs neighbours be able to adjust their metabolisms to deal with the climate change?

Sea Monsters

During our long voyage from Panama to Hilo, we indulged in a lot of chat relating to sea life. Being the most spectacular of creatures, in our view, whales initiated many of our lively debates and if a whale happened to be cruising alongside at night, he/she invariably put on a great show. Whenever we sailed parallel to the waves, and if a whale was in the next wave beside the boat, and if there was phosphorescence, we were treated to such a display of light and agility that we would almost quit breathing. Cetacean visits are about as good as it gets at sea.

We both knew stories about the early days of whaling and the heavy-haul trade when mariners used the largest sailing vessels ever built. The recorded history contains many sea monster tales. Sailors, since time immemorial, are a superstitious lot. Any living, aquatic creature, large and unknown to man, slithering and diving, its intent unknown, was labeled a monster. In the past, prior to the popular press and prior to modern science researching the multitude of lifeforms inhabiting the oceans, sailors would understandably be frightened by these manifestations. The Kraken, that horrible, large, multi-tentacled monster of Caribbean folklore, is an excellent example. This beast was said to rear up out of the sea, wrap its arms around an entire ship and drag it to the bottom. A horrendous fate indeed.

In my travels, I had yet to see a Kraken, but if you were to ask me about mermaids, I would answer, "Absolutely!" Mermaids are not sirens of the sea waiting to trap sailors and put them under a spell. Mermaids are beautiful, ocean ladies with graceful bodies, alluring smiles and no wiles.

Having never encountered a sea monster and with the on-going rage over UFOs, I had redirected my self-education regarding phenomena, from the sea to the heavens. I have seen meteors, man-made satellites in orbit, the Aurora Borealis, high flying aircraft and almost anything else you might think of, but no unidentified flying objects so far. I won't quit gazing expectantly skyward and the ocean will never cease to fascinate me. Similarly, myth and sailor superstition continue to intrigue me. I love this stuff and I'm always watching for the miracles of the unknown.

In the midafternoon, I was snoozing in my bunk with Forestay who liked to sleep with her back to my neck. I was shocked by Hilt's loud voice. "SEA MONSTER!"

Without thinking, I untangled myself from the sleeping bag and lunged for the hatch, gouging my head in the process. "What? Where?" I asked, landing on deck and bleeding.

"You'll see in a minute, Skip," he said. "I can't believe my eyes."

Over the past hour, the wind had turned northeast and our course was approximately north. We were close-hauled at four knots. Hilton said the monsters were just below the surface and riding the waves. I went forward and held on to a shroud for safety. I didn't have long to wait.

As *Ancestor* breasted a sea, I saw my first two foot wide, six foot long, enormous, rusty-coloured, sausage-shaped monster undulating through the water, rising and sinking in the troughs and very much alive! Well, this 'beast' had no fangs or tentacles or stingers but it was positively fascinating. There were more like him, too. We saw as many as five at once. What a spectacle! Some appeared to exceed half a mile in length, perhaps even longer. I knew instinctively that these were not sea monsters. I also knew we were witnessing a phenomenon, a living thing we had never heard of or read about.

I made my way aft and grabbed a heavy plastic, mason's mud bucket with twenty feet of knotted rope attached to it. "Hilt," I yelled, "we have to get a sample. Grab some kind of weight to put in the pail." It just so happened that we had a seven pound sounding lead on deck, which Hilt removed and hastily passed to me. With the weight in the bucket and the bucket rope tied off to a cleat, I dropped to my knees and scanned the water. *Ancestor* came to the top of the next roller and I saw the 'monsters' in the trough. Perfect. I cast the bucket well ahead of my deck position and watched it sink. *Ancestor* rose on the next wave. I dragged the bucket through one of the monsters and brought the sample aboard. Thousands of plankton were wriggling in every direction. The bucket was teeming with life!

Having lashed the container on deck, we searched for more "coils of life." There were dozens of them, lengths unknown. We sailed on for a mile before leaving their domain. Hilt said, "Hey Skip, they are obviously going somewhere, otherwise why would they be in that formation and following the waves?" He was right. If these small creatures were simply feeding, they would most likely be in no organized pattern. Rather, they would probably spread themselves over a wide area and stain the water's surface with their distinctive red-tide colour. A new mystery for us!

We placed a small number of specimens on a metal dish where we could separate and study the tiny creatures with a three power magnifying glass. Hilt and I identified two distinctive forms. One was shrimp-like. The other was a round blob. We saved some samples, hoping to dry and preserve them for analysis and classification by a marine biologist back on the coast. Our discovery was exciting. We spent many happy hours talking about Hilt's sea monsters.

I noted the latitude and longitude of the plankton sighting: 39 degrees 28 north, 156 degrees 48 west.

* * **

We were on the outer fringes of the North Pacific High. The unstable northeast wind was tending to veer but not with any serious intent. The charts showed the Great Circle Course in the North Pacific and as we approached the highway between Los Angeles and the Philippines, we spotted several freighters following an east-west course. Had any radio operators on these ships tried to contact our little vessel on VHF? It would have been fun to gam with other seafarers.

A day later, we encountered several more sea monsters, though the plankton did not appear as a cohesive mass like the previous group. These coil formations were altering and losing shape as if the whole 'monster' was about to disintegrate. Our enthusiasm was renewed. We engaged in long, friendly arguments about whether or not any other mariners had ever witnessed this spectacle. Would ocean science provide explanations? Our dried samples were safely sealed in an envelope and stowed with the charts for later analysis.

Due west of Cape Mendocino, California, the air temperature remained a chilly fifty-seven degrees Fahrenheit. The sky was overcast. The region of high pressure was centered at 46 degrees north and 152 degrees west and *Ancestor* was not exactly flying across the ocean. A hardly legible note was scribbled on the log margin: "So – who is in a hurry?"

Summer solstice found us becalmed on an oily, slick sea, with sails slatting. We waited for wind. The ocean emitted a foul smell, as if we were downwind from a fish plant. There was also the usual sea life about and the occasional skim of oil, similar to the surface water of a duck pond.

And tiny, unidentifiable, star-shaped objects, like mussel shells connected to a central hub were floating past. Hundreds of them! Each organism measured one inch across. What were they? It was best to be patient. We could only bide our time and see.

Hilt caught a four pound mahi mahi for everyone's breakfast, i.e. for Hilt, me, Forestay and our four, huge feathered friends who were cruising along with us. The usual morning brouhaha developed. Forestay stalks albatross. Birds clumsily land on moving deck. Persistent and brazen birds dine despite humans' loud laughter and ship cat's hisses. On this morning, we also sighted our first shearwaters and fairy terns. We would see a lot more of them near the coast since we were now wandering into their domain.

According to the WWVH weather bulletins, which notified seamen about the location of gales and the centre of the high pressure area in our part of the world, we assumed we were in for more light and variable breezes. Sadly, our assumption was correct.

Coincident with the approach of nightfall, the cloud cover - our constant daylight companion - dissipated at last. And we were blessed with a fantastic sunset. On midnight watch, after I had poured a cup of tea and peeled one of the remaining bananas, I heard a great 'poof' sound. The fin of an Orca cut through the water ten feet off the starboard side. He stayed nearby for twenty minutes, torpedoing toward us from many different angles, diving under the boat and generally making a fuss. Forestay, our cat on guard duty, raced from side to side on deck. "Watch him, Forestay. Don't let him come onboard." The cat heeded the captain's instructions and the whale stayed in the water where he belonged.

Mars and Jupiter were patrolling the eastern sky. I scanned the heavens looking for meteors and comets, which often streak through the atmosphere on any night watch. Hilt and I made a habit of counting these 'streakers' and reporting on how many each of us had seen. I once saw thirty-three in three hours. At 0300, before going below, I routinely observed the altitude and approximate azimuth of any stars which could be used in the morning navigation, when both the star, or planet, and the horizon were visible. This sort of preparation proved useful when I tried to locate these heavenly bodies as night turned into day.

On this particular occasion, Hilt came on deck at 2100. He turned on the radio and picked up a CKNW news broadcast announcing floods in southern Alberta, a threatened waterfront strike in Vancouver, numerous traffic accidents, a robbery, and a shooting in Surrey. Normal stuff. But we preferred our dull life out here, floating across the Pacific Ocean, eating too many fish and waiting to fill our sails.

At midnight the wind veered to the east and then to the south east. Precisely what we had been hoping for! Neither of us felt sleepy: a transition time. Hilt asked me to play some tunes on his guitar and so we drifted for the next few hours. Our songs were clear but subdued in the magic of that tranquil night.

Seal of Approval

For a few hours, we'd been becalmed and fretting about where the next wind would come from. Early on the morning of June 24th, although it was as delicate as pipe smoke and barely ruffled the whiskers on my chin, our first northwesterly breeze arrived. In whispers, we asked one another, "Do you think we've finally reached the westerlies?" "Is this really it?" "Can we aim for the coast?" We needn't have worried about keeping our voices low. Our questions would not have scared these zephyrs away but we needed more wind and I suppose we were overly anxious. As it turned out, this faint northwesterly was sent to titillate us poor sailors, and within a few hours, we were hardly moving and whatever breezes we did have, were mostly from the eastern and southern coordinates, with plenty of calms in between.

The first rays of the sun reflected off the oily water, limiting our vision and it seemed that clouds wanted to rule the day. Since these conditions were beyond our control, we might as well make cinnamon pancakes. Hilt fired up the stove and mixed the batter. A tasty breakfast was the very best antidote to a grey morning with the air temperature at fifty-seven degrees.

Our noon position was 42 degrees 44 north, and 156 degrees 55 west latitude. We were 1,538 nautical miles from Hilo and 1,550 from Victoria, with sufficient provisions for another month. Great! We would deal with whatever the planet had to throw at us. *Ancestor* rolled and pitched in the sloppy sea and we hung on, pumped the bilge and debated the evening meal's menu.

Later on, Hilt noticed activity to the south. *Ancestor* crested a wave and through the binoculars, I identified a clump of fish net moving very slowly. Something was caught in it.

Eager to investigate whatever it was, we attempted to manoeuvre ourselves closer to the object but there was insufficient wind to give us steerage. To solve that problem, we hove-to. "Hilt," I said, "we have seen lots of junk lying around out here. Fish floats and plastic garbage are one thing but chunks of fish net are a no-no, in my opinion. Let's get that net and haul it on deck. If there's something trapped inside, we can release it or eat it: one or the other." Hilt lowered the dinghy. I stuffed a knife in my belt, grabbed a short handled gaff hook and climbed aboard.

The net and its contents were three hundred yards away. I rowed and kept an eye on Hilt, who was guiding me in the right direction. Soon, I was able to rotate the dinghy to get a visual fix on our target. There was definitely something alive and trapped in there because the net's movements intensified as I approached. It took a few minutes for me to realize it was a harbour seal! I was surprised, to say the least, although I correctly recognized the brownish-grey coat, round head, large eyes and the V shaped nostrils. I had observed hundreds, if not thousands, of this species on the BC coast. This fellow looked to be between five and six feet long and he certainly had a lot of fight in him.

My initial plan was to get as close as possible, cut the net and free the seal from his prison. Not a simple task. I rowed with the transom of the dinghy facing the seal, in order to push the net thither and yon. The seal attacked and bit a chunk out of the transom's thin plywood. When he dove to avoid my approach, I could see that the net mesh wrapped about his head and shoulder had caused black welts and white pus. The pitiful sight made me extremely upset. I directed my silent anger toward all drift net fishing operations, wherever they might be.

Calming myself, I tried to figure how I might save this guy. The seal considered me an enemy and he was reacting accordingly. How could I free him? If he was alongside *Ancestor*, we might have a chance but how do we get him there? That was the immediate concern. I could not estimate how much netting was involved, considering the way it was ballasted by the seal and by the marine growth clinging to it. An idea came to me. I cautiously backed the dinghy up to the net. Once in position, I used the gaff hook to grab the mesh and then I wedged the five foot handle of the gaff under the dinghy's centre seat. The gaff pole was also resting atop the transom and it was well secured. Satisfied that I had a good purchase on the netting material, I took the strain on the oars, using a quick, dipping stroke, and I tried to row the entire mass toward the boat. It wasn't working.

Time to re-think and re-plan. Everything was okay except I needed help with my propulsion system. Because our vessel was becalmed, Hilt couldn't sail over to help me. While I was still searching for a solution to this predicament, the seal resurfaced and when he saw the transom of the dinghy, he lunged full speed ahead at *Full Speed Ahead*. Fortuitously, his forward lunge increased the slack on the net! I quickly adjusted the tension! The seal's leap had narrowed the distance to the boat by at least three feet. In order to encourage the seal to repeat his surprisingly useful manoeuvre, I taunted him with the end of one oar. He charged again. And I rowed as hard as I could. Progress! We were getting there.

Ages later, we were finally beside *Ancestor*. I was exhausted. Hilt reached down, grabbed a section of net, pulled it over the bulwarks and lashed it onto a cleat. I clambered aboard and together we pulled the dinghy on deck. The twilight sky still afforded good visibility so we reviewed the seal's situation and what to do next. We didn't have much of a plan. We would lift the net until the seal was unable to fight and use a sharp blade to cut the cording away. "Piece of cake," said Hilton.

Except it was a struggle lifting the net and the seal high enough to liberate the animal but we persevered until finally, the seal was half out of the water. Even though he was still thrashing about, his neck was within reach. I leaned over the bulwarks and ran the knife, backside against the seal's neck, down and down, slicing until the knife tip touched the netting. One more thrust and there was a loud 'snap'. The net ripped apart. The seal slipped into the water and disappeared. We gave three cheers and congratulated ourselves on the great Pacific prison-break. Then we hauled the netting on deck. It was cluttered with the bones of other less fortunate creatures, mussels and marine growth. The mess had to be pulled to the bow to flake it and get it out of our way while we worked the ship. Afterward, a well-deserved meal and a small libation of Grand Marnier were mandatory in celebration. I was still pretty shaky and suffering from muscle fatigue. Hilt had to be our chef, but I needed no assistance bending my elbow for the alcoholic toast.

I relaxed while Hilt cooked. We talked more about harbour seals. Were they pelagic? Or was this seal just out here roaming around, getting fat, and enjoying the good life until tragedy struck? How long had he been in this predicament? How come he was so fat and sassy and full of energy? How could a net-entangled seal catch food? He couldn't. Could he? I thought harbour seals are not pelagic. They inhabit coastal waters. In our combined years of sailing, my friend and I had never encountered this species offshore and definitely not 1,500 miles from the nearest land. We pondered our latest mystery,

A harbour seal was tangled in a section of drift net and needed rescuing

munched our meal and agreed that we would like to learn more about these mammals when we reached port.

Night settled over the boat. While Hilt was washing up, we heard recognizable sounds to the north. "Ouunck. Ouunck." The noise came closer and Forestay became agitated. Trembling, she stood on the rail, prepared to pounce on anything that dared to threaten her home. The three of us searched the ocean ripples. Incredibly, there was 'our' seal. He was unmistakable, with those dark, collar-like markings around his neck. Then we saw a second seal. "Hey Jon, she's a female! Same colour and shape but slightly smaller than her mate."

Our visitors came nearer, until they were alongside the hull, diving and surfacing, grunting and staring at us, with their huge, round eyes. We could have touched them. Their antics continued for five minutes and we laughed and spoke to them in what we hoped was comprehensible seal language. There seemed to be real communication between the four of us. Hilton and I were amazed and intrigued by this very unusual event, which was unlike anything we had ever experienced. The hair on the back of my neck was standing on end. My whole body tingled with excitement. Then, without warning, the performance ended. The seals leapt clear of the water, dove, and made a beeline for Vancouver Island!

This had been a very emotional day for us. We sat under the stars, shaking our heads and crying. Granted, such behaviour definitely does not present an image of tough sailors out to challenge the world. But we were overwhelmed by the interactions of two entirely different life forms helping one another and communicating.

Near midnight, we were still talking about the incident. We guessed that the female seal had remained with her partner to catch fish and feed him as the net drifted in the Pacific High. Did seals mate for life? Didn't they have to dry out and rest on rocks?

During the seal rescue and now, after everything had quieted down, including the light breeze, we could see again those tiny, star-shaped lifeforms floating on the water. There certainly were a lot of them. Why had they gathered? What was that all about? So many unanswered questions!

Jelly Sea

The rising sun graced the world with light and energy. Meanwhile, *Ancestor's* skipper and first mate ate oatmeal with raisins and honey and occupied themselves with a dialogue about the physical changes they were witnessing among those star-shaped creatures which were evolving into jellyfish. Some were small and growing larger. The bigger and more mature jellies were deep blue, with stiff sails, about an inch in height, spanning the surfaces of their bodies. They were gorgeous and there were thousands of them. Hilt figured he counted two hundred of them in a three foot square area. Dense indeed.

By noon, no matter where we looked, the sea was literally covered with jelly fish. Right to the horizon! *Ancestor* rolled in the light airs and the sloppy swells and the jellies sloshed through the boat's drain scuppers, causing slick, hazardous decks. We marvelled and cursed their presence in the same breath.

For seven days across six hundred miles of ocean, we would sail through this teeming expanse of life.

* * *

On that same day, we began to slope toward land as much as the inconsistent, southeast wind would allow. Its direction suited our purpose. The following afternoon, having plotted our position on the chart, I was pleased to note in the log that we were 'finally east of Hawaii!' I also recorded the flocks of terns wheeling around us. Their behaviour did not make sense. They weren't feeding and it was difficult to determine if they were heading toward some specific destination or only hovering above *Ancestor* temporarily. We assumed that we were on the flight path of a huge Fairy tern migration. By day the terns were silent but at night they were so raucous, we could not believe that they were the same birds.

In the distance, guillemots flew in circles but unlike the terns, *Ancestor* did not interest them. Our four Black-footed Albatross continued to cruise with us and land on deck to share our food. An albatross's awkward attempts to get airborne are always amusing. Often a bird has to make three or four tries before he is successful. Some of our albatross would jump off the rail and hit the ocean with a loud belly flop. Beating their wings frantically to gain lift, they would 'run' on the water and occasionally bash into an oncoming wave, stop and gaze about sheepishly and look embarrassed. We delighted in their company for over two thousand miles.

The winds stayed in the south and the southeast and we logged daily distances that were much better than we had done for awhile. We covered eighty miles one day and one hundred and fifteen the next. Ours was a slow trip, but a good one.

X Marks the Spot

*T*he *jellyfish spawn had transformed the sea. Evidently, Neptune, or another prankster, wanted to have some fun by dipping the largest paintbrush imaginable into an enormous bowl of jelly and slathering the ocean from horizon to horizon. The prankster created an impressive work of art which, unfortunately, produced an extremely unimpressive smell. Wind-produced waves were smoothed and modified. They undulated, shining in the sunlight and glittering in the moonlight. An eerie world. Ancestor was sailing through strange and unfamiliar waters.*

That evening, on my watch, the wind increased to Force 4. *Ancestor* steered herself with confidence while the Fairy terns raised their usual ruckus. Forestay ran everywhere possible, merrily attempting to bat the birds from the sky. The racket was natural but annoying and I made every effort to annoy them too by singing silly, nonsensical sounds as forcefully as I could. Without success. So I packed the bowl of my pipe with Hawaiian leaf and puffed the night away.

Our wind dropped to a faint breeze in the early hours of the next day and a heavy fog developed and painted the world white. Visibility was reduced to one hundred yards. I considered taking air and water temperature readings in order to learn something from the exercise but it began to rain and I forgot about science.

At 0600 when the watch changed, Hilt asked, "Where's Forestay, Skip?"

"I think she has finally caught one of those noisy terns and she has sneaked down into the hold to eat the thing in your bunk, mate!" We thought no more about her since the ship's cat had a habit of overeating and then sleeping for hours, hidden away somewhere. When Hilt went below he searched the hold but there was no sign of the ship's cat.

Forestay did not appear by noontime and we were worried. For more than an hour, we searched every corner and hiding spot on the boat, expecting a meow to greet us at any minute. We refused to accept the fact that she might have fallen overboard.

From the log:

We have just discovered that Forestay is missing! I saw her at about 0300h when Hilt came on deck for his early watch. Hilt did not see her at any time during that watch and I had not enjoyed her neck-warming company during my off-watch. She is gone! She must have taken a flying tackle at a tern and fallen over the side. We have lost a good friend and shipmate.

Forestay's disappearance was awful. We were shocked. We reprimanded ourselves. We should have tethered the little puss during the night watches, or at least made sure she was below with the hatches closed. I used an indelible pencil to draw a large cross on the chart on our noon position: 45 degrees 20 north, 152 degrees 18 west.

Hilt was particularly saddened. He and the cat were best buddies. Whereas I had always been the one who fought and played rough games with Forestay, Hilt had become her cuddle pal. They were always curled up together, the cat purring happily in his arms. There was no joking around on *Ancestor* that afternoon.

I dreamed about Forestay that night. She was floating vertically in the water, her nose just breaking the surface amongst the jellies, her body skirted with tentacles like her neighbours. I thought that I could see a jelly-like sail forming on her nose.

Wind and Fog

The atmospheric fog, and the fog in our minds, persisted into the following day. When the skies cleared, we were bathed in sunshine. Its brightness eased our sorrow. I occupied myself with sun sights and position lines. Hilt played his guitar and sang and smiled occasionally.

The south winds were tending to veer more into the southwest. This was encouraging. I listened to WWVH radio and tracked the region of high pressure and also the location of tropical storm Bridget, currently located at sixteen degrees north and 127 west. Fortunately, Bridget (not my friend, Brigid) was moving northwest and we could only hope that she would peter out before threatening us.

The weather didn't vary a great deal. Either it rained, or the rain stopped only to be replaced by fog. We sailed slowly on our way, through the unchanging jelly ocean, always believing that the next day would bring a surprise and that surprise would be finding ourselves, boat and all, back in warm tropical waters. I didn't know how our downstairs neighbours, the cockroaches, crickets and centipedes were doing, but on night watches, Hilt and I wrapped ourselves in every stitch of clothing we had.

The fog stayed with us for fifty hours. Visibility ranged from one hundred yards to half a mile. There were no stars, not even our sun, for navigation. Dead reckoning was the only option in order to track our route. Hilt and I both experienced the strange sensation that *Ancestor* was somewhat elevated above the water. No matter which way we looked, we were going downhill!

On July 1st, at noon, the sailing jellies began thinning out and by twilight, the sea was clear again.

Once, I had sailed through the Sargasso Sea, in the Atlantic, to deliver a yacht. The density of the sargasso weed in those waters baffled me. I had learned that this was a spawning area for eels which birthed here before moving toward eastern shores and rivers to complete their life cycles. Now here we were in the northeastern Pacific, watching sea jellies spawn. Where might they be sailing to and why? Perhaps my ignorance was a good thing, like propping a door open with a stick, so that knowledge, when passing by, might enter for a cup of tea and an enlightening discussion.

* * *

The wind held in the south and strengthened to Force 4 and even Force 5. *Ancestor* loved it and roamed happily along toward the Strait of Juan de Fuca. On July 2nd at noon, I plotted our position and discovered that we had made one hundred and seventy-four miles in the past twenty-four hours. Our best day's run! We were thrilled by *Ancestor's* performance. She preferred to have a bone in her teeth and she was heading for somewhere. Despite our exhilaration, we missed our feline sailing mate but we avoided talking about her.

As we approached another great circle shipping route, caution prevailed. On July 3rd, in the middle of the night, the wind moderated. Again we were enveloped in fog. And of course, this was also when we encountered a ship, whose heart-stopping foghorn blared, "Beware! Beware!" The sound's source was unclear but the blasts were awful and they seemed to surround us. My reaction was to light our kerosene running lights, futile as that seemed.

How would a multi-ton vessel spot our pitiful flames in the pea soup murk? And even if the ship's crew did see us, by then, at such close proximity, an evasive manoeuvre would be out of the question. I extinguished the port and starboard lights, but left the stern light burning. Its gleam offered companionship at least, despite our bleak situation.

Within twenty minutes - or an eternity - the clamorous horn diminished and we could relax, alter our course to the north, and hope to escape the shipping lane before any more alarming incidents came our way.

After what we believed to be a near collision, we were relieved but I could not go below and sleep. The wind was turning to the southwest, there was outstanding phosphorescence and the sickly-strong odour of fish oil filled the air.

* * *

> *The wind that sang of trees uptorn and vessels tost.*
>
> - Wordsworth

Thirty days out of Hilo, the wind finally moved to the northwest. Our location was 48 degrees north and 135 degrees 42 west. In the morning, the fog dissipated and our world was suddenly gifted with blue skies and sunshine.

With the change of wind direction, it was possible to set our course for the Strait of Juan de Fuca, allowing about twelve degrees of drift. The wind was encouraging but as soon as our celebratory beer had been consumed, I became aware of abnormal wave heights and swells. I shared my concerns with Hilt. We had to seriously consider that heavy weather might be in the offing. WWVH reported Hurricane C, packing winds in excess of seventy knots, located at 16 degrees north and 109 degrees west, and moving northwest by west at fifteen knots. In our vicinity, we were experiencing the lesser winds on the periphery of that system.

Our heavy weather preparations were simple. Lash down anything that can be blown overboard. Have lots of small cordage and spare rope at hand. Get the storm trysail ready to hoist. Make a pot of soup and a stack of bannock. That was it.

By mid-afternoon, the wind had increased to Force 7 (fresh gale – 34 knots) and in one hour it had reached a Force 8 gale (forty knots). The cloud-crammed sky snarled. Fortunately, the gale did not get any wilder. At first, we put a double reef in the mainsail and let *Ancestor* scud to the east, but in the night, when the seas increased, the main boom was dipping into the ocean as we roared along. When this happened, there was too much water force on the boom and the lower mainsail. We had to furl the main and set the storm trysail. Double sheets were installed on the staysail and we set it as well. This seemed to be the correct rig for the conditions and *Ancestor* steered herself on a safe course until dawn. It was bitter cold. Hilt and I stood one hour watches. The off-watch descended to the galley, closed the hatch, and kept the Primus stove and a kerosene lamp fuelled so we might be able to dry our soggy clothes and warm our hands and bodies before the next watch.

Before daybreak, having relieved Hilt on deck, I went to the bilge pump, cursed the high seas, braced myself and pumped three hundred strokes. When the pump started sucking air, I was exhausted, but also alerted to the possibility that we may have loosened a seam with all this heavy working of the hull. With a flashlight, I lowered myself into the hold, closing the hatch tightly behind me and I did a hull inspection. Several seams on the waterline were letting in a bit of water, but the main culprit was on deck. Whenever we plunged into a trough, the leeward deck was momentarily submersed and the ocean spray gushed through between the planks. Not a pretty sight, but at least the hull was un-compromised and that gave me confidence in the boat's integrity. We were not sinking. *Anyway, pumping the bilge is good exercise.*

The blow continued, with howling winds, flying spray and cold, hour after hour. I estimated the seas at eighteen to twenty feet. Not life-threatening but the wave heights did impress the crew. "What I like best about a gale," I assured Hilt, "is the anticipation of the peace that will follow when the storm has worn itself out."

Hilt's retorted, "Thanks, Skip. That's a comforting thought to carry around in my head while I'm pumping the gale out of the bilge or trying to dry my clothes after a one hour watch that never seems to end."

From experience, I knew very well that in a gale at sea, the ocean's power is formidable but it is a mistake to think of this vast watery expanse as an adversary. On the contrary, one can never combat the sea. One can learn to live with the ocean's moods and tempests, accept their interactions, and with acceptance, fright is rarely an issue for a seaman. The sailor can relax as much as the conditions will permit and be dazzled by awesome, raw power of nature. Well – that is what I had learned. A gale might be 'inconvenient' in relation to maintaining one's charted course or one's arrival date at some predetermined destination, or a vessel's position to a lee shore. Nevertheless, in my view, extreme weather systems are to be appreciated and not feared.

Sometime that night, in the thick of it, I tried to explain my heavy weather philosophy to Hilt. We were both as cozily tucked in as it was possible to be, with safety lines snugged and our backs to the wind. I'm not sure if my mate bought my idea or not, but he did say that he couldn't imagine being out in these conditions without his skipper's stalwart attitude and without the laughs I threw into the face of the storm. "Hell!" he said. "You are happy out here!" Hilton was right. I was shivering and groaning and loving it.

Forty-eight hours later, the gale force winds began to moderate. We un-lashed the trysail and set the full main. The seas decreased too, leaving *Ancestor* to be shoved around by the leftover slop of that intense gale. Before midnight, the wind dropped even more and we made only minimum speed on our course.

Hilt managed to get a fairly good signal from CKWX that evening and the first item on the news was the eruption on the south slope of Mauna Loa on the Big Island! Hilton commented that Madame Pelée was five weeks late with her fire show.

A noon fix placed us approximately 250 miles from Cape Flattery. The wind continued to die off, the seas continued to be bouncy and at twilight, Hilt was feeding Ritz crackers to a couple of seagulls who had recently arrived on the scene from the east. "Welcome to the *Ancestor*," my friend said. "Have some crackers. You're looking kind of pooped."

The Flotsam and Garbage Blues

*A*s the gale hurled one final, tremendous blast at us and as *Ancestor* slid down a towering sea, we nearly collided with a twenty foot, wooden ladder! It was in good shape. We speculated on where it had come from and where it might end up. That ladder was almost the last piece of flotsam we were to come across on this trip. The North Pacific High is a great, clockwise, twisting gyre. We had just sailed through it and we were alarmed by how much man-made debris cluttered the water including sections of fish net, chunks of Styrofoam, lengths of polypropylene rope, bottles of every shape and size, and glass fish floats covered in mussels and barnacles! The gyre was a water-bound junk mall.

Ever since the incident when we had rescued the tangled harbour seal from its net-prison, we deliberately and diligently collected any scraps of fishnet we found and pulled them onto our forward deck. We had quite a collection which produced an interesting and undesirable odour but we were able to avoid the stench because the wind was usually from astern. (When we arrived in Victoria, we had a hard time getting rid of this killer heap of junk but happily, someone hauled it away after hearing our story of the Gyre).

In this section of the North Pacific, there was never more than a ten minute gap between sightings of floating rubble, and when we considered that most of the time the sea had been coated in jellyfish, we worried about the amounts of garbage we had not seen. Fish nets were our primary concern, but the bobbing masses of Styrofoam came a close second. Perhaps if we had a large vessel, low in the water, with acres of deck space, we could clean up this outrageous mega-mess. That was our dream, brought on by the disgust we directed both at our fellow humans who had produced these non-biodegradable materials and those people who had dumped these polluting substances into our once pristine oceans. *Why does this happen?*

* * *

Our approach to the Strait of Juan de Fuca was slow and slower. Calms and fickle and feeble breezes were the norm.

From the log:

0130 Becalmed in mist.

0600 Hilt counted seven orcas during his morning watch.

0800 Freighter Eastern Hill, Uma Jima, passed half mile off starboard side. Hoisted our "V"

flag, hoping they will report our position. Don't think they saw us.

0830 Force 2 breeze from SE. Course is 30 degrees, close-hauled. Water temperature 51 degrees, air temperature 61 degrees. Lovely summer morning!

1000 Made up a new fish lure using the last of the feathers from the Bay of Panama. Hilt

found them in a plastic bag. Caught a salmon. Coho, I think.

1200 Position is 48, 40 north, 129, 12 west. Made 38 miles since noon yesterday.

1600 Becalmed.

1945 Heard a prop-plane above the clouds. Sounds like a four engine job.

2400 Still becalmed.

At 6:00 a.m., the wind awoke, beginning in the north and then backing into the north-north-west by afternoon. At about 9:00 a.m., we launched the dinghy, to row a short distance and retrieve a twelve inch diameter metal fish float. That was the most exciting event of the day, except in the evening, the sea grew very rough, likely due to indiscriminate currents and we had to hand-steer. My mate and I admitted that hand steering was an immense hardship but we were both happy to have some activity to occupy our spare time.

On this day, we cracked open the last of the macadamia nuts. It was great sport trying to hold the nuts firmly while whacking them with a claw hammer. One definitely needs a proper nut cracker for this job. When Forestay was still with us, nut cracking provided her with endless amusement and exercise. Waiting for the hammer to strike, she would crouch on deck, her little body like a coiled spring. As the shell bits (and often nut pieces too) went flying off in all directions, Forestay would make a flying leap to catch them. She never tired of this sort of activity. Remembering our lost shipmate, we ate the last of the nuts and cast their shells into the water in a salute to her memory.

Dawn arrived without theatrics, while I made myself useful by replacing the staysail sheets, one of which had chafed through during the night. Nor did the sunrise provide dramatic or special effects and the northwest wind did not have to push the clouds away. Visibility was excellent. I scanned the horizons knowing we must be vigilant now that we were nearing the Strait of Juan de Fuca, where many shipping lanes converge and ship traffic increases considerably.

We were getting excited about our arrival in Victoria and the conversation about Hilt's purchase of the *Ancestor* was on going. He was jotting down notes and planning my Carriacou sloop's life on the waters of Lake Huron. I still could not picture *Ancestor* on an inland lake. The image was completely unappealing. I found it repugnant to even think about tourists, with their pastel-coloured clothing and fashionable boating shoes, crowding the decks of my sea-going vessel. I had a feeling that this was not to be her future, although the idea of selling her to Hilt so easily was attractive. *Jon, let the future take care of itself. Just concentrate on reaching Vancouver safe and sound – that's all.*

1830 Hilt saw an unusual shape on the horizon. Off to the northeast, the mountains of Vancouver Island had come into view. In unison, we shouted "Land-ho!" shook hands and acknowledged our third landfall together. According to the latest update, plotted on the chart, we were sixty miles from the Vancouver Island coast.

Later, on the same evening, at precisely 2030, the sun's upper limb touched the horizon and we saw a perfect green-flash! The thin, brilliant, green column of light shot vertically into the sky for one second and vanished. This rare sighting called for a celebratory tot of Grand Marnier, and as we drank, we couldn't suppress our happiness. It was one thing to see the green flash in the tropics but here we were, at forty-nine degrees north latitude, viewing a sunset phenomenon. Second sips were obligatory.

The night sky did not disappointment us either. When darkness claimed our world, the Aurora Borealis unfolded in the north. Pink curtains of light danced above, shimmering and waltzing to the music of the sun's energy. We were overwhelmed by these displays and by the not-too-distant landfall off our bow.

Early next morning, we passed over the one hundred fathom contour of the ocean floor. The water, no longer the cobalt blue of the deeps, was green and teeming with marine life. Guillemots and puffins dropped onto the sea, passionately pursuing their breakfast. Three types of diving, feasting seagulls added to the cacophony. On the northern horizon, a fleet of fishing vessels went about their daily routine. We were crossing the La Pérouse Bank and *Ancestor* and her crew were grateful for the fine weather instead of the fog that usually pesters this area in the summer months.

More activity. Shipping entered and left the strait. What a steady stream of traffic! We were constantly on the lookout, ready to change course to avert a collision. The wind held in the northwest and our boat carried us toward her next port of call. At 1900, I took compass bearings on both Pachena and Carmanah Points. We were now on visual bearings and would remain so all the way to Vancouver.

I wiped my sextant with a damp cloth and dried the instrument carefully. I placed it in its protective case and said, "Thank you." *Will I ever use it again?*

* * *

In the morning, sixty miles from Victoria, we agreed to make every effort to reach port today. I had learned, that despite the light north westerly breezes, we could anticipate stronger winds in the afternoon. We opted to finesse the sheets to gain as much headway as possible and dodge the marine traffic. At noon, the wind freshened and backed into the south west. *Ancestor* surged forward, with the bone in the teeth bow wave that all sailing vessels love to demonstrate.

By mid-afternoon, another wind change occurred. In order to maintain our course, while running under full sail and pushing toward Victoria harbour, we performed a rather poorly executed gybe. Normally, we would have reefed or furled the main under these conditions but on this occasion we were into what Hilt calls 'full speed ahead and damn the torpedoes' mode. My friend was tending the mainsheet and I was steering carefully, to bring the stern into and through the eye of the wind. Murphy must have had something to do with the shape and height of the seas, for as soon as the mainsail caught the wind on the new tack, an arbitrary wave picked up our transom and flung it over, causing Hilt to release the sheet, which zipped through his bare hands and caused a painful rope burn. The gybe succeeded and we didn't break anything, but Hilt had suffered. I shouted, "Fetch a bucket of salt water and put your hands in that."

At 1800, Sheringham lighthouse was abeam. The wind had risen to Force 6. Our vessel was scudding and surfing past Race Rocks. At 1900, the wind gusts exceeded Force 7 (30 knots plus). *Ancestor* was flying. With every surge and plunge, we expected something to give, but we were protected by the many Hawaiian good-luck charms still adorning our rigging.

Finally, making our port turn into Victoria's outer harbour, we found respite from the heavy seas. We rounded-up. Dropped the mainsail. Even though the wind's velocity had not diminished, here the wind seemed blissfully calm. Luckily, it was also late at night and there was no traffic approaching from any quarter. We sailed in. Hilt was steering. I prepared the anchor. Before long, we were rounding the headland and entering the inner harbour, aglitter with the lights of the Parliament Buildings on our starboard bow and the Empress Hotel directly ahead of us.

Hilt insisted on doing his usual anchor handling, even though his hands were injured. I took the helm. Because the winds inside the harbour were unsettled, I hoisted the mainsail again to give us maneuverability. I saw an ideal spot for us at the outer end of a float and steered for it. Hilt waited for my signals.

When the geometry looked just right, I gave the sign to lower away. Hilt did so, took control of the anchor line and waited for my instructions. With the helm hard over, our mainsheet in, and the jib sheet flying, *Ancestor V* glided to the float and stopped as Hilt adjusted the anchor rode.

2300. We had arrived. I stepped onto the finger and made the spring line fast to a convenient cleat. The sails were furled and our other mooring lines were attached to the dock in short order. Hilt gritted his teeth against the pain of his damaged hands.

There were two couples approaching us when we landed. One person said, "We couldn't believe how quiet your engine is. You must have an excellent exhaust and muffler system."

"Yes," I replied, "it is a good system. Thanks. And it's so efficient simply because there is no engine." They were incredulous and for a moment, they thought I was joking.

"Where did you come from?"

"Hilo, Hawaii was our last port, thirty-eight and a half days ago."

These folks were vacationing in Victoria from Missoula, Montana. Clearly taken with our brief history of sailing, the couples invited us to breakfast at the Empress Hotel in the morning before they left the city. We thanked them and I explained that first, we would have to do the Customs and Immigration thing but I anticipated getting our clearance by 0900. The Missoulans disappeared into the night, speaking excitedly together. Hilt and I went below, he to make a cup of tea and I to bring the log up to date. We were tired and hungry. *What a hell of a day!*

'Statistics'

Hilo to Victoria - 3,103 nautical miles

Travel time - 38.5 days

Becalmed - 70 hours total

Average day's travel - 81 miles (including calms)

Fresh water consumed - 38 gallons

Provisions remaining - 3 potatoes, 3 onions, 10 pounds of rice, 5 pounds of flour, 1 packet of crackers, 7 bottles of beer

We were in much better shape regarding our remaining provisions in Victoria than we had been on our arrival at Hilo.

Midnight. Hilt was asleep below. I made certain our obligatory Canadian courtesy and quarantine flags were displayed from the starboard flag halyard. I knew perfectly well that maritime law requires a visiting foreign vessel to notify Customs and Immigration immediately. But I was pooped and I only wanted to find my bunk. I chose to fudge our arrival time in the morning. *Oh no. Here you go again!*

Victoria to Vancouver

Although Hilt's rope-burned hands looked bad next morning, he was ready for action. I offered to escort him to a clinic or a hospital once we cleared customs, but being a trooper, he said, "Fresh fruit, bacon, eggs, toast and coffee first. Then hands. I'll be okay."

I launched the dinghy and rowed over to the customs dock, with the necessary papers in my back pack, ready to answer the usual questions. At 8:00 a.m., I used the telephone on the float to contact the customs office. It was gratifying to have someone pick-up immediately on the other end.

The question and answer ritual went well until I confessed to the gentleman that *Ancestor* was not moored at the dedicated customs float, because we had chosen a slip in front of the Empress Hotel. After a lengthy explanation, I convinced him that it was a decision I had to make because we were powered by sail only and if we were tied to his customs dock, we might have been unable to leave again until there was an appropriate wind. Etcetera. The guy seemed to understand my situation. When he asked about our Grenadian registered vessel, I assured him that it was my intention to communicate with his colleagues when I reached Vancouver. At which time those officials could evaluate my vessel for import customs duties. *Ancestor V* would be staying in Canada.

On and on it went. The man on the phone line provided me with the name and number of the customs people in Vancouver and he advised me that I would be expected call them by, or before, July 17th. I thanked him sincerely. I was surprised to receive our clearance number then and there, along with a very civil, "Have a nice day, sir."

So simple. I could hardly believe it. He didn't even want to confiscate our potatoes and onions! Back on *Ancestor*, I recounted my story to Hilt before lowering *Ancestor's* quarantine flag. We were legitimate. Breakfast time.

Our Missoulan welcoming committee was on the quay when we stepped on deck, wearing our last, semi-clean clothes, which consisted of fresh T-shirts and not-so-fresh trousers. Hilt wore a pair of rather mouldy shoes and I had my favourite flip-flops. We invited our breakfast benefactors aboard and shook hands all round.

Ancestor V's guests, all Missoulans, wrote their names in our log: Warren and Vicki Drew and Tom and Moira Payne. Warren was a broker. Tom was a professor of political science. One of them was also a violin teacher. Visit and tour complete, the six of us disembarked and walked to the Empress. Except Hilt and I were not walking but staggering, as we had done when we took our first steps ashore in Hawaii. Hilt was being extremely careful. Taking no chances. Our new friends got a kick out of our sailors' swagger. "Would we be denied entry to the restaurant," I asked, "since we are definitely not attired for any prestigious dining establishment?" The Payne's and Drews, having anticipated this possibility, had already briefed the hotel staff. The restaurant crew would be notified prior to our arrival and we wouldn't be turned away.

In the dining room, trying to ignore the curious smiles and stares of the other diners, we selected a table conveniently close to the buffet. Hilt said, "Skip, we have sailed all those miles, thinking we were in paradise, or very close, at least, when actually paradise is here in Victoria!" He was partly correct. Before us lay a cornucopia of food. And we could eat all we wanted. I don't recall the details of that grand feast. The hotel's ambiance was exotic, as were the fruits, baked goods, beverages and the crème de la crème, Double Devon Cream. I scooped large dollops onto flaky, crusted scones. The circumstances could have been embarrassing. But they weren't.

Our presence at the restaurant was the focal point of the morning chit-chat. A fellow came to our table and asked, "Are you, by any chance, the sailors off that strange sailboat down on the docks? If you are, may I take some photos of you and your vessel for the Times Colonist newspaper?"

We consented to his request. After breakfast, shadowed by the newsman and his photographer, who materialized on the sidewalk beside us, we were accosted by a throng of people asking questions and shaking our hands. It was not easy to find a free moment to thank and say good-bye to our generous, Missoula, Montana friends.

While the newspaperman was interviewing Hilt, I phoned home. Good news. Todd would fly across to Victoria later today. I also dialed my friend Hajo Hadeler, the skipper of *Nausikaa*. Hajo offered to come to Victoria on Monday and tow us, as necessary, to Vancouver.

When I returned to *Ancestor*, the crowds had not diminished. I had to politely elbow my way through the crush of bodies just to board my boat! I paused to praise Hilt. "You are doing a fine job managing our public relations. Carry on." With that taken care of, I escaped through the hatch and hid for an hour. My stomach was uncomfortably full. I needed to be prone for awhile.

The day passed. The garbage fish net vanished from the forward deck and someone else loaned us a hose to wash down the decks. I used biodegradable soap that yet another thoughtful person had given us. The soap erased the gunk and the foul odours forward and the salt water residue from the decks and topsides. *Ancestor* smelled clean and wherever she was not scuffed-up, she looked pretty fine. At least to me.

Todd arrived that afternoon. He hadn't been on *Ancestor* since Balboa and he was thrilled to join us. The Times Colonist requested more photos for their article on that 'strange West Indian smuggling boat' in the harbour. Todd, wearing my fancy handmade hat, posed with me and the photographers clicked their shutters. Afterward, my

(Times Colonist photo)
Todd and his dad in Victoria harbour

(Times Colonist photo)
The crew at Victoria

son threw his bag into the hold, and eagerly waited for whatever might happen next.

And what happened next was a deck party on *Ancestor*. Hilt surprised me by serenading us despite his bandaged hands. Hilton's voice was wonderful too. We had quite an evening and by 2200 there were some wasted characters sprawled about under the stars and a few more had gone to sleep in the hold.

At midday, on Monday, *Nausikaa* motored in and her skipper manoeuvred her to an inner harbour float like a professional. Hajo's boat became another 'eye-catcher' vessel in front of the Empress.

Hajo and I shared a history way back to 1963. He was a film editor then at CBC Television on Georgia Street in Vancouver and I had recently launched the first trimaran ever to be built in Canada. I had her moored at the Georgia Street Marina, near Stanley Park. Hajo taught me how to use a sixteen millimetre movie camera. As I recall, we both enjoyed a Broma pipe. Every time we got together, we produced clouds of smoke. When he first rigged the *Nausikaa*, I was invited to accompany him and his wife on the vessel's maiden voyage. Here in Victoria, I was very pleased to see him again.

Our Monday night party was a repeat of the Sunday night. I nursed my usual one beer while monitoring the festivities to ensure that my guests refrained from falling into the water. I am proud to say we suffered no casualties. Good fun!

After everyone had gone, Todd crawled into my bunk. I unclipped the staysail to make myself a nest on the foredeck. The harbour was peaceful. There was very little traffic. I awoke that night and replayed a dream I'd had. *Ancestor is at anchor at Puyades Island in the San Blas. The moon is climbing through the palm trees on Ancestor Island. I can hear the roar and hiss of waves on the windward reef.* I lay there, with Todd asleep below, wondering if Ancestor or I would ever drop anchor there again. I hoped to sail to Puyades Island once more, someday, but I was unable to visualize *Ancestor* with her hook down in those Caribbean waters. My mood was a mixture of happiness and sadness. In the morning, when I awoke, garbage trucks were roaring toward the full dumpsters lining a nearby paved city street.

* * *

Nausikaa towed us out of Victoria harbour early the next day. Predictably, my emotions were bittersweet, knowing that this would be the last leg of what had been a thrilling and joyfully adventurous voyage. Hilt was content. He had rung his wife to say that *Ancestor's* new skipper couldn't wait to return to Ontario to start the ball rolling for the purchase of the boat. Todd, always a happy traveller, was enjoying the finishing strokes of our voyage.

The Strait of Juan de Fuca was, in the words of Stefan, my Greek sailing friend, "As flat as piss on a plate." Windless conditions are common in mid-July on the west coast of British Columbia. Without the tow, which we accepted without hesitation, our crossing to Vancouver could easily have taken a week. Our course took us south of Trial Island, then northward, passing Sidney to port. With Beaver Point, on Salt Spring Island, showing us her modest navigation light, we angled northwest into Trincomali Channel, then proceeded eastbound to Porlier Pass and into the Strait of Georgia. From there, we had a straight shot to Point Grey and Vancouver Harbour. When the tides were with us we made good time, but when the ebb tide started, its outward flow really slowed us down. The *Nausikaa* chugged along. *Ancestor* followed like a faithful companion. During the tow, *Ancestor's* crew indulged in a nostalgic musical evening. Hilt and I belted out our entire repertoires, trying our best not to break any guitar strings. Many glances and grins were exchanged with the memories of sea miles shared. We sang eulogies for Forestay. Todd steered most of the time and he didn't seem to mind eating his meals while he tweaked the tiller.

The lights of Vancouver painted the night sky. Stars and planets faded into the background. At 0130, Wednesday July 16th, we reached

Mosquito Creek Marina on the north shore of Vancouver's inner harbour. There we tied up to our finish-line float. On deck, not saying much, we shook hands, hugged, and smiled. *Ancestor V* had arrived.

Final 'Statistics'

Victoria to Vancouver - 80 nautical miles

Grenada to Vancouver - 10,174 nautical miles

Total travel time - 5 months and 3 days

Provisions remaining - 3 bottles of beer

* * *

On a fine summer morning, two friends, Bill Reaume and Walter Bradshaw, came to the marina to help us remove the ballast rock from *Ancestor's* hold. They were keen to engage in this enterprise and after we had warped the boat to the mouth of Mosquito Creek, we formed a chain gang. Soon we could hear the constant and satisfying 'plop' sound of rounded, granitic ballast stones splashing into the water.

In five hours, the job was complete and for the first time, I could see the bilges and the inside bottom of the hull. My first discovery was hundreds of cockroach carcasses. Great windrows of them between the frames. I had expected roaches but I had also thought there would be the remains of crickets and centipedes. However, there were only a few, scattered, empty shells. Had the cockroaches eaten them all during the voyage? I was sad, in a way, to think of these hearty creatures devouring one another before they finally succumbed to the frigid waters of the North Pacific Ocean. These critters did not have a pleasant voyage.

A second, and initially, a more agreeable discovery revealed the condition of the hull planking. It looked sound. But on closer examination, I could see that the planking had been eroded by rock particles being sloshed back and forth in the bilge water whenever the vessel pitched and rolled over ten thousand miles. The maximum, measured depth of this erosion was one eighth of an inch.

My inspection of the inside of the hull was interrupted by the arrival of a large straddle lift contraption. The machine was already in the process of dropping slings into the water so that we could centre the boat on straps for the haul out. Without mishap, we and our boat were efficiently deposited on land. Shoring devices were placed to stabilize our hull. The straddle lift rumbled away and there she was, *Ancestor V*, naked for all to see.

Unburdened, *Ancestor* continued to reveal her magical persona. When the lift operator placed her on land and shored her up, we noticed that she was not aligned with the other boats in the yard. She sat at an angle to all of them. I was curious. I pondered this mystery while gathering my charts for safekeeping. When I gave the rolled charts to Bill, I went below and found one chart that I had missed! Surprised, I opened it and saw a very old gnomonic map of the Northern Hemisphere. How had that map remained hidden for the entire, long voyage? What was the significance of this? I couldn't put a mental finger on it. After my pipe was loaded, I sat alone, meditating for half an hour, until a hunch disturbed my peace. I climbed up and spread the map on deck. A neighbour, on the boat beside us, was trying out a new hand-bearing compass. I asked to borrow the instrument. Amidships, I aligned his compass's sight along the central axis of my boat and took a reading. I converted the magnetic reading to 'true'. Then I used a short wooden batten to draw a pencil line on the map on the corrected azimuth. The pencil line intersected towns, mountains and cities but what was of immense interest to me was the fact that the line pointed exactly to the Caribbean island Carriacou! Was *Ancestor* trying to tell me something? Did she want to go home? Was I abandoning her?

* * *

One afternoon when Todd was aboard, we heard a familiar voice calling my name. We were elated to see Jenny, the cook from the *Jens Juhl*, standing at the bottom of the ladder, smiling up at us. She climbed aboard. We hugged and I asked, "What are you doing here in Vancouver?"

"I'm on my way to Singapore. I rerouted because I wanted to see *Ancestor* and her crew again, so far away from the Windward Islands." Our visit would be short. Jen was catching a red-eye flight to Asia that night.

I would soon be travelling too, having just accepted a contract for a project in Iran. My departure date was also drawing near.

Hilt contacted me from Sarnia. He could not take the boat to Lake Huron after all. My shipmate was sad and I was sorry for him. Yet I was relieved to know that *Ancestor* would be staying here, in the mother ocean. I made the decision to advertise her for sale.

Epilogue

After writing this story about finding the 'ancestor of all sailing ships', and preparing and equipping her, and sailing her from the Caribbean to Vancouver, I began researching her 'post Jon' adventures. I spoke with other people/owners who loved Ancestor as much as I. The search was good fun. With her Canadian registry, the V had been dropped from Ancestor's name. In this epilogue, the information I discovered is cherished and special. As you will read and see in the following pages, Ancestor has been rebuilt and re-rigged a number of times. She continues to inspire sailors.

When I collected and reviewed my material, I was saddened to think that I did not take very many photographs during my time with the boat. And having read my book, you will know I'm not a clever money manager. In retrospect, I realize that my cruising kitty never seemed to be adequate. I never had more than barely enough cash to get by. When it came to a toss-up between provisioning and photography, food was more important than film.

Leif Arntzen

Leif purchased my boat in 1975. In my opinion he was young, enthusiastic, and a good sailor. He possessed the right qualities to become *Ancestor's* next skipper.

Leif now lives in New York where he makes music. He is working on a new project: *Polaris*, a 41 foot, Concordia Sloop. Of course, she's a wooden boat.

The following are unedited extracts from Leif's recent letters:

I rebuilt Ancestor in Lynn Valley and then took her back to Mosquito Creek. The top mast was broken by the trucker when he pulled her out of the boat shop. The hull had been totally reefed and re-caulked by a retired caulker from Vancouver Shipyards. He was a real character. He showed this eager teenager how to use caulking irons, how to prep the seams, how to loop the cotton, how hard to hit the irons, what a bad section of seam felt like when it needed work. He was a great teacher and a positive influence to me in my youth.

Back at Mosquito Creek we installed lead ballast between the frame timbers. After launching she tightened up quickly and then didn't leak a single drop. There was still no engine or electronics of any kind. The only bilge pump I had was the original wooden column pump, which I never used and a whale gusher that I installed. I don't remember ever having to use either pump. I put a trunk cabin to increase the living accommodations.

I always regretted losing the flush deck beauty and simplicity of *Ancestor's* design. Gorgeous work boat lines and construction system; iron-drifted, hand-hewn and mind's-eye shape. Such ancient perfect ideas. I think the green heart backbone was mainly four pieces: single piece stem with an S end-to-end wow in it, scarfed into a solid one piece bomb-proof keel timber (also with a noticeable end-to-end wow in it), a sternpost and a crazy grown horn timber that reached up to the transom timbers somehow.

Along with my brother Arnt and Brad Simmons we sailed to Cortes Island, a distance of 100 miles, taking one week to do so in the gentle breezes of the Salish Sea in mid-summer. We had a lot of fun and used a seventeen foot long sweep oar to help with propulsion along the way.

On a circumnavigation of Vancouver Island with Peter Pierobon and Kathleen Gabelemann. I remember *Ancestor* riding like a duck in the westerlies from Cape Scott, all the way past Cape Cook and into Kyoquot in a single glorious shot. We got stuck in Kyoquot for seven days waiting out a southeast gale, playing with the shop keeper's pet seal.

She sailed like a dream downwind, or any other point for that matter. The only hard part was getting up that heavy canvas mainsail you made in Bequia when preparing for your voyage from the Grenadines to B.C.

I remember there were no electronics or engine onboard, and a Primus stove, two bunks made of Purple Heart tongue and groove board, flush fore deck with cargo hatch, and that amazing grown tiller that I could stand on the top of without fear of breaking. The rudder post was about six inches thick solid grown timber with a slot cut through for the tiller that was housed in a solid timber log that ran from the horn timber straight up through the deck. It was simple and strong.

I had installed a Mercedes diesel engine, along with living quarters forward, with wood stove and about 8,000 pounds of lead strapped in the bilge.

Lief and crew sailing to Cortes Island (Lief Arntzen photo)

As I said, she rode like a duck on a pond, very stable and easy sailing. She self-steered wing on wing with the staysail sheeted flat centre all the way up from the Gulf Islands to Lund, B.C. in a strong southeast wind.

In 1978, Leif sold *Ancestor* to Hillel Wright.

Hillel Wright

How is this for a character description?

"*Hillel Wright is the product of the 60s and 70s. American, Canadian, hippy, wastrel, womanizer, fisherman, poet, teacher and masterful storyteller.*"

- Rotary Sushi: Many Kinds of Stories. February 2004

Hillel Wright bought *Ancestor* in 1978, and my West Indian boat continued to work for a living. Hillel installed a three cylinder Isuzu diesel engine. He wasn't able to get a fishing license but he did acquire a D license for the boat. Hillel ended up packing shellfish in Georgia Strait for three years.

The following are unedited extracts from Hillel's memoirs of *Ancestor* in his publication, *Allah's Radio*.

22 October 1979, Baynes Sound, Denman Island Wharf,

0300 hours, wind Southeast, 30-40 knots.

0345 hours, wind Southeast 15-20 knots, rainy.

0600 hours, wind Southeast 10-20 knots, hard rain.

Oystering time and tide wait for no one. It's now or never. I get up and light a fire in the wood burning cook stove

0715 hours, wind Southeast 10-15 knots, rain.

The crew, Achmed Kassim Sirouk, deckhand and Richard Clarke, oysterman with the Fanny Bay Oyster Company arrived from Buckley Bay. I meet them at the ferry landing and get the latest forecast from the ferry skipper. Strong southeast winds, 25 knots to gale force winds of 35 knots are predicted.

Ancestor is a good sea boat. A 40' wooden sailboat, she was built in the Eastern Caribbean and sailed in the Windward Islands and the Guianas, freighting and smuggling. She was sold to a Canadian, Jon van Tamelen. In 1975, he sailed her to British Columbia with stone ballast via the Panama Canal, the Galapagos and Hawaii. Shortly after arriving on the BC coast he sold her to fisherman Leif Arntzen and I bought her from him in December of 1978. In the spring of 1979, I equipped her with a three cylinder Isuzu diesel engine linked to a 17" wheel. This was, at best, auxiliary power. Ancestor was not built with engine power in mind, but was powerfully rigged as a gaff cutter with a 600 square foot mains'l, a club-footed stays'l and a working jib on a 10' bowsprit. We steered by a tiller joined to a hardwood rudder-post, pumped by hand and had no electronics, not even a radio.

But she was sound and seaworthy and we were a crew of three strong men. Kassim was known around the docks as "the hydraulic winch," and spent a lot of time wrestling in pubs. We had about 40 miles to Cortes Bay, where we would hole-up overnight. With a strong wind, even a gale behind us all the way, we should make it in six hours. Besides, Comox harbour, 10 miles northwest up Baynes Sound, there was no other reliable shelter until we crossed the Strait of Georgia.

We spent a couple of hours, stowing and securing the gear needed for a 10 day oystering trip to the southeast side of Cortes Island. We left the wharf at 0945. The wind was down to a moderate breeze, 8-10 knots southeast, but the sky was dark and the cloud bellies ragged. We ran up Baynes Sound under full mains'l, stays'l and jib. We had Union Point on Vancouver Island abeam to port at 1015. A strong sudden gust struck the sails and I had to lean hard into the tiller to prevent a jibe. Kassim and Richard went forward to take in the headsails. By 1045, as we approached Comox Bar, the wind had increased to a steady 25 knots and was beginning to gust higher. We lined up the range lights for crossing the bar and steered north-northeast to keep us in the narrow passage between the shoals off of White Spit on the Denman Island side and the rocks off Willemar Bluffs approaching Cape Lazo on Vancouver Island. We started the engine for auxiliary power. We were on a beam reach and Ancestor rolled heavily into the choppy channel, but "a rolling boat will always see you through" and by 1145 we had passed Buoy P 57 off the cape and were steering northeast by compass for Sutil Point on Cortes Island, 20 miles away.

Now was the time to take a deep reef in the main. We had broken a skylight window in the cabin roof while crossing the bar and we had a leaky thru-hull fitting below. The wind in the gulf was now gale strength and Ancestor was getting harder and harder to keep on course. I worried about whether the rudder-post would hold and I wanted to patch the skylight, plug the thru-hull fitting, and pump.

We came into the wind, using the engine to hold us in place while we cast off the main halyard and the two gaff halyards. When the huge sail was half way down the mast, big trouble struck. One of the gaff halyards kinked and stuck itself in a doughnut shaped fairlead on a spreader bar, about 30' above the deck. I gave Richard the helm and ran up the ratlines to free the line, while Kassim attempted to bag the wet heavy sail. I was a few feet below the spreader bar when a strong gust hit the sail belly, which snapped Kassim over the side into the cold grey choppy sea.

The next 15 minutes seemed like half an eternity. I shouted for Richard to "keep pointing!" at Kassim as I shoved the engine up to full throttle and took over the helm. We were just able to lower Ancestor's monstrous boom into a carved notch in the boom gallows and throw Kassim a life jacket. He got the life jacket on, but he had drifted beyond the range of the life ring. We had to turn Ancestor and try again.

At this point, Kassim told us later, he feared that the ship would run over him. His whole life literally flashed before his eyes and he was filled with love for both Richard and I as he prayed that we would be alright and survive the storm.

"I can't see him!" I heard Richard shouting.

Miraculously, the whole time our ordeal was going on, a small private floatplane was hastily retreating to Courtenay to land on the river. I guess we all saw Kassim in his yellow Helly Hansen rain gear and orange life-vest at the same time. Richard waved at the plane and pointed to Kassim in the water and then the plane dipped its wings in response. We threw the life ring again and this time Kassim scrambled into it and we began to pull him back to the boat.

A few minutes later a red and white C-113 Labrador helicopter from CFB Comox appeared above us. The floatplane had deciphered Richard's signals and radioed for help.

We soon had Kassim alongside Ancestor. He weighed 240 lbs. dry, but now soaking wet and numb with cold, he was a dead weight in the water. We signalled the helicopter and began to let out our lifeline. Kassim drifted away from us in the ring until he was far enough away for the chopper to hover and send down a rescuer on a cable to pick Kassim up. Seconds later he was lying beside another rescuer in a sleeping bag and was heading for St. Joseph's Hospital in Comox.

To make a very long story short, Richard and I managed to get the mains'l down and lashed, and to reset the heavy, self-tending canvas stays'l. With the gale blowing harder all afternoon it was about all the power we needed, although we ran the engine at cruising speed to assist while we had the dangerous shoals off Mitlenach Island as a lee shore. I managed to nail a piece of plywood over the broken skylight pane, plug the leaky thru-hole with the right shaped piece of wood from a box of wood scraps, and pump out enough water from the bilge to stop the nerve-wracking sound of sloshing below decks.

At 1400 hours the wind was gusting above 50 knots, the sea was smoky and furious, and there was a vicious lump over Mitlenach shoals. This was about the worst of it, except that the wind was blowing so hard ahead that we couldn't get into the channel between Cortes Island and Twin Islands and into Cortes Bay. We anchored for the night in 15 fathoms in the lee of Twin Islands and made it into Cortes Bay during a brief lull the next morning. The following day, after being watched for signs of hypothermia, Kassim returned, and soon it was back to work, oystering.

A week later, loaded down with 7,000 lbs. of oysters, we got ready to return to Baynes Sound. On October 30th, at 1235 hours we again pass buoy P 57 off Cape Lazo. The wind is northwest, 10-15 knots, the sea slightly choppy, and the sky overcast in the south and clearing in the north. Kassim begins, in Arabic, a Muslim thanksgiving chant, "Allah hu! Allah hu." Richard, a

Christian, and I, a Jew, join in. "Allah hu! Allah hu! Allah hu!" We are all chanting and dancing joyfully around the deck.

31 October 1979, 1500 hours; moored, Denman Island wharf.

Hillel is famous for his novels, short stories and poetry.

Michael Clarke

Michael acquired *Ancestor* in 1981 and applied his energies, talent, and materials to renovating the aging vessel. She was quite run-down.

Michael has a love for wood in all its forms. He has constructed beautiful buildings on Lasqueti Island and elsewhere. Boats have also been his passion, and when he took ownership of *Ancestor*, he applied his talents well. Between 1983 and 1986, he replaced the decks (red cedar): rebuilt two trunk cabins (cedar and fir) and added yew stanchions for safety. In Nanaimo, the lead ballast was removed and recast in interlocking, v-shaped ingots. Brent Swain made the molds. The newly shaped ballast was reinstalled, creating more headroom below decks.

The majority of *Ancestor's* repairs were done in Scottie Bay on the north side of Lasqueti Island. In order to continue working through the winter months, Michael erected a shelter, using long, pliable battens which were milled timber off-cuts. Plastic sheeting made a serviceable roof.

Michael Clarke with crew at Scottie Bay

Summer fun, on and off Ancestor

Michael and his wife Cindy used *Ancestor* to earn a living as much as possible. He recalled a trip to Vancouver with two and a half tons of clams and forty sacks of oysters aboard! They pursued another money making venture when they attended the Renaissance Fair in Courtenay, where they unloaded their cappuccino machine from the boat and sold fresh coffee to the masses. Eventually they formed Karma Coffee and went into the business.

Michael and Cindy continued living aboard, sailing, working and planning further improvements to the boat.

At Scottie Bay (Michael Clarke photo)

With lug sail and bowsprit (Jeff Potter photo)

On Lasqueti Island, there was a great deal of interest in the Chinese junk rig. Allen and Sharie Farrel built *China Cloud* and rigged the vessel using this sail plan: Rubin, D.S. (2002). *Salt on the wind*, Horsdal & Schubart.

Michael was not impressed with *Ancestor's* gaff rig. He thought it was cumbersome and labour-intensive in heavy weather. Consequently, he removed the existing rig and installed a single, un-stayed mast, which carried a 700 square foot sail! The modifications were a success. Their main advantages were the ease of manoeuvring and easier reefing. *Ancestor* was changing her appearance. No one in the Grenadines would recognize her now.

Prior to the sail plan's alterations, I had the opportunity to do another trip on *Ancestor*. The old rig and the mouldy and weary cotton sails I had stitched-up in Bequia long ago were able to capture a light westerly breeze as we departed Scottie Bay and headed to Jedidiah Island for a picnic lunch. Changes to the boat were indeed necessary.

We neared Jedediah. The wind stopped for a rest. I was starting to help furl the sails when a thundering racket assailed my eardrums. I was in shock. An engine growled and thumped, a propeller churned the water and *Ancestor* surged forward! What? An engine? On *Ancestor*? I shook my head in disbelief, having known before now that she had an engine but until the contraption actually came to life, my memory always focused on of her earlier years. A new reality set in.

One would have to write another book to accurately describe all the work Michael did on the old vessel, but a few more words will have to do.

I particularly like Michael's story about being anchored in False Bay while Cindy was busy below decks giving birth to their first born. When their daughter, Tillicum, was twenty minutes old, Michael carefully made his way up the ladder, baby in his arms, stood on deck and showed her the star-filled universe!

* * *

Godfrey Stephens was building boats, carving and painting on Lasqueti in those days. He fell in love with *Ancestor* and Michael once heard him say, "I'd kill to have that boat." Well, he didn't have to kill anyone and eventually he did take over the helm of this magical vessel. Michael and Cindy acquired property at Mine Bay because their family was growing and new opportunities were on their horizon.

Godfrey Stephens

This chapter of *Ancestor's* life may seem slightly mixed-up.

I sat across from Godfrey inside his latest vessel, a 22 foot Aquarius, with a three-masted junk rig, stainless steel, wood-burning stove, a four foot long, underwater window and wood shavings everywhere. A bottle of tequila sat within easy reach. We discussed Godfrey's and *Ancestor's* shared history.

"Jon," he said, "time twists memory."

I quoted Anthony Burgess. "The truth is what you think you remember." This was our starting point.

The tequila bottle passed back and forth while Godfrey attempted to reconstruct the chronology of his love affair with *Ancestor*. I concentrated on my own memories, hoping to find my own chronologies. Not easy.

Godfrey first saw *Ancestor* in 1975. She was ashore at Mosquito Creek, her stern poking out from a boat shed. His brain plunged into sensory overload and he announced, "That boat was made for me!" Clearly, it was love at first sight, and I knew that love was still alive in his breast in 2017.

(Godfrey Stephens photo)
At Becher Bay, Vancouver Island, Aija rowing out to Ancestor

If one wishes to look into Godfrey's heart, do so by peering into the pages of Gurdeep Stephens's Wood, Storms and Wild Canvas: The Art of Godfrey Stephens. (D & I Enterprises, Victoria, 2014).

My words, by comparison, are weak and insufficient. Although I will try to retell my close friend's story. His tale of *Ancestor* drifted between us through the wood smoke and tequila haze.

The following is an excerpt of Godfrey's story, transcribed as well as this author can remember it.

I sailed into Hot Springs Cove with the Pookmis one day and there was the Ancestor at anchor.

Leif was aboard with a lady friend and someone else. They were on a trip around Vancouver Island, I think. He told me that *Ancestor* sailed like a witch.

She had a three cylinder Isuzu diesel engine. I considered that fact and wondered what you would have thought about *Ancestor's* iron jib? I wanted that boat so bad I could taste it!

Remember that time at Gibsons Landing when I was carving a red cedar door for Bruno Gerussi? You came sailing in on a 36 foot steel boat, the Pilot's Dream. I was having a drink when I saw her come in and anchor under sail. I said to the guys, 'That's got to be Jon van

Waiting for the underwater window installation

Tamelen on that boat.' It sure enough was. Your guests were June and John Poulsen and I ended up selling Poulsen a carving for a thousand dollars.

"Pookmis was anchored in the southern part of the bay, so I quickly went aboard, upped the anchor and the canvas and sailed over to you. Man, it felt good. That night you convinced me that if I wanted to go offshore I should build a steel boat. Tougher, safer than a wood boat and all that. So I sold Pookmis and built Mungo, a steel boat and I took her offshore – and lost her down on the southern Baja peninsula in 1989. Another chapter of my life. She was a good boat but I left her bones in Baja.

When Hillel Wright owned *Ancestor*, Michael Clarke was working with him. I was on Lasqueti then, building boats and carving – and lusting after *Ancestor*. I almost scored then. Hillel was having trouble with the bank and seemed agreeable to selling her to me. I went to Vancouver and sold a carving for 3,500 dollars. This was to be the down-payment. When I got back I found that Michael had scooped me and he was the new owner. I was devastated, but Michael is a good guy and he quickly got into rebuilding her.

When I bought *Ancestor* in 1995, she was tied-up in Sooke. I was heading over from Vancouver, but stopped to visit friends before taking the ferry. I had ouzo and retsina. What a night. What a week. There was this fantastically beautiful woman. When everyone else had gone to sleep we sat and talked until morning. Next day we climbed into to her BMW and went to Sooke. *Ancestor* welcomed us aboard. We were awake for 190 hours! We made plans in a daze of exhaustion from making love and lack of sleep. When Margot did go to sleep, I was still talking to her. It was unbelievable. She snored gently and answered my questions in her sleep! We were compatible.

One day she suggested that she would pay for the boat if she could have a 50% share in *Ancestor*. My response was, 'No. *Ancestor* can have only one owner. I can't share her with you.'

She was going to take my wildness away! I couldn't do it. We had been together for six months.

Then she was gone. I still love her. I can't help it.

When Michael owned *Ancestor*, he needed to install a new mast. Your old 'telephone pole' had been broken off above the crosstrees. The broken mast had been sleeved, but she needed a new spar. Michael and Alan Farrell cut down a tree, dressed it to shape and painted it. Something you or I wouldn't do.

Michael also changed her rig. She looked impressive with a single 700 square foot junk sail. Handled like a dream. No more struggling with that gaff main. She was still junk-rigged when I bought her. When the plastic sail started to get ratty, Alan offered to coat it with linseed oil!

I worked on *Ancestor* at Sooke. Carved the cap rail with knot designs and a lot of stuff. You've seen her. Maybe that's how I learned to tie a bowline. No, I just made that up!

I loved to go below into *Ancestor's* womb of wood. There was bark on some frames. Nobody had bothered to fancy-up the timbers! Gotta love that.

Have a puff, Jon. When I was in Jamaica once I met this guy. He said, 'Come and have a little smoke with I.' When you first arrive there they call you a 'white snake.' After you get a tan they get friendly and drop the snake handle.

I managed to run aground a few times. Always got floated again so no harm done. I remember letting her dry out at Deep Bay once. Real low tide, so no problem. There were quite a few folks on the beach. I had this porthole which I wanted to install as an underwater window. I was inside. Selected a good spot for the window, flashed up the chainsaw and went to work. Imagine the beach-walkers' surprise when they saw the end of a chainsaw buzzing through the hull! I made

Go figure!

a few cuts for a square hole then rounded it out until it was a good fit for the porthole. Bedded it and bolted it in place just as the incoming tide was lapping the hull.

At one point I decided to re-rig the *Ancestor*. Give her back her old look. Her persona. It was a lot of hard work, but worth it. Did I send you a photo of her underway with that new rig?

We entered a gaff-riggers race at Sidney one time. It was a party. The wind died, but we kept truckin'. We were the last boat to finish and Katherine Robinson accepted the booby prize, which was a box of turtles! Fun days.

"The Isuzu diesel engine was OK but the fuel tank wasn't, so I replaced it with a Saab tank, mounted against the transom.

I can't remember who installed the new tiller. I kept the old one, which your hand massaged a million times. I also kept the original gaff. I did an amazing sculpture. Big. The mermaid holds the tiller. It's her spear-thrower. The gaff is her spear. Haven't finished it yet. Dead body parts of *Ancestor* getting new lives!

"Ralph Hull liked her new rig, but there were some things he didn't like, for sure. I was ranting one day that I should take her out of the water, remove the keel, which would give her a shallow draft, add a centreboard, and sheath the hull to the waterline with steel bedded in Stockholm tar, through-bolted on all frames. She would be bullet and reef proof! I'd lower the deck to just above the engine and build an

Ancestor's tiller becomes a spear-thrower, gaff is a spear and boom jaws hold it all together. Godfrey Stephen's art.

African Queen. I'd have my carving studio up there. And Ralph said, 'No, no, no. I'd buy her from you before I'd let you do that.'

I still think it's an excellent idea. And Ralph did buy the *Ancestor*.

I had a nine and a half foot fibreglass dinghy on the float. I'd replaced her gunwales with yellow cedar. She was upside down on the float and one aft corner was barely in the water. One day I rolled her over and found that the yellow cedar gunwales were riddled with worms!

After Ralph bought *Ancestor*, he noticed quite a lot of punk wood. The transom was rotten. Tony Lyons rebuilt it. The name-plank was OK so it was reused. Brent Swain called *Ancestor* a 'mulch-boat'. Bad man, Brent. He was right though. She always needed work.

I finally realized I was an old man on an old boat. Everything changed. I was still in love with *Ancestor*, but I had to move on. It was tragic.

Ralph Hull

Ralph Hull is a Leo. He says that old age starts in the next decade. Godfrey and I sat down in Ralph's new home overlooking Sooke harbour. As I looked our mutual friend over, I could see Ralph was an active guy. Actually, kind of a notoriously active guy.

Godfrey once told me that Ralph had worked for twenty-three radio stations in the USA and managed to get fired from nine of them. Reason: He was pushing the Blues on white radio stations! My kind of guy. Ralph has owned many boats and loved them all. Now he is in retirement, surrounded by walls, bookshelves and a lifetime of photo albums.

Ralph first saw *Ancestor* in 1975 when he sailed into Mosquito Creek Marina with a friend. Her wonky bow appealed to him. He could feel her spirit, even though she was so far from her Grenadian home.

He was thrilled when he bought *Ancestor* from Godfrey in 1995. Ralph proceeded to refit and revamp her to his liking. He loves to have fun. He decided to enter *Ancestor* in the famous Swiftsure Race to show all those fancy mega race yachts how to race properly. When he approached the sponsors, he was told that even the handicap rules would not qualify his vessel for the competition. Being a very persistent person, he hounded the race organizers and his protest resulted in a change in the handicap assignation, which was raised to 336. *Ancestor* was in.

(Godfrey Stephens photo)
Ancestor with a bone in her teeth, Ralph Hull on the helm

So, in 1996 *Ancestor* sailed with the fleet, adding a bit of fun and becoming the subject of many jibes and well-intentioned jokes among the sailors. The starting flag went down and the flotilla headed south to take advantage of tides and breezes. *Ancestor* sailed south across the strait and when she neared Port Angeles, the wind was indulging in an extended holiday, leaving *Ancestor* flogging about and doing her best to whistle up the summer breeze. To no avail. *Ancestor* retired from the event and Ralph started dreaming almost immediately about next year's race, when surely they would have suitable gaff-rigger winds.

In 1997, *Ancestor* had her breeze. Ralph recalls trying to reef the mainsail. Unfortunately the reefing winch had not been bolted down and the crew discovered this oversight rather too suddenly, much to their despair. While running down the strait later that day, the conditions were still what Ralph called 'interesting'. Two men were on the tiller for two hour watches while *Ancestor* scudded toward the finish line. Ralph didn't mention how they placed in the race. He was only participating for the fun of it. He wasn't expecting to win.

Ralph continued to make improvements to the boat. At one time, he had her out of the water for several weeks to repair her twisted stem. Nothing worked. He also had her re-registered from the Grenadian to the Canadian flag. This process caused the V to be dropped from *Ancestor's* official name. She was no longer a part of my family!

Ancestor was entered in the Port Townsend wooden boat show. Ralph said there were more than ten thousand visitors that year and there was always a large crowd around the old 'West Indian smuggler.' She was still mystifying sailors.

Ralph, Godfrey, and I reminisced on sailing in general and *Ancestor* in particular. It was a rowdy time with good friends, lots of humour and some sadness.

Ancestor was sold to Brad Simpson in February of 2002 and she sailed into American waters in search of new adventure.

Brad Simpson

In June of 2016, I rode the Black Ball Ferry from Victoria to Port Angeles, Washington to visit *Ancestor*. Brad and I had spoken by phone and because he was working on a construction job, he couldn't join me at the boat.

* * *

Post Script

*W*hile I followed Brad's directions to Ancestor's new home, I reflected on that evening in 1974, when I'd first seen that no-name vessel plowing her way into Kingstown harbour. Long-dormant images leaped into my memory and I experienced again the awe I felt when I saw her and I remembered knowing immediately that she and I had to meet, and that my decision to purchase Ancestor was unwavering. When I first saw her, I was compelled to sail Ancestor somewhere, anywhere, and soon.

I drove south on Taylor Cuttoff Road, watching for the large open field which was supposed to give me my first glimpse of *Ancestor*. Suddenly I was there. I stopped and saw the vessel across a green pasture. She looked, from a distance, as if she was quietly grazing!

(Sara Miller photo)

The author and Ancestor in 2018

I was excited, but I cautioned myself to go slowly and follow Brad's directions if I wanted to get within walking distance of her.

Ten minutes later, I parked the camper van and made my way through the open woods to *Ancestor's* dry-land mooring. She looked like the *Ancestor* of my dreams: the same shape and the wonky stem. Her mast and standing rigging were resting on deck. I was overcome by the love and affection I still felt for this old Carriacou boat. Then I became aware of many distressing details. The planking displayed wide gaps and major shrinkage. She had sprung butt ends and rust-bleed from old, tired fastenings.

I touched her hull. In three languages, I whispered, "Hi, *Ancestor*," and waited for my boat to recognize me. Nothing. Her spirit had escaped through the gaping seams of the hull.

I hugged *Ancestor's* bow. I'm a foolish optimist who never gets depressed but here I was, crying and my stomach churned. My enthusiasm and my expectations for this rendezvous had been scuttled by fate.

Under a shroud of sorrow, I began to inspect my old sailing partner. The decks appeared to be in reasonable condition. Below decks, I identified a long lump of rust which used to be an engine. The internal ballast had been removed as well as most of the bulkheads and any sheathing that may have obscured the planking or frames. Brad had mentioned that two of the frames were punk and would have to be replaced. These were easy to spot.

My internal and external examination continued. I was convinced that the entire hull needed to be re-planked. She had been out of her natural element far too long and the existing planks would never swell to their original dimensions.

Although I remembered our history - our partnership - something indefinable was bugging me. I sat on the deckhouse, lit my pipe, relaxed and meditated. My instincts were telling me that there was a message here. Unexpectedly, I had a hunch.

I found my small compass in the van, went back onboard and took the old lady's bearings. Why was she facing in that direction? I had to know. Later, back on Moya, I laid out that old gnomic chart and plotted my boat's compass course. *Ancestor's* bow was pointing directly at Carriacou!

What will our next chapter be?

Miscellaneous Receipts

Canvas for new sails

Spice Island Charters (G'da) Ltd.

CASH BILL

Phone: 4-342   L'ANCE AUX EPINES,
                     ST. GEORGE'S, GRENADA,

Nº 6269   1/2/ 19 75

M Ancestor

1 Pt seam # cement Brown # 7570	4 18
2 Paint Roller covers @ 3.15	6 30
1 Roll masking tape	3 57
1 - 3" Paint Brush	7 20
1 Gal Thinners	8 95
Hauled 40 ft @ 2.75	110 00
2 Lay days @ $1.00	80 00
	220 25

$220.25

The Tenth of Next Month.

Invoice for haulout

Glossary

Athwartships - Describes beam to beam on a boat.

Baggywrinkle - Anti-chafe gear, made from rope and attached to standing rigging or other areas of sail contact on a vessel. Minimizes wear on sails and looks cool too.

Backing - Relating to directional wind change, when one faces the existing wind and the wind shifts to the left. Veering is when the wind shifts to the right.

BEAUFORT WIND FORCE SCALE

FORCE	KNOTS	CLASSIFICATION	APPEARANCE
0	Calm		Sea surface is smooth
1	1 – 3	Light air	Scaly ripples
2	4 – 6	Light breeze	Small wave crests, no breaking
3	7 – 10	Gentle breeze	Crests begin to break
4	11 – 16	Moderate breeze	Waves 1 – 4 ft. White caps
5	17 – 21	Fresh breeze	Waves 4 – 8 ft. White caps and spray
6	22 – 27	Strong breeze	Waves 8 – 13 ft. White caps and spray
7	28 – 33	Near gale	Waves 13 – 20 ft. White foam & streaking
8	34 – 40	Gale	Waves 18 – 25 ft. Streaking & spindrift
9	41 – 47	Strong gale	Waves 23 – 32 ft. Rolling seas, poor visibility
10	48 – 55	Storm	High waves, overhanging crests
11	56 – 63	Violent storm	Waves to 55 ft. Foam streaked seas
12	64 plus	Hurricane	Huge seas, sea completely white, driving spray

Blue Peter - Code flag P. When displayed alone it means, "This vessel is about to leave port."

Bobstay - A chain or cable and runs from the end of the bowsprit to the stem of the vessel at or near the waterline.

Bolt rope - Rope sewn around edges of a sail to prevent tearing and stretch.

Bowsprit - A spar projecting from the bow used as an anchor for the forestay and other rigging.

Bullseyes - Circular blocks of wood with a single hole, used to fairlead sheets or other lines at deck level.

Cathead - A wooden beam located athwartships, forward, on a vessel. The beam protrudes outward from the hull and provides a place to secure an anchor while at sea.

Carénage - An area in a harbour traditionally used for careening vessels, to facilitate repairs or painting on the hull.

Cleat - T-shaped devices used to control and secure sheets and lines on a boat.

Cranse - A fitting, mounted at the end of a bowsprit to which stays are attached.

Crosstrees - On a gaff rigged boat, cross trees are equivalent to spreaders on a Marconi rigged vessel.

Cringle - A ring, or eye, sewn into a sail for rope attachments. Sometimes known as a grommet.

Deadeye - A circular wooden block with a groove around the circumference, with three holes through the block. Used for tensioning of standing rigging.

Fairlead - A device often a hook or a ring, to guide a rope, line or cable around an object.

Foot - The bottom edge of a sail.

Forestay - A cable between the masthead and the end of the bowsprit.

Gaff rigged - A sail plan in which the mainsail has four corners.

Greenheart - A dense rot-resistant wood. Native to northern South America.

Gudgeon - A metal, female fitting, fixed to the bottom end of the keel, into which the rudder shaft is installed.

Gybe (or jibe) - A sailing manoeuvre. The stern of the vessel passes through the wind, putting the vessel onto a new course.

Halyard (or halliard) - A line that is used to hoist a sail (from the old term 'haul yards').

Head - The top point of a Marconi sail. On a gaff sail, head refers to the top from the throat to the peak. A marine toilet is called the heads.

Jib - Triangle-shaped foresail at the bow.

Jump up - A Caribbean party, with dancing and carousing.

Leach - The tailing (rear) edge of a sail.

Lizard - A block of wood, usually teardrop shaped, with a circumferential groove and a single hole through the centre. Used to fairlead a sheet from a jib or staysail, above decks, to the cockpit.

Kedge anchor - A small anchor used to reposition a boat (or haul it off a reef or sandbar).

Masthead - A platform partway up the mast. Used by a lookout or by crew working on the rigging.

Marconi-rigged - A sailing vessel rigged with only triangular sails.

Parrels - Mast hoops, normally made from split bamboo, onto which a sail is attached. Parrels slide up and down the mast on a gaff rigged boat.

Purple heart - A very dense, water-resistant wood, native to Surinam, Guyana and Brazil.

Ratlines - Short pieces of rope tied between the shrouds to form a ladder up the mast.

Sampson post - A heavy, vertical timber, projecting through the fore deck, used for anchor management.

Shrouds - Vertical rigging lines from the deck to the masthead.

Stays - Rigging lines that run from the masthead to the bowsprit and aft to the stern.

Staysail - A sail with the luff attached to the inner stay.

Taffrail - The rail across the top of the transom on a boat.

Taffrail log - A mileage counting device which mounts on the taffrail and is connected by a non-twist rope to a spinning rotor which is pulled behind a boat.

Tack - A manoeuvre to change course by letting the bow pass through the eye of the wind.

Topping lift - A rope or cable attached to the after end of the boom and passed through blocks on the upper mast, then to the deck. Used to control the set of the boom and the shape of the mainsail.

Transom - The aft end of a boat above the waterline.

Watch - A period of time. When on watch a crew member is on duty and in control of the vessel.

Wearing ship - An old term for gybing in square rigged ships.

Whisker stays - Cables or chains attached from the cranse iron leading aft to the hull sides where they are secured. Otherwise known as bowsprit shrouds.

Acknowledgements

Many thanks to Alix Whitfield (friendly editor) for her careful reading and sorting out of my words. How many cases of wine do I owe you now?

Sara Miller, first mate of the Moya. I'm so pleased you are in tune with the digital age and that you like playing in Photoshop. Good work on the images and the cover suggestions.

Hillel Wright for permission to use his *Ancestor* story from Allah's Radio.

Douglas Pyle wrote Clean Sweet Wind, Sailing Craft of the Lesser Antilles. A hearty thanks to you. Your book offered inspiration: the cover brought back pleasant memories.

About the Author

Water and wilderness are the fuels of life for Jon. He has logged over 300,000 miles on the ocean and has paddled thousands of miles by canoe on rivers and lakes in Canada.

He and his mate Sara live on Moya, a 36-foot sailboat. They have circumnavigated the planet on Moya and now spend their time on the west coast of British Columbia.

The 'lost' logbooks from Ancestor recently re-appeared and prompted Jon to share this carefree adventure with other sailors.

Also written by Jon van Tamelen, *Canadian Canoe Expedition: 5200 Miles from British Columbia to Quebec.*

Jon van Tamelen can be contacted through svmoya@gmail.com.

www.ingramcontent.com/pod-product-compliance
Lightning Source LLC
Chambersburg PA
CBHW070538160426
43199CB00014B/2286